THE GO MANUAL

Global Opportunities in Youth With A Mission

YWAM Publishing
A Ministry of Youth With A Mission
Seattle, Washington 98155

The GO Manual: Global Opportunities in Youth With A Mission

Seventh Edition 1993

ISBN 0-927545-62-4

Data entry & layout: YWAM Publishing - Seattle, WA

Scripture quotations are from the King James Version of the Holy Bible unless otherwise noted.

Printed in the United States of America.

Foreword

The doors of opportunity for us to share the gospel of Jesus Christ have never been so wide open. From Eastern Europe to the jungles of the Amazon, from the crowded cities of Asia to the villages of Africa, beyond to the Pacific and North America, the Lord is calling forth an army of workers.

This new Macedonian call is not just for seminary-trained missionaries, but for anyone who will take up the challenge of bringing Christ to the nations. There are a multitude of ways to be part of God's new missions army. Whatever your skill, talent or vocation, God can use you in missions.

The GO Manual helps show you the places of service that are available in Youth With A Mission. Workers are urgently needed for many of these positions. As you study the list of opportunities available worldwide, I want to encourage you to pray about how you can be a part of what God is doing throughout the world.

No matter where you may be in life - young or old, single or married (with families too!), skilled or unskilled, or from any nation or denominational background - God has a calling for your life. By asking God where he wants you to serve, and moving out in obedience to His calling, you will experience firsthand His faithfulness and the joy of seeing His Kingdom extended.

As we near the 21st century, we want to move forward - through every door of opportunity that God opens.

Loren Cunningham
President
Youth With A Mission

Acknowledgments

This manual continues to be produced because of a desire to see Christians from all walks of life and from all the countries of the world involved in missions. Information has been gathered from many of the YWAM operating locations worldwide.

Thank you to those YWAMers throughout the world who sent in their specific information for this edition of The GO Manual. This book is dedicated to all those who serve faithfully in world missions.

Thanks to Joe Portale and his team in Hawaii for their work on past editions of The GO Manual and to Loren Cunningham, from whom the vision for The GO Manual originated.

Special thanks to Mark Markiewicz for his input and suggestions which were integrated into this edition of The GO Manual. Thanks also to Jim Hagman for his help on the data base.

This edition would not be possible without the help and support of my husband Jim and the staff at YWAM Publishing. Thank you!

Your input will help us greatly as we prepare for the 1995 edition of The GO Manual. Please write to me c/o YWAM Publishing with suggestions or comments.

Michelle Drake
YWAM Publishing

Table of Contents

How Do I Use The Go Manual?

The GO Manual is designed to help you find specific training and mission opportunities in Youth With A Mission (YWAM) that correspond with your interests and abilities. It is divided into seven main sections:

Youth With A Mission (YWAM) - SECTION I

This section is a brief overview of YWAM's programs and emphasis. Three ministries are highlighted to let you see some of the variety of mission opportunities available in the world. If you are not familiar with Youth With A Mission, spend some time reading through this introductory section.

Whether your calling is short or long-term, there are many opportunities available to you in almost any region of the world. Pray and ask God to lead you as you read and consider the global opportunities found in this manual.

YWAM Opportunities & Addresses - SECTION II

YWAM operating locations worldwide are involved in a variety of ministries which fall under three main categories: evangelism, mercy ministry and training. This section contains an overview of each operating location. The ministry emphasis of a particular location as well as their current staff needs, addresses, and phone numbers is provided.

YWAM Training Schools - SECTION III

YWAM has a variety of training programs to prepare you for missions work. You'll find an alphabetical listing of schools by course title, followed by columns giving information about the country and city in which the school is located, the starting dates, length of the school and the language the course is given in. After determining the school and country of your interest, locate the address for that school (in Section 2) and write to them for specific information and an application form.

YWAM Base Ministry Focus - SECTION IV

If you have an interest in a particular area of ministry, such as campus evangelism or medical ministry, you can determine which countries have listed these areas of ministry as one of their priorities. This section is most helpful for those who know what area of ministry they would like to be involved, but are unsure of exact geographic location they would like to serve.

YWAM Short-Term Outreach Information - SECTION V

If you are interested in a short-term mission experience, consider being a part of one of YWAM's outreaches. Outreaches may take place in your own country or in another culture and nation. The length of time, dates and minimum age requirements vary. Outreaches are listed first by name, and then by the country and city from which the outreach is being organized. You will also find information on the destination, starting date, length of the outreach, and necessary and/or helpful languages to be spoken on a specific outreach. For more detailed information, write to the particular operating location sponsoring the outreach.

YWAM Camp Information - SECTION VI

This section will help you locate YWAM-sponsored camps taking place in your vicinity. There are a variety of camps for families, teens, and children. Camps are listed by country and city first and then by camp name. For more information and requirements, contact the specific base listed by code.

YWAM Seminar/Conference Information - SECTION VII

There may be a YWAM-sponsored seminar or conference near you this year! Seminars and conferences are listed first by country and then by seminar/conference name. Information on starting dates, length, language and minimum age of participants is also provided. Write to the particular operating location sponsoring the seminar or conference for full details.

NOTE: For ease in locating the particular operating location address, use the Ctry/City code provided. Ctry/City codes begin with the country and then list the state/region and the city or operating location name in an abbreviated form. See the appendix for the code key.

When you write to the YWAM location, please mention that you saw that opportunity in THE GO MANUAL.

SECTION 1

Youth With A Mission (YWAM)

Some Statistics

Year YWAM founded	1960
Long-Term staff	over 7,000
Short-Term workers	over 20,000
Permanent YWAM bases	480
Countries with YWAM bases	over 120

Statistics provided by Research and Information, Youth With A Mission International Office, Colorado Springs, Colorado, USA.

Who is YWAM?

Since our founding in 1960 by Loren Cunningham, Youth With A Mission (YWAM) has seen thousands involved worldwide in fulfilling Christ's command: "Go ye into all the world and preach the gospel to every creature" (Mark 16:15).

Youth With A Mission draws people from a variety of backgrounds to work in a vast spectrum of evangelistic activities. Young people, families, retired persons, recent high school graduates and Ph.D.'s are among our ranks. People from more than 100 nations and many denominations are included, from the new babes in Christ to church leaders and missionaries with many years of experience.

Each year, over 20,000 people are involved in YWAM's short-term projects. Mobile ministries have gone into every country of the world. Over 7,000 work as permanent staff at 480 centers in 120 nations.

Three Methods of Action

YWAM embraces three methods of action - ways which we believe God has given us to be a part of the goal of taking the gospel to all the world:

- Evangelism - spreading God's message.
- Training - preparing workers to reach others.
- Mercy Ministries - showing God's love through practical assistance.

Evangelism

From Sweden to Saipan, YWAM workers are announcing salvation in dozens of creative ways: ministry to the needy inner cities of the world, reaching university campuses, outreach at international sporting events, participating in drama and music, sharing door-to-door in an African village or an American town, or being part of a ship ministry. In each evangelism effort, we follow up new Christians, linking them with established churches or fellowships wherever possible. We also help these converts form a Christian fellowship where none exists.

Training

We are engaged in various training programs in a number of locations on every continent.

The Discipleship Training School (DTS) or Crossroads Discipleship Training School (CDTS) make up the basic program for most YWAM bases around the world.

In addition there are special schools including schools of Christian counseling, preschool teacher training, missionary paramedics, foreign language studies, missions and biblical studies. We have schools focusing on the Muslim world, creative ministries, nutrition and agriculture.

University of the Nations (U of N) has a unique international and missions-oriented emphasis. Courses and seminars are being offered through the following colleges: Christian Ministries, Communication, Counseling and Health Care, Education, Humanities and International Studies, Performing Arts, and Science and Technology.

Mercy Ministries

Our mercy ministries seek to demonstrate the love of God to the poor and needy in practical ways.

These include medical, dental, and counseling teams; vocational rehabilitation; agricultural training; nutrition services; building and maintenance services; language and cultural adjustment classes for refugees; food and clothing distribution.

YWAM's first ship, the Anastasis (Greek for "resurrection") is an 11,695-ton ship, 522 feet long, with living quarters for 476 people. Equipped with three cargo holds for relief materials and food, and an 18-bed hospital, this ship is a "Special Delivery" system taking the Gospel of Jesus Christ and His practical works of love to many needy port areas.

The Good Samaritan, a small cargo/passenger coastal carrier, has delivered relief goods to Haiti, Mexico and refugees in Honduras.

The Pacific Ruby serves the islands of the Pacific bringing medical aid to isolated peoples.

Together, these three ships have delivered millions of pounds of relief supplies, performed hundreds of surgeries, and preached the Gospel to thousands.

Note: If you are interested in knowing more about Youth With A Mission, we would encourage you to read the book "Is That Really You, God?" by Loren Cunningham with Janice Rogers. (See YWAM Publishing resource materials in the Appendix.)

Youth With A Mission
STATEMENT OF PURPOSE

Youth With A Mission (YWAM) is an international movement of Christians from many denominations dedicated to presenting Jesus Christ personally to this generation, to mobilizing as many as possible to help in this task, and to the training and equipping of believers for their part in fulfilling the Great Commission. As Christians of God's Kingdom, we are called to love, worship and obey our Lord, to love and serve His body, the Church, and to present the whole Gospel for the whole man throughout the whole world.

We in Youth With A Mission believe that the Bible is God's inspired and authoritative word, revealing that Jesus Christ is God's Son; that man is created in God's image; that He created us to have eternal life through Jesus Christ; that although all men have sinned and come short of God's glory, God has made salvation possible through the death on the cross and resurrection of Jesus Christ; that repentance, faith, love and obedience are fitting responses to God's initiative of grace towards us; that God desires all men to be saved and to come to the knowledge of the truth; and that the Holy Spirit's power is demonstrated in and through us for the accomplishing of Christ's last commandment" . . . Go ye into all the world, and preach the gospel to every creature" (Mark 16:15).

Four Profiles

Evangelism:

Brazilians in Africa

Youth With A Mission is growing as an international movement. Most Western nations are represented in our ranks and increasingly we see dynamic involvement from countries which aren't traditionally missionary senders. One such group are the Brazilians working in Africa.

Five African countries were Portuguese colonies until 1975. The Gospel is present in them all, but is usually a very tiny minority of the population, with many people groups unreached.

In 1987 Robson Soares, a Brazilian YWAMer, heard Loren Cunningham say that Sao Tome & Principe, a Portuguese-speaking island country off the coast of Gabon, was one of the two countries in which YWAM had never worked. Robson took this as a challenge and decided to change it.

Sao Tome was a country with only one church at that time. Soon Robson and his team helped form new congregations. National workers assumed responsibility for leadership over the new churches, and they believe the ten new works will multiply into many times that number.

This team served as an example to YWAMers in Brazil, and other teams were soon forming to confront other challenges in Africa. The next team went to Guinea-Bissau, a country split between Animistic and Moslem tribes, with a tiny minority of Christians. Cooperating with the government and the existing church, education and health care were brought to the Fulani tribe. The Fulanis were the people who brought Islam to West Africa. The first Christian school in the history of Guinea-Bissau has been established for more than 100 children. Health care clinics are being formed in the outlying villages as well, and churches planted in a region where there have never been any.

In the spring of 1991, YWAM established a permanent presence in Angola. A training school for the churches was launched along with primary health care, since there are no doctors available. The Mercy Ship Good Samaritan joined forces with a team in an effort to further alleviate the suffering of the people and bring them the light of the Gospel.

Current plans are to establish a work in Mozambique and in Cape Verde Islands. The first African missionaries are now starting to work in these countries, and they are targeting new countries.

Brazilians have moved out of a difficult economic situation in their own country and displayed great courage, competence, and initiative in their efforts in Africa. It's something God is doing all over the world with many national groups. Come and join some of the truly international teams as they push back the frontiers of darkness and multiply churches where there have never been any before!

Training:

University of the Nations

University of the Nations (U of N) is YWAM's global university dedicated to be a multiplier for missions in fulfilling Christ's Great Commission. It is one university but located in many countries on every continent. Each U of N location is committed to instructing men and women in the ways of God, while equipping them with the professional skills necessary to serve in a wide variety of disciplines and reach the world for Christ.

U of N has many opportunities for those wanting to discover their place of service and potential as evangelists, missionaries, or Christian servants in government, business, education, communication, performing arts or science. The U of N vision is to send missionaries from every nation into these geographic and vocational fields.

Through seven developing areas of study, the U of N provides global opportunities for university education and training to people of every race, nation, denomination and economic background. Schools are now being offered in the areas of:

Christian Ministries
Communication
Counseling and Health Care
Education
Humanities and International Studies
Performing Arts
Science and Technology

A U of N education offers a student the maximum in options, opportunities and flexibility for international, cross-cultural learning experiences. The doors to leadership in the

21st century will be wide open to men and women with international experience, who know the world and have the tools to function across cultural boundaries. That's why U of N students are constantly challenged with a global outlook through both academic studies in multi-cultural settings and pursuing their studies in several nations.

A student might begin study in Switzerland or Singapore and move on to take schools in the USA, Canada, Belize or any of the more than 150 locations in over 70 countries.

The U of N faculty is a global network of experienced resource professors and lecturers. Many come in from professional work to instruct in U of N classrooms around the world.

U of N is developing a multi-faceted program of degrees and diplomas that fulfill regional requirements. For those needing only a few schools in a specialized area of study, U of N also offers an ideal opportunity to reach that goal.

As we count down to A.D. 2000, the church may be entering its greatest era in reaching and influencing the world for Christ. We invite you to join us at a U of N location as we prepare to meet this challenge.

Mercy Ministries:

Mercy Ships - Anastasis

Youth With A Mission operates three ships under the ministry of Mercy Ships: the Anastasis, the Good Samaritan, and the Pacific Ruby. Mercy Ships provides practical assistance through disaster relief and emergency medical help while ministering the love of Christ and sharing the Gospel.

YWAM's first ship, the Anastasis (Greek for "resurrection"), is an 11,695 ton ship, 522 feet long, with living quarters for 450. It is equipped with four cargo holds for relief materials and food, and a hospital with three operating rooms.

In the past year, the Anastasis has been involved in two major projects:

- Sierra Leone, West Africa (November 16, 1992 - April 7, 1993)

The staff of the Anastasis conducted Primary Health Seminars in Sierra Leone. Over 7,600 patients were treated for such ailments as malaria, skin diseases, and respiratory disorders. The dental clinics treated over 3,175 patients. 409 operations were performed during the ship's stay in Sierra Leone including cleft lip and palate, facial reconstruction, tumor removal, skin and bone grafts, and cataracts.

The ship delivered 410,000 pounds of relief cargo, consisting of construction and agricultural supplies and tools as well as a mobile hospital unit and medical supplies and equipment. A construction crew built a 1500 square foot medical facility as well as making improvements in the YWAM training center and Sierra Leone Children's Home. Development projects were also completed including latrine facilities and freshwater outlets in the poorest districts of Freetown.

• Lithuania (July 23 - August 16, 1993)

Three years ago, Lithuania broke the yoke of Soviet communism. Free at last, she struggles to throw off the past, but it takes time to learn how to be free. The day after the U.N.'s recognition of the nation in 1991, Dr. Juoxas Olakas, Lithuania's Minister of Health, drafted a letter to Mercy Ship's President, Don Stephens. He described the nation's desperate health care conditions and appealed to Mercy Ships for help.

Two years later, the Anastasis sailed into Klaipeda loaded with supplies donated from around the world. The medical team found increasing disease and insufficient medications. Standard medical equipment lay in disrepair.

While hundreds of people waited for dental or medical treatment, they heard the Gospel through preaching and the "Jesus" video. Daily Bible studies grounded new believers in their faith. Klaipeda Mayor Benediktas Petruaskas echoed the words of many, "We are thankful for the materials you brought, but, more important for our nation is the spiritual help. Our world is in turmoil. It is our obligation to listen to your message." The 350 Anastasis crew members from 30 nations and many denominations visibly demonstrated a message of reconciliation, forgiveness and love.

YWAM Staff Person Profile

Louise Tolmie, a New Zealander, currently serves on staff with Youth With A Mission in Lakeside, Montana. For Lou, the process of becoming involved in missions did not happen overnight.

Lou was just beginning nurses training in New Zealand when she first heard about YWAM. Although intrigued, she set the idea aside to finish three more years of nurses training. After working in the medical field for 4 years, God brought YWAM to her mind again and challenged her to take steps toward fulfilling this long-time dream to go into all the world with the Gospel.

Completing the process of correspondence and application with YWAM bases in the United States, Lou was accepted for the Discipleship Training School (DTS) program at YWAM Montana. After working an additional six months to save enough money for her trip and schooling, she left her home in New Zealand, arriving at the YWAM campus nestled in the mountains that surround the beautiful Flathead Valley in Northwest Montana.

During her DTS, Lou was completely surprised by the revelation of truth that God brought to her each week. Her realization that she could have a intimate relationship with God and that He had specific plans for her was life-changing!

Lou's DTS outreach took her to the Ukraine for two months. During this time, she experienced the faithfulness and power of God as the outreach team shared with people on the streets and worked alongside Christians to build a new church facility. The 13 team members shared in children's camps (formerly used for communist training), seeing over 300 people come to the Lord, including one of the camp leaders.

Returning from this exciting time of outreach, Lou decided to apply for staff at YWAM Montana to work with DTS students that she might multiply in others those things God was developing in her. Lou continues to be involved in training and releasing people for the work of the Kingdom. While leading a DTS outreach team to Puerto Rico, her team was able to minister God's love to some of the spiritually and physically needy street people and AIDS victims of this self-governing commonwealth.

YWAM staff members often wear more than one hat, and Lou is no exception. She has served in the food service division of the YWAM Montana campus and is currently working in the administration office for the training schools. Lou helps in the planning of future schools as well as in the day-to-day operation of current schools. Her home is in dormitory style housing along with students who are training for short and long term missions. She provides support and friendship to those around her, continuing to challenge people of all ages to take steps in fulfilling the calling God has placed on their lives.

Lou and thousands like her make up the full-time staff at over 480 locations in 120 countries. Ordinary people, doing extraordinary things as they follow God's call "to know God and to make Him known" to all nations.

How Long A Commitment Do You Require?

Short-Term

What is a short-term mission opportunity?

A short-term missionary is one who commits from two weeks to two years of his or her time to spread the Gospel.

Some of the short-term opportunities include:

EVANGELISM:CHILDREN
BUILDING/MAINTENANCE
ADMINISTRATORS
COOKS
SUMMER OF SERVICE
EVANGELISM:STREET
KING'S KIDS OUTREACHES
BOOKKEEPERS
PERFORMING ARTS TEAMS
MEDICAL ASSISTANTS
TEACHERS
SECRETARIES
COMMUNICATION DEPT. STAFF
INTERCESSION TEAMS

Most operating locations have openings for both long and short-term personnel. Some of these opportunities involve outreaches in which you work on a team led by a full-time YWAM staff member. Group intercessory prayer is an integral part of outreach, and often during that time God reveals His strategy for reaching a particular city, island, or group of people

What are the requirements?

The general requirements for participation in a short-term program are:

1. You must have committed your life to Jesus Christ and desire to see His life shared with others.

2. For overseas work, you must have a valid passport and be a high school graduate or at least 18 years old. For work in your own country, you must be at least 16 years old. (Some exceptions apply, see minimum age column under Outreach Section and Camp Section.) Though we are called Youth With A Mission, you need not be young in age, just young at heart.

3. You must complete and send in the appropriate application form (obtained from the YWAM base offering the opportunity) accompanied by a non-refundable registration fee. Allow plenty of time for correspondence. Upon approval by the program director, you will be notified where and when to arrive.

4. You are responsible for your transportation to and from the mission location. (Round-trip tickets are required.)

5. For outreaches, a fee is due upon arrival for the program. Fees, which vary for each program and country, cover your food, housing, and other basic expenses during outreach. Laundry, postage, medical and other personal expenses are your own responsibility. Write to the specific YWAM base for more information.

Long-Term

Those interested in long-term mission opportunities desire to see specific goals reached in the overall task of world evangelism. They give at least two years, or the rest of their lives, in ministry.

Youth With A Mission is rapidly expanding and has opportunities for long-term missions in almost any area.

Just some of the long-term opportunities are:

- MECHANICS
- COMPUTER DATA ENTRY
- EVANGELISTS
- RECEPTIONISTS
- ADMINISTRATORS
- CHURCH PLANTERS
- TEACHERS/EDUCATORS
- PHYSICIANS/NURSES
- COOKS/BAKERS
- CARPENTERS

Prerequisites for long-term missions

The successful completion of a Discipleship Training School (DTS) is required in order to prepare one for missions work. DTS, a five to six month course, serves to introduce you to YWAM and is a time of building relationships which have long-reaching benefits in your ministry.

Special training, education or skills will be used whenever possible, however, adaptability is always important in missions.

Placement decisions are made through prayerful cooperative consideration between you and the leadership of the particular YWAM ministry to which you are called.

Financial support

Since YWAM is a fully volunteer organization, no one

receives a salary. Each worker, from the International Director to the newest recruit, looks to God for his or her own needs. God's faithfulness in providing comes in many ways. Some staff members receive regular support from a home church, friends, and/or families, while others rely on God's provision through other ways.

Lifestyle of a long-term missionary

Long-term workers must be prepared to make adjustments. The diet and lifestyle are simple and often international. Community living is the norm. Singles are often housed in dorms, married couples in a single room, and families in two or three rooms.

As YWAMers, we are not trying to be ascetics. We enjoy the blessings of God, but we economize where necessary in order to free up more resources for the extension of God's Kingdom.

I Want To Go - What Do I Do Now?

1. Prayerfully consider the various opportunities listed in the following sections.. Choose two or three options.

2. Consult with your pastor or spiritual leader about your desire to go to the mission field. Pray with him about your intentions.

3. Request information and an application form from the location sponsoring the opportunity of your choice. Complete application and return it.

4. Upon acceptance for the opportunity, you will be sent details describing what to bring, where and when to arrive and any other necessary information.

5. Make arrangements for necessary finances, air transportation, visas, shots, passports, and other details.

6. Start praying for the ministry in which you will take part. Remember: every ministry opportunity is dependent upon prayer to see God's maximum accomplished.

I Don't Speak 'YWAMese!"

These are common expressions or ministry names (YWAMese) used to facilitate communication within Youth With A Mission:

- **Crisis Center**: ministry reaching out to troubled youth, often in the inner city.
- **Crossroads Discipleship Training School (CDTS)**: this course is a special discipleship training program for men and women from all walks of life - those who are at

a crossroads in life and are seeking new direction, new vision, and renewal in the Lord. Most students are over 35 years of age, and the program is suited to their particular needs.

- **Discipleship Training School (DTS)**: YWAM's foundational training school aimed at preparing messengers of the Gospel, helping people to know God in depth. The goal is to encourage a daily walk with God rather than to accumulate information. Usually a five to six month program consisting of three months of classroom teaching and two or three months in active evangelism.
- **FEET**: a ministry involving mobile evangelism teams using the tools of drama and music, and taking its name from Romans 10:15: "How beautiful are the feet of them that preach the gospel of peace . . ."
- **Field Ministry Internship Program**: hands-on field experience for college students during the summer, integrating one's college major with an on-going cross-cultural ministry in community development, computer science, fine art, international law, medicine, performing arts, public administration, social work, television journalism, and youth ministries; offered by the U of N for credit to students from other colleges. (DTS not required)
- **HANDS - Helping a Neighbor Develop & Serve**: a ministry of King's Kids in which kids have an opportunity to meet the needs of those they are ministering to through practical service.
- **Hospitality**: the act or practice of being friendly and showing care and concern towards guests and new arrivals.
- **ICS - International Christian Schools**: a network of indigenous preschool, primary and secondary schools run by YWAM with the purpose of equipping children with the knowledge of God and developing their academic, spiritual and physical potential.
- **Impact - International Missions Program for Assembling Consulting and Technical Teams**: coordi-

nating people who desire to be a witness on the mission field through short-term use of their profession, skill, or specialty field.

- **Impact World Tour**: an evangelistic outreach to rural America. The three goals of the Impact World Tour are to serve and help strengthen the existing local church ministries, to help reach the unreached in rural communities, and to challenge rural America with a call to missions.
- **King's Kids International (KKI)**: trains and mobilizes children, teens and families into missions outreach locally and internationally, using performing arts, service skills and sports as modes of expression.
- **Living Alternatives**: ministry to girls with unwanted pregnancies through Pregnancy Crisis Testing Centers and Homes for Unwed Mothers.
- **Mercy Ministries**: ministering to the practical and spiritual needs of the poor and needy people of the world.
- **Mercy Ships**: using ships to take the Gospel of Jesus Christ and His practical works of love to needy port cities. The ministry began with the M/V Anastasis.
- **Muslim Ministries**: evangelism and mercy ministries to Muslims in the Middle East and Europe.
- **NIKO**: a Greek work which means to conquer and subdue. NIKO camps are a ministry of King's Kids designed to help youth discover their physical, social and spiritual strengths and weaknesses through survival skills and physical endurance. Team-building and dependence on God is a primary focus.
- **Pioneering**: a continuous process toward establishing a permanent ministry. It can include outreach ministries and centers, tentmaking, student missionaries, mercy ministries, growth groups, new fellowships, schools, YWAM bases or other full time ministries.
- **Slavic Ministries**: evangelism and missions work among the Slavic people of the world.
- **Spheres of Influence**: seven areas that have major influence in every society; the family, school, church,

media, performing arts, business and government. These were previously called the Mind Molders.

- **Summer of Service (SOS)**: a short-term summer outreach involving training and evangelism.
- **Tentmaker**: a person who finds entry to a seemingly closed country through opportunities for professional people to use their skills in a regular paying job. The word comes from the Apostle Paul's example of occasionally working in his profession as a tentmaker on his missionary journeys.
- **Trailblazing**: a continuous process leading toward pioneering. It includes a significant time of ministry and intercession by a YWAM team within a country, city or people group with the desire to discover its needs, to respond to those needs as led by God and to prepare for future ministries.
- **Urban Ministries**: a ministry aimed at reaching people in large cities with a message appropriate to their circumstances and needs.
- **University of the Nations (U of N)**: YWAM's global university dedicated to be a multiplier for missions. One university, but with 150 branches in 70 nations. The U of N vision is to send missionaries from every nation into geographic and vocational fields -- from towering glass office buildings in world-class cities, to remote grass huts in steaming jungles.
- **Volunteer**: a person who works at a YWAM location for a period of 2 weeks to 3 months (maximum). DTS not required.
- **YWAM base**: a permanent ministry facility run by local YWAM leadership within a country.

* For other common YWAM abbreviations and codes used in this manual, please see the Appendix at the end of this book.

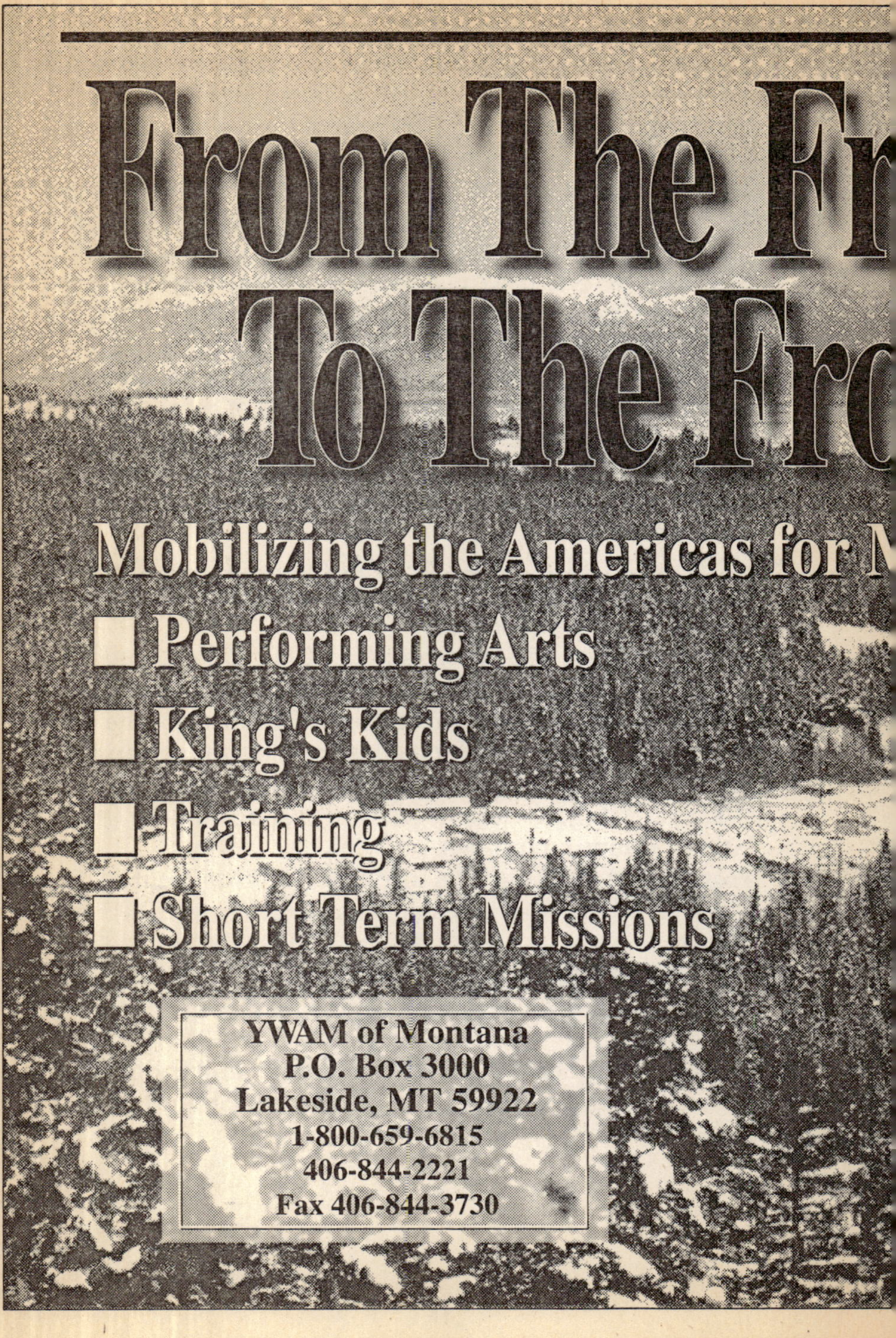
From The Fr
To The Fro
Mobilizing the Americas for
Performing Arts
King's Kids
Training
Short Term Missions
YWAM of Montana
P.O. Box 3000
Lakeside, MT 59922
1-800-659-6815
406-844-2221
Fax 406-844-3730

ontier
ntiers
lissions Worldwide:
Yes! I'm interested in YWAM Montana!
Name
Address
City State Zip
I would like more information about...
☐ School of Worship
☐ School of Biblical Studies
☐ Summer of Service
☐ Vacation With A Mission
☐ King's Kids
☐ Sports Ministries
☐ Musician's Summer of Service
☐ YOUth A.T.T.A.C. (teen camp & outreach)
☐ Discipleship Training School
☐ Crossroads Discipleship Training School
☐ IMPACT Ministries
☐
YWAM Montana • P.O. Box 3000 • Lakeside, MT 59922 • 1-800-659-6815

Section II

YWAM Opportunities & Addresses

This section is designed to give you an overview of all the YWAM operating locations according to the information received. Contact the specific location for more detailed information.

Explanation of Information in Section II

Country/State/City:

Operating locations are listed alphabetically by country. The mailing address follows. Addresses and phone numbers are current as of October 1993.

PLAIN ENVELOPE!! (Mail Warning):

Please take note of these warnings! This warning after the address indicates the specified address is in a sensitive country requiring your confidentiality. Please observe the following guidelines when sending any mail to addresses where a PLAIN ENVELOPE warning appears:

1. No "YWAM" or other Christian logo or name should apear on the envelope!!
2. To be safe, do not include such addresses in mass mailings!!
3. Please write the address on the envelope in handwritng.
4. Do not mention sensitive information in the letter as it may be censored!!

5. Do not mail valuable items such as cash.

Director or Contact Names:

One or several may be listed after their corresponding title.

Ministry Focus/Emphasis:

The main ministry priorities for this particular operating location. The list is not all-inclusive. This category is meant to give a general idea of the ministries a particular location is involved in.

Language:

The primary languages spoken at this location are listed in order -- with the main language spoken listed first. In many cases, only one language will be listed.

Avg. # Staff:

This number indicates the average number of people currently on staff at this location.

Schools:

Schools which are currently scheduled to take place at this operating location are listed. See Section III (Training Schools) for abbreviation meanings.

Main Outreach Locations:

Operating Locations have listed their six main outreach locations. This is where they send the majority of their outreach teams for ministry. Again, this list is not all-inclusive.

Priority Staff Needs:

These staff needs are not listed in any particular order. The staff opportunities may be short or long-term. Please note that ALL operating locations have a need for logistical staff on a continual basis. Logistical staff would include: food service, maintenance/grounds, secretarial, housekeeping, and hospitality.

YWAM INTERNATIONAL
and
REGIONAL OFFICES

International Office

YOUTH WITH A MISSION
(Office of the President)
75-5851 Kaukini Hwy
Kailua-Kona, HI 96740-2199 USA
Tel: 1-808-326-7228
Fax: 1-808-326-4453
President: Loren Cunningham

Field Offices

YOUTH WITH A MISSION
(The Americas Field Office)
PO Box 4600
Tyler, TX 75712 USA
Tel: 1-903-882-5591
Fax: 1-903-882-7673
Americas Director: Leland Paris

YOUTH WITH A MISSION
(Europe, Middle East & Africa Field Office)
13 Highfield Oval
Ambrose Lane, Harpenden
Herts AL5 4BX
England, U.K.
Tel: 44-582-76-54-81
Fax: 44-582-76-80-48
EMA Director: Lynn Green

YOUTH WITH A MISSION
(Pacific & Asia Field Office)
PO Box 61
Watson, A.C.T. 2602
Australia
Tel: 61-6-241-55-00
Fax: 61-6-241-60-98
Pacific & Asia Director: Tom Hallas

Regional Offices

YOUTH WITH A MISSION
(North America Office)
PO Box 55309
Seattle, WA 98155 USA
Tel: 1-206-363-9844
Fax: 1-206-363-9845
Regional Director: Denny Gunderson

YOUTH WITH A MISSION
(Central America & Caribbean Office)
PO Box 970471
Miami, FL 33197-0471 USA
Tel: 1-305-388-2589/5187
Fax: 1-305-388-0903
Regional Director: Rick Allegretto

JOVENS COM UMA MISSAO
(South America Office)
PO Box 832555
Miami, FL 33283 USA
Tel: 1-305-892-1346
Fax: 1-305-892-1346
Regional Director: Gerson Ribeiro

YOUTH WITH A MISSION
(Europe Office)
Heidebeek
8181 PK Heerde
Netherlands
Tel: 31-5780-16755
Fax: 31-5780-15399
Regional Director: Jeff Fountain

YOUTH WITH A MISSION
(Middle East & North Africa Office)
Contact the EMA Field Office
Harpenden, England, U.K.

YOUTH WITH A MISSION
(Africa Office)
13 Highfield Oval
Ambrose Lane, Harpenden
Herts AL5 4BX
England, U.K.
Tel: 44-582-76-54-81
Fax: 44-582-76-80-48
Regional Director: Iain Muir

YOUTH WITH A MISSION
(South Asia Office)
PO Box 127
Pune 411 001, Maharashtra
India
91-212-659-601
91-212-659-601
Regional Director: Steve & Elizabeth Cochrane

YOUTH WITH A MISSION
(East Asia Office)
10 Borrett Road
Hong Kong
Tel: 852-524-6057
Fax: 852-810-5198
Regional Director: Gary Stephens

YOUTH WITH A MISSION
(SE Asia, Australia & New Zealand Office)
PO Box 61
Watson, A.C.T. 2602
Australia
Tel: 61-6-241-55-00
Fax: 61-6-241-60-98
Regional Director: Tom Hallas

YOUTH WITH A MISSION
(Pacific Office)
74-5606 Pawai Place, Suite 201
Kailua-Kona, HI 96740-2199 USA
Tel: 1-808-329-0588
Fax: 1-808-329-0580
Regional Director: Sosene Le'au

International Ministries

YOUTH WITH A MISSION
(Mercy Ministries)
PO Box 2020
Lindale, TX 75771-2020 USA
Tel: 1-800-424-SHIP (within USA)
Tel: 1-903-882-0887
Fax: 1-903-882-0344
International Director for: Don Stephens

YOUTH WITH A MISSION
(Evangelism & Frontier Missions)
Caixa Postal 2024
30.161 Belo Horizonte, MG
Brazil
Tel: 55-31-398-1488
Fax: 55-31-398-1166
International Director for: Jim Stier

YOUTH WITH A MISSION
(Training & Education)
75-5851 Kuakini Hwy
Kailua-Kona, HI 96740-2199 USA
Tel: 1-808-326-4454
Fax: 1-808-326-4453
Int'l Director for:
Darlene Cunningham

International Coordinating Offices

YOUTH WITH A MISSION
(Slavic Ministries)
PO Box 4213
Salem, OR 97302 USA
Tel: 1-503-363-1571
Fax: 1-503-363-2417
International Director of: Al Akimoff

YOUTH WITH A MISSION
(King's Kids International)
PO Box 117
Kailua-Kona, HI 96745-0117 USA
Tel: 1-808-329-5745
Fax: 1-808-329-6323
International Director of:
Dale Kauffman

YOUTH WITH A MISSION
(French Ministries)
3 Place de la Tour Neuve
26130 St. Paul-Trois-Chateaux
France
Tel: 33-75-04-75-51
Fax: 33-75-04-51-30
International Director of: Daniel Schaerer

JUVENTUD CON UNA MISION
(Spanish Ministries)
1303 Grandview Ave
Waterloo, IA 50703 USA
Tel: 1-319-233-3943
Fax: 1-319-235-1808
Int'l Director of: Wedge & Shirley Alman

JOVENS COM UMA MISSAO
(Portuguese Ministries)
Caixa Postal 2024
30.161 Belo Horizonte, MG
Brazil
Tel: 55-31-398-1488
Fax: 55-31-398-1166
International Directer of: Jim Stier

YOUTH WITH A MISSION
(WORD for the World)
PO Box 7
Elm Springs, AR 72728 USA
Tel: 1-501-248-7229
Fax: 1-501-248-1455
International Director of: Oren Paris

YOUTH WITH A MISSION
(University of the Nations)
75-5851 Kuakini Hwy
Kailua-Kona, HI 96740-2199 USA
Tel: 1-808-326-7228
Fax: 1-808-329-2387
President: Loren Cunningham
Vice Pres. Acad. Affairs:
Howard Malmstadt

YOUTH WITH A MISSION
(Mercy Ships)
PO Box 2020
Lindale, TX 75771-2020 USA
Tel: 1-800-772-SHIP (within USA)
Tel: 1-903-963-8341
Fax: 1-903-963-7300
International Director of: Don Stephens

YOUTH WITH A MISSION
(Family Ministries)
Eden
W14580 County D
Weyerhaeuser, WI 54895 USA
Tel: 1-715-353-2280
Fax: 1-715-353-2935
International Director of: Larry Ballard

YOUTH WITH A MISSION
(Urban Missions)
PO Box 296
Sunland, CA 91041-0296 USA
Tel: 1-818-896-1589
Fax: 1-818-896-2077
International Director of: John Dawson

ALBANIA

YWAM - Albania
National Office:Albania
c/o MAF Mail for Tirane
Wiesenweg 39
CH 5102 Rupperswil,
Switzerland

Phone: 355-42-34708
Fax: 355-42-34708

- Ministry: Church Planting, Training, Short Term, Evangelism
- Language: Albanian, English

AMERICAN SAMOA

Taputimu

Youth With A Mission
National Office:American Samoa
PO Box 2608
Taputimu, Pago Pago
American Samoa 96799 USA

National: Tua Meafua
Phone: 1-684-688-2235
Fax: 1-684-688-2325
Avg.# Staff: 3

- Ministry: Training, Discipleship
- Language: English, Samoan
- Schools: DTS
- Outreach Locations: Western Somoa, Canada, Fiji
- Staff Needs: DTS Staff, General Base Staff, Evangelism Team

ANGOLA

Jovens Com Uma Misao
Cx Postal 11
Ganda - Benguela,
Angola

Director: Marcos Antonio Azolin
Phone: 244-72-230-65
Fax: 244-72-234-73

ARGENTINA

Buenos Aires

Juventud Con Una Mision
National Office:Argentina
Casilla de Correo 595
1000 Correo Central
Buenos Aires,
Argentina

Director: Alejandro Rodriguez
Phone: 54-1-621-2480
Fax: 54-1-325-1446

Resistencia

Juventud Con Una Mision
Casilla de Correo 477
3500 Resistencia, Chaco,
Argentina

Director: Jose Maria Liste
Phone: 54-722-35262

AUSTRALIA

A.C.T., Canberra

Youth With A Mission (Canberra)
Field Office:Pacific & Asia
PO Box 61
Watson, ACT, 2602 Australia

Director: Merv McDermid
Field: Tom Hallas (Pacific/Asia)
Phone: 61-6-241-5500
Fax: 61-241-6098
Avg.# Staff: 100

- Ministry: Training, Frontier Missions

- Language: English
- Schools: DTS, CDTS, SBS, SOFM, CBVM, IBC, FMS, FTS, HS, RIE, ETTC
- Outreach Locations: Indonesia, India, Central Asia, Balkans, Australia, Malaysia
- Staff Needs: Graphic Artist, Journalist, Administrator, Academic Advisor, Secondary Teacher, Primary Teacher, Pre-School Teacher, Schools Staff, Operations Mgr, P.R. Manager, Missions Communc., Construction Wrkr

VIC, Melbourne - Surrey Hills

Youth With A Mission - Melbourne
National Office:Australia
1 Kent Road
Surrey Hills, VIC, 3127
Australia

Director: David Lawton
National: Stephen Aherne
Phone: 61-3-836-0011
Fax: 61-3-836-9231
Avg.# Staff: 50

- Ministry: Evangelism, Training, Kings Kids, Evangelism:Mobile
- Language: English
- Schools: DTS
- Outreach Locations: VIC towns/cities, Pune, India, East Malaysia, Asia

Staff Needs: Secretarial, Maintenance, Kings Kids Staff, DTS Staff, Evangelism Teams, Accounts, Food Services

A.C.T., Canberra

Lighthouse Ministries
GPO Box 548
Canberra, ACT, 2601
Australia

Director: Darrell Furgason
Phone: 61-6-241-5500
Fax: 61-6-241-6098
Avg.# Staff: 7

- Ministry: Campus Evangelism, Training
- Language: English
- Schools: Humanities and Science: A Christian Perspective
- Outreach Locations: Australia, Asia
- Staff Needs: Humanities Staff, Evang:Chinese

Northern Territory, Darwin

Youth With A Mission
PO Box 290
Darwin, NT, 0801
Australia

Director: Joe Sheehy
Phone: 61-89-81-2424
Fax: 61-89-81-2424
Avg.# Staff: 8

- Ministry: Hosting Teams, Evangelism, Indigenous Groups
- Language: English
- Outreach Locations: Aust. Outback, Indonesia, Aboriginal, Burma
- Staff Needs: Kings Kids Dir., Kings Kids Staff, Aboriginal-Evang., Kitchen Staff, Maintenance, Accountant/Clerk, Desk Top Publ., Evang.:High School, Evang.:University, Evang-Children, Hospitality, Communications

NSW, Albury

Youth With A Mission Albury
PO Box 354
Albury, NSW, 2640
Australia

Director: David Skeat
Phone: 61-60-25-8217
Fax: 61-60-40-1618
Avg.# Staff: 7

- Ministry: Training, Evangelism, Country Towns, Kings Kids, Mercy Ministry
- Language: English
- Schools: DTS
- Outreach Locations: Country Australia, Thailand, India, Laos

- Staff Needs: DTS Director, Evangelism:Children, Evang:High School, House Parents, Farmer, Accountant, Puppeteer, Radio/TV Announcer, Evang:Mobile Team, Evang.:Kings Kids, DTS Staff, Youth Worker

NSW, Goulburn

Youth With A Mission
52 Mundy Street
Goulburn, NSW, 2580
Australia

Director: Timothy Coates
Phone: 61-48-21-2477
Phone: 61-48-21-2274
Fax: 61-48-21-9006

NSW, Kotara Fair

Youth With A Mission - Newcastle
PO Box 66
Kotara Fair, NSW, 2289
Australia

Director: Rod Thorpe
Phone: 61-49-56-24-70
Fax: 61-49-52-86-18
Avg.# Staff: 5

- Ministry: Urban Ministry, Youth Ministry, Training, Communication, Mobilization, Evangelism
- Language: English
- Schools: DTS (Urban Outreach Apprenticeship)
- Outreach Locations: India, North Coast Aust.
- Staff Needs: Coordinator/Youth, Youth Workers, School Evangelism, Communication, DTS Staff, Evangelism Team

NSW, Ryde

Youth With A Mission
PO Box 116
Ryde, NSW, 2112
Australia

Director: Brent Williams
Phone: 61-2-808-3293
Fax: 61-2-808-3301

NSW, Sydney

Youth With A Mission
PO Box 492
Mount Druitt, Sydney, NSW, 2770
Australia

Director: Robert Westwood
Phone: 61-2-835-2000
Fax: 61-2-835-2003
Avg.# Staff: 22

- Ministry: Training, Evangelism, Church Planting, Youth Ministry, Urban Ministry
- Language: English
- Schools: DTS, BLS, PDS, Korean/English DTS
- Outreach Locations: Thailand, Japan, Malaysia
- Staff Needs: DTS Leader, Receptionist, High School Ministry, Urban Church Planter, Youth/Community Wrkr, Kings Kids Staff, Accountant, Worship Leaders, Counsellors

NSW, Sydney

Indo-Chinese Mission Training Centre
PO Box 1025
Cabramatta, NSW, 2166
Australia

Director: Peter Davis
Phone: 61-2-823-5743
Avg.# Staff: 5

- Ministry: Training, Mobilization, Evangelism, Mercy Ministry
- Language: English, Khmer, Vietnamese
- Schools: Vietnamese DTS, Cambodian DTS
- Outreach Locations: Cambodia, Vietnam, Thailand, Laos, Australia

- Staff Needs: Secretarial, DTS Staff/Vietnam., Maintenance Wrkr, House Parents, Coord. Relief/Dev, Social Worker, Youth Worker

NSW, Sydney

King's Kids
PO Box 492
Mount Druitt, Sydney, NSW, 2770
Australia

Phone: 61-2-835-2000
Fax: 61-2-835-2003

- Ministry: Primary and high school work.
- Language: English
- Outreach Locations: Australia, South Pacific
- Staff Needs: Administrator, Secretary, Choreographer, Worship Leader

NSW, Sydney

Youth With A Mission
Northern Peninsula Ministry
54 Delmar Parade
Dee Why, Sydney, NSW, 2099
Australia

Contact: David/Janelle Tidey
Phone: 61-2-971-8053
Avg.# Staff: 4

- Ministry: Evangelism, Mercy Ministry, Training:Church
- Language: English
- Schools: Life Audit School
- Staff Needs: Community Outreach

Queensland, Ashgrove

Frontiers and Communications Center
Int'l Prayer Events Coordination:YWAM
309 Waterworks Rd.
Ashgrove, QLD, 4060
Australia

Director: Roger McKnight (QLD)
Phone: 61-7-366-6126
Fax: 61-7-366-3111
Avg.# Staff: 18

- Ministry: Prayer Networking, Mobilization, Pioneering
- Language: English
- Schools: School of Intercession Worship & Warfare
- Outreach Locations: Central India, Australia, South East Asia
- Staff Needs: Accounts, Campus Evangelism, Evangelism:India, Administration, Graphic Arts, Desk Top Publ., Journalism, A/V Specialist

Queensland, Carbrook

Carbrook Training Centre
799 Redland Bay Rd.
Carbrook, QLD, 4130
Australia

Director: David Way
Phone: 61-7-287-6511
Fax: 61-7-287-6510
Avg.# Staff: 27

- Ministry: Training, Evangelism
- Language: English
- Schools: DTS, SOE
- Outreach Locations: Nagpur, India, Australia
- Staff Needs: Receptionist, Secretary, Maintenance, Grounds, Cook, Hospitality, Building Devel., Accounts, Workers:Children

Queensland, Townsville

Youth With A Mission - Townsville
PO Box 7568
Townsville, QLD, 4814
Australia

Director: Ken Mulligan
Phone: 61-77-726-358
Fax: 61-77-724-414
Avg.# Staff: 7

- Ministry: Campus Evangelism, Communication
- Language: English
- Outreach Locations: Pacific, Asia, Australia
- Staff Needs: Evangelists, Secretarial, Accountant

Queensland, Townsville (Mercy Ships)

Mercy Ships Australia
PO Box 6221
Townsville Mc
Townsville, QLD, 4810 Australia

Contact: Ken Mulligan
Phone: 61-77-721-342
Fax: 61-77-724-414
Avg.# Staff: 7

- Ministry: Mercy Ministry
- Language: English
- Outreach Locations: Pacific, Asia, Australia
- Staff Needs: Secretarial, Accountant, P.R. Officer, Medical Coordinator, Graphic Artist

South Australia, Adelaide

Youth With A Mission
G.P.O. Box 1029
Adelaide, SA, 5001
Australia

Director: Mark Brokenshire
Phone: 61-8-390-1040
Fax: 61-8-390-1041

Tasmania, Sandy Bay

YWAM Tasmania
National Kings Kids Office
PO Box 428
Sandy Bay, Tasmania, 7005
Australia

Director: Tim Winslade
Phone: 61-02-250-332 (Int'l)
Phone: 002-250-332 (in Aus
Fax: 61-02-250-332
Avg.# Staff: 9

- Ministry: Youth Ministry, Children's Ministry, Kings Kids, Training, Constru
- Language: English
- Schools: DTS, PCYM
- Outreach Locations: Indonesia, Pacific Islands, Australia
- Staff Needs: Accounting, DTS Leader, DTS Staff, Maintenance, Kitch Supervisor, Secretarial, PCYM Staff, Child Care, Kings Kids Staff

Tasmania, Sorell

Youth With A Mission Tasmania
PO Box 55
Sorell, Tasmania, 7172
Australia

Director: Matthew Colwell
Phone: 61-02-651-053
Fax: 61-02-651-053
Avg.# Staff: 15

- Ministry: Children's Ministry, Youth Ministry, Church Ministries, Country Towns, Media, Music
- Language: English
- Schools: Discipling Kingdom Musicians School
- Outreach Locations: Indonesia, India
- Staff Needs: Farmer/Grazier, Builder, Gardener/Orchard, Evangelism, Evang: Kings Kids, Builders, Administrator, Tradesman, Journalist, Graphic Designer, Radio Announcer, Clerk

Victoria, Collingwood

Youth With A Mission
(Singleton Lodge)
18-22 Islington St.
Collingwood, VIC, 3066
Australia

Director: Peter Waters
Phone: 61-3-419-7244
Fax: 61-3-416-0361

Victoria, (Island Breeze)

Youth With A Mission
Island Breeze
1 Kent Road
Surrey Hills, VIC, 3127
Australia

Western Australia, Perth

Youth With A Mission
Western Aust/North Territ. Reg'l Office
PO Box 8501
Stirling Street
Perth, Western Australia, 6849
Australia

Director: Peter Brownhill
Phone: 61-9-221-1217
Fax: 61-9-325-1830
Avg.# Staff: 75

- Ministry: Frontier Missions, Training, Evangelism:Mobile
- Language: English
- Schools: DTS, CDTS, PHC, SOW, CCDTS, SOFM, FCD, Poor & Needy D
- Outreach Locations: Indonesia, Australia, Pakistan, Thailand, India
- Staff Needs: School Staff/Leader, Accounts, Admin. Secretaries, Com

Programmer, Hospitality, Mercy Ministry Wrkr, Kitchen Staff, Target-2000 Staff, Builder/Carpenter, U of N Development, Communication/Media

AUSTRIA

Vienna

Juegend Mit Einer Mission
National Office:Austria
Herklotzgasse 14 12
Wien (Vienna), 1150
Austria

Director: Gavin Farley
National: Bruce Clewett
Phone: 43-1-83-02-71
Phone: 43-1-812-98-44
Fax: 43-1-812-76-58
Avg.# Staff: 20

- Ministry: Youth Ministry, Family Ministry, Kings Kids, Evangelism
- Language: German, English
- Schools: DTS
- Outreach Locations: Uganda, Poland, Slowahia-Rep., Tschech-Rep., Vienna, Austria
- Staff Needs: Administrator, Secretaries, Youth Evangelist, Worship Leader, School Leader, Bookkeeper

AZERBAIJAN

YWAM Azerbaijan
c/o Strategic Frontiers
PO Box 25490
Colorado Springs, CO, 80936
USA

Director: Nathan Wagner

BANGLADESH

Chittagong

YWAM Chittagong
PO Box 822
Chittagong 4000
Bangladesh
PLAIN ENVELOPE !!!

Director: Ick Mo Jung
Phone: 880-31-225-953
Fax: 880-31-225-785

Dhaka

Silo Schmidt
PO Box 5038
Dhaka, 1205
Bangladesh
PLAIN ENVELOPE !!!

Director: Silo Schmidt
Phone: 880-2-891-411

BELGIUM

Brussels

Jeunesse En Mission (YWAM)
National Office:Belgium
Avenue des Celtes 19
1040 Brussels
Belgium

National: Jan Piet de Visser
Phone: 32-2-736-33-63
Fax: 32-2-732-52-36
Avg.# Staff: 10

- Ministry: Youth Ministry
- Language: French, Dutch, English
- Schools: King's Kids
- Staff Needs: Administrator, Bookstore Sales, Bookstore Mgr., Counselor:Unwed Moth., Hospitality, Maintenance, Personnel Mgr., Secretary, Translator, Worship Leader, Evangelism:Urban, Evangelism:KK/Youth

Flanders

Jeugd Met Een Opdracht-Vlaanderen
YWAM-Flanders
Sisal Straat 2
B-9000 Gent
Belgium

Director: Ignace Verreth
Phone: 32-91-236-38-08
Avg.# Staff: 4

- Ministry: Church Planting, Kings Kids, Family Ministry, Evangelism
- Language: Dutch, English
- Schools: King's Kids
- Outreach Locations: Hungary, Roemenia, Flanders, Belgium
- Staff Needs: Youth Leaders (KK), Secretary (KK), Church Planters, Evangelists, Housekeeper, Construction Wrkr

BELIZE

Belmopan

Youth With A Mission
Caribbean Regional Office
Box 78
Belmopan
Belize

Director: Glenn Martin
Phone: 501-82-2677
Fax: 501-82-2622
Avg.# Staff: 15

- Ministry: Serve the Body of Christ, equipping them to participate in the Great

Commission., Providing a cross-cultural experience for North American Christians.

- Language: English
- Schools: DTS
- Outreach Locations: Belize, Mexico, Caribbean
- Staff Needs: Secretarial, Accountant, Preschool Teacher, Communications Dir., Maintenance Wrkr, DTS Staff, Personnel/Pastoral, Evangelists, Youth Ministry Wrkr, Church Ministry Wrkr

BOLIVIA

La Paz

Juventud Con Una Mision
National Office:Bolivia
Casilla 4663
La Paz
Bolivia

National: Oscar Lima
Fax: 591-2-786753
Avg.# Staff: 8

- Ministry: Urban Ministry, Kings Kids, Church Planting
- Language: Spanish
- Schools: School of Cross-cultural missions
- Outreach Locations: Boliviano, Brasil
- Staff Needs: Childrens:Teachers, Schools/Base Staff, Performing Arts, Musicians, Preachers/Teachers, Nurse, Graphics Designer, Hospitality Worker, Evangelism, Church Planters, Secretarial, Kings Kids Staff

Santa Cruz

Juventud Con Una Mision
Casilla 1607
Santa Cruz
Bolivia

Director: David Hulford
Phone: 591-3-42-86-94
Fax: 591-3-42-86-94
Avg.# Staff: 22

- Ministry: Street Kids, Training, Training:Church, Evangelism:Mobile
- Language: Spanish, English, German
- Schools: DTS, SBS
- Outreach Locations: Bolivia, Paraguay, Brazil
- Staff Needs: Administrator, Accountant, Secretarial (bi), House Parents, Cook, Mobile Team, SBS Tutors/Staff, Kings Kids Staff

Trinidad

Juventud Con Una Mision
Casilla 339
Trinidad, Beni
Bolivia

Director: Kevin Stabler

BRAZIL

Belo Horizonte

Jocum Contagem
National & Area Office:Brazil
Caixa Postal 2024
Contagem
Belo Horizonte-MG, 30.161-970
Brazil

Director: Jim Stier
Phone: 55-31-398-1488
Fax: 55-31-398-1166
Avg.# Staff: 180

- Ministry: Evangelism, Training, Mercy Ministry, Children's Home, Preschool
- Language: Portuguese

- Schools: DTS, Mission School
- Outreach Locations: South America, Brazil
- Staff Needs: Secretarial, Construction, Teachers, Administration, Daycare Helpers, Children's Home Wrkr, Evangelism, Communication, Kitchen

Belem

Jovens Com Uma Missao
Caixa Postal 1186
66.000 Belem, Para
Brazil

Director: Alcir Cavalheiro
Phone: 55-91-255-2192

Belem

Jovens Com Uma Missao
(Ct. Valorizcao da Crianca)
Caixa Postal 1186
66.000 Belem, Para
Brazil

Director: Naum Dias De Freitas
Phone: 55-91-255-2192

Belo Horizonte

Jovens Com Uma Missao
Rescue and Restore Urban Missions
CP 438
Belo Horizonte M.G., 30161.970
Brazil

Director: Johannes Lukasse
Phone: 55-31-444-0912
Fax: 55-31-442-7567
Avg.# Staff: 80

- Ministry: Urban Ministry, Mercy Ministry, Street Kids, AIDS Victims, Training, Homeless
- Language: Portuguese, English
- Schools: PCYM, CDTS, Urban Health Care, School of Video Productions
- Outreach Locations: Brazil Cities, South America
- Staff Needs: Administrator, Accountant Clerk, Carpenter Teacher, Community Develop., Cook, Maintenance, Hospitality Wrkr, General Physician, CDTS Staff, Secretary (bi), Pastoral Worker (bi), Driver:Van

Belo Horizonte (Daycare)

Jovens Com Uma Missao
(Daycare)
Caixa Postal 2024
Belo Horizonte, MG, 30.161
Brazil

Director: Ramona Azevedo
Phone: 55-31-398-1488

Belo Horizonte (Luzeiro)

Jovens Com Uma Missao
(Luzeiro)
Caixa Postal 438
Belo Horizonte, MG, 30.161
Brazil

Phone: 55-31-283-1539

Belo Horizonte (Recanto)

Jovens Com Uma Missao
(Recanto)
Caixa Postal 438
Belo Horizonte, MG, 30.161
Brazil

Phone: 55-31-444-6932

Belo Horizonte (Rescue House)
Jovens Com Uma Missao
(Rescue House)
Caixa Postal 438
Belo Horizonte, MG, 30.161
Brazil
Phone: 55-31-442-5436

Blumenau
Jovens Com Uma Missao
(Amiguinho Feliz)
Caixa Postal 1473
89.100 Blumenau, SC
Brazil
Director: Ursula Richter
Phone: 55-47-323-1426

Curitiba
Jocum Curitiba - YWAM Curitiba
PO Box 6180 (cx.p. 6180)
Curitiba, Parana, 80011.970
Brazil
Director: Laurenildo R. Santana
Phone: 55-41-222-7774
Fax: 55-41-232-6690
Avg.# Staff: 61

- Ministry: Urban Ministry, Hosting Teams
- Language: Portuguese
- Schools: KK, DTS, Preschool Training
- Outreach Locations: Parana, Santa Catarina, Sao Paulo, Mato Grosso
- Staff Needs: Communications, Construction, Secretarial, Maintenance, Children's Wrkr, Kitchen Director, Administrator, Plumber/Electrician, Nurse, Mechanic: Vehicle, Evangelism Team, Short Term

Florianopolis
Jovens Com Uma Missao
Caixa Postal 1367
88.000 Florianopolis, SC
Brazil
Director: Carlos Leitzke
Phone: 55-48-243-2094
Fax: 55-48-247-3778

Manaus
Jovens Com Uma Missao
Caixa Postal 2800
Manaus, Amazonas, CEP 69001-970
Brazil
Director: Mario da Silva
Phone: 55-92-233-8658
Fax: 55-233-9036/233-2840
Avg.# Staff: 30

- Ministry: Evangelism, Street Kids, Mercy Ministry, Training, Education
- Language: Portuguese
- Schools: DTS
- Outreach Locations: Amazon, Peru, Colombia, Venezuela, English Guinea
- Staff Needs: Computer Programmer, Administrator, Journalist, English Teacher, Portuguese Teacher, Telephone Operator, Receptionist, Translator, DTS Staff, Street Kids Staff

Maues
Jovens Com Uma Missao
Caixa Postal 1419
69.190 Maues, Amazonas,
Brazil
Director: Eliane Hanzen Valderra
Phone: 55-92-542-1394

Port Velho
Tribal Ministries
Director: Reinaldo Cazao Ribeiro

Caixa Postal 441
Porto Velho, Rondonia, 78.900.970
Brazil

Phone: 55-69-223-1553
Fax: 55-69-223-3750
Avg.# Staff: 100

- Ministry: Indigenous Groups, Unreached Peoples
- Language: Portuguese
- Schools: Crosscultural Ecuation/Literacy, Linguistics, Ecology/Envir., PHC, DTS
- Outreach Locations: Acre State, Rondonia, South Amazon, Bolivia, Tribes, Labrea/Purus River
- Staff Needs: Cattle Manager, Farming, Boat Crew, Kitchen, Kindergarten, Office/English Wrkr, Teachers: DTS, Computer, Bible Translators, Long-Term Tribal Wrkr

Porto Alegre

Jocum - Jovens Com Uma Missao
Southern Brazil Office
Caixa Postal 224
Porto Alegre - R.S., 90.001-970
Brazil

Director: Paulo de Barcellos
Phone: 55-51-488-1633
Fax: 55-51-488-1633
Avg.# Staff: 40

- Language: Portuguese, Spanish
- Schools: DTS, School of Early Childhood Education, KK
- Outreach Locations: South Brazil, Uruguay
- Staff Needs: Secretarial (bi), Food Service Staff, Construction Wrkr, Children's Wrkr/Teach, Communications, Maintenance Worker, Farm Wrkr - Animals, Farm Wrkr - Garden, Mercy Ministry

Recife

JOCUM - Recife
Northeast Brazil Office
Caixa Postal 1278
Recife, PE, 50.001-970
Brazil

Director: Jaime Araujo
Phone: 55-81-222-3111
Fax: 55-81-222-3111
Avg.# Staff: 70

- Ministry: Training, Evangelism, Mercy Ministry, Church Planting
- Language: Portuguese, English, Spanish
- Schools: DTS, IBC, SCPL, SOE, Community Development
- Outreach Locations: NE Brazil
- Staff Needs: Secretary (bi), DTS Director, Schools Staff, Public Relations, Base Administrator, Street Children Wrkr, Work With Beggars, Drama Players, Musicians, Preschool Teacher, Medical Workers, Agriculturalist

Recife

Jovens Com Uma Missao
(Lar de Criancas)
Caixa Postal 1278
50001 Recife, PE
Brazil

Rio de Janeiro

Jovens Com Uma Missao
Caixa Postal 3724
20001 Rio de Janeiro, RJ,
Brazil

Director: Wellington de Oliveira
Phone: 55-21-776-1378

Sao Paulo

Jovens Com Uma Missao
Caixa Postal 7040
Sao Paulo, SP, 01064-970
Brazil

Director: Alberto Tavares
Phone: 55-11-267-4696
Fax: 55-11-267-4696
Avg.# Staff: 20

- Ministry: Street Kids, Evangelism, Urban Ministry, Worship/Prayer
- Language: Portuguese
- Schools: DTS
- Outreach Locations: Sao Paulo City, Sao Paulo State, Brazil
- Staff Needs: Food Service Staff, Musicians/Worship, Accountant, Street Kids Wrkr, Mercy Ministries, Training Staff, Graphic Artist, Evangelism Staff, Church Planters

Tapaua

Jovens Com Uma Missao
(Nova Esperanca - Tapaua)
Caixa Postal 2800
69000 Manaus, Amazonas
Brazil

BULGARIA

Youth With A Mission - Bulgaria
PO Box 81
6200 Chirpan,
Bulgaria

Director: Hristo Cholakov
Phone: 359-416-5633
Fax: 359-416-5633

BURKINA FASO

Jeunesse En Mission
01 B.P.4
Ouagadougou 01
Burkina Faso

Director: Issa Xavier
Phone: 226-30-24-23

BURUNDI

Burundi
c/o YWAM Eastern Africa
PO Box 76046
Nairobi
Kenya

Director: Method Kamanzi
Phone: 254-2-71-42-46
Fax: 254-2-71-42-45

PLAIN ENVELOPE !!!

- Ministry: Evangelism, Training, Church Planting
- Language: French, English
- Outreach Locations: Eastern Zaire, Rwanda, Tanzania
- Staff Needs: Team Leader, Accountant, Evangelism Leader, DTS Staff, Nurse, Comm. Devel. Wrkr, TESOL Teacher, Secretary (bi)

C.I.S.

Russia, Barnaul

YWAM - Barnaul (C.I.S.)
(c/o YWAM Amsterdam)
Prins Hendrikkade 50
1012 AC Amsterdam
Netherlands

Phone: 31-20-626-92-33 (Neth)
Fax: 31-20-620-18-23

Belarus

YWAM Belarus (C.I.S.)
PO Box 4213
Salem, OR, 97302
USA

Phone: 1-503-363-1571
Fax: 1-503-363-2417
Avg.# Staff: 5

- Ministry: Training, Evangelism, Discipleship, Mercy Ministry
- Language: Russian, English
- Staff Needs: DTS Leader, DTS Staff, Coord. Outreach, Hospitality Wrkr, Bookkeeper, Church Planters, Youth Workers, Secretarial

Russia, Krasnador

YWAM Krasnador (C.I.S.)
PO Box 4213
Salem, OR, 97302
USA

Phone: 1-503-363-1571
Fax: 1-503-363-2417
Avg.# Staff: 45

- Ministry: Training, Evangelism, Discipleship, Mercy Ministry
- Language: Russian, English
- Schools: DTS, School of Church Ministry
- Outreach Locations: Kamchatka, Arctic People, Siberia, Caucasus
- Staff Needs: Coord. Outreach, DTS Staff, Secretarial, Bookkeepers, Youth Workers, Church Planters, Translators

Russia, Murmansk

YWAM - Murmansk (C.I.S.)

Phone: 47-625-72-333 (Norway)

(c/o YWAM Norway)
(Grimerud Gaard)
2312 Ottestad
Norway

Fax: 47-625-72-972 (Norway)

Ukraine

YWAM Ukraine (C.I.S.)
PO Box 4213
Salem, OR, 97302
USA

Phone: 1-503-363-1571
Fax: 1-503-363-2417
Avg.# Staff: 16

- Ministry: Training, Evangelism, Discipleship, Mercy Ministry
- Language: Ukrainian, Russian, English
- Schools: DTS, Russian/Ukrainian Language School
- Outreach Locations: Central Asia, Mongolia, Turkey, Siberia, Russia, Ukraine
- Staff Needs: DTS Leader, DTS Staff, Coord. Outreach, Hospitality Wrkr, Secretarial, Bookkeepers, Translators, Church Planters, Youth Workers

CAMBODIA

YWAM Cambodian Desk
(Cambodian Inquiries through Thailand)
G.P.O. Box 177
Bangkok, 10501
Thailand

Contact: G. Stephen Goode
Phone: 66-2-212-6060
Phone: 66-2-212-6061
Fax: 66-2-212-6062
Avg.# Staff: 20

- Ministry: Relief, Community Development, Medical Ministry, Education, Children's Ministry
- Language: English, Khmer
- Staff Needs: Administrators, Medical Coordinator, Secretary, English Teacher, Vocational Teachers, Kings Kids Leaders

CAMEROON

Jeunesse En Mission
(Relief & Development)
B.P. 11086
Yaounde,
Cameroon

Director: Annelies Ndebele
Phone: 237-221873 Attn:JeM

CANADA

BC, Winfield

Youth With A Mission
Regional Office:British Columbia
PO Box 922
Winfield, BC, V0H 2C0
Canada

Director: Paul Martinson
Contact: N. Reid
Phone: 1-604-766-3838
Fax: 1-604-766-2387
Avg.# Staff: 30

- Ministry: Training, Mercy Ministry, Indigenous Groups
- Language: English
- Schools: DTS, CDTS, SBS, Children in Need
- Outreach Locations: Guyana, Native Canadians, Mexico, Caribbean, Guatemala
- Staff Needs: Maintenance, Hospitality

Alberta, Calgary

Youth With A Mission - Calgary
King's Kids Alberta
#212, 110-11 Avenue SW
Calgary, Alberta, T2R OB8
Canada

Director: Russell Sanche (Alberta KK)
Phone: 1-403-266-8669
Fax: 1-403-265-7737 Attn:YWAM
Avg.# Staff: 6

- Ministry: Kings Kids
- Language: English
- Schools: King's Kids
- Outreach Locations: Alberta Towns, Prairie Province, Native Reserves, Eastern Europe, Dominica
- Staff Needs: Secretary, Coord. HANDS Outreach, Coord. Sports Outreach, Child Advocate, Coord. Intercession, Coord. Native Outreach

Alberta, Edmonton

Youth With A Mission
5328 - 89 St. (2nd Floor)
Edmonton, Alberta, T6E 5P9
Canada

Director: Allan McBryan
Phone: 1-403-466-0519
Fax: 1-403-466-0680
Avg.# Staff: 6

- Ministry: Urban Ministry
- Language: English
- Staff Needs: Urban Ministry, Family Ministry, Receptionist, Urban Min. Leader

Alberta, Turner Valley

Youth With A Mission Training Centre
Box 730
Turner Valley, Alberta, T0L 2A0
Canada

Director: Allan Burney
Phone: 1-403-933-5623 (Off.)
Phone: 1-403-933-2423 (Ctr)
Fax: 1-403-933-5080
Avg.# Staff: 26

- Ministry: Training and releasing Christians into their ministry calling in missions.
- Language: English
- Schools: DTS
- Outreach Locations: Dominica (Carib), Mexico, USA, NW Terr/Canada, Canada, C.I.S.
- Staff Needs: DTS Staff, Fundraiser, Outreach Staff, Maintenance, Mechanic, Cook, Hospitality, Child Care Wrkr, SOE Director, SOE Staff, Graphic Artist, Secretary

BC, Richmond (YWAM Associates)

YWAM Associates International
PO Box 94187
Richmond, BC, V6Y 2A3
Canada

Director: Peter M. Jordan
Phone: 1-604-274-9926
Fax: 1-604-271-5000
Avg.# Staff: 5

- Ministry: Maintain relationships with former YWAMers worldwide through communication., (Need names and addresses of former YWAMers)
- Language: English
- Schools: School of Hospitality
- Outreach Locations: South Pacific, Guyana
- Staff Needs: Administrator

BC, Vancouver

Youth With A Mission

Director: Randy Parizeau

Greater Vancouver Ministries
Box 21507
1850 Commercial Drive
Vancouver, BC, V5N 4AO
Canada

Phone: 1-604-255-5262
Fax: 1-604-255-9670
Avg.# Staff: 10

- Ministry: Urban Ministry, Mercy Ministry, Discipleship, Hosting Teams
- Language: English
- Outreach Locations: Vancouver, Mexico, Vancouver Island
- Staff Needs: Administrator, Secretarial, Communications Dir., Mission Bridge Dir., Perform. Arts Staff, Urban Workers, Music Band Members, Short Term Workers, Street Evangelists

BC, Vancouver (King's Kids)

King's Kids Canada
Box 3303
Vancouver, BC, V6B 3Y3
Canada

Director: Todd Rutkowski
Phone: 604-850-5437
Fax: 604-850-9271
Avg.# Staff: 8

- Ministry: Leadership Training, Kings Kids, Frontier Missions, Family Ministry, Youth Ministry
- Language: English
- Schools: Principles in Child & Youth Ministry
- Outreach Locations: Canada, USA, Latin America, Middle East, Asia
- Staff Needs: Accountant, Computer Data Entry, Dir.:Youth Centre, Evang.:Child/Youth, Fund-Raiser, Graphic Designer, Pastoral Worker, Public Relations, Researcher, Secretary, PCYM School Staff, Writer:Publications

BC, Victoria

Youth With A Mission - Victoria
Commonwealth Games 1994 Outreach
PO Box 922
Winfield, BC, V0H 2CO
Canada

Director: Graham Jackson
Phone: 1-604-766-3838
Fax: 1-604-766-2387

- Ministry: 1994 Commonwealth Games outreach coordinating office.
- Language: English
- Outreach Locations: Common. Games

Nova Scotia, Granville Ferry

Youth With A Mission
Box 9
Granville Ferry
Annapolis Co., Novia Scotia, B0S 1K0
Canada

Director: Cameron Albright
Phone: 1-902-532-5554

Ontario, Cambridge

YWAM Academy of Performing Arts
Po Box 1150
Cambridge, Ontario, N1R 6C9
Canada

Contact: Rob/MaryAnn Parker
Phone: 1-519-622-0545
Fax: 1-519-622-2008
Avg.# Staff: 80

- Ministry: Training, Creative Arts
- Language: English
- Schools: DTS, AIM, CDTS, Performing Arts, Focus Nine Sixteen
- Outreach Locations: Central America, South America, Europe

- Staff Needs: Computer Programmer, Cook, Kitchen Wrkr, Groundskeeper, Librarian, DTS Staff, Seamstress, Accounting Clerk, Secretary/Recept.

Ontario, Toronto

Youth With A Mission - Toronto
280 Sheppard Ave, Suite 208
North York, Ontario, M2N 3B1
Canada

Director: Soon Ho Kim
Phone: 1-416-221-8109
Fax: 1-416-221-9863
Avg.# Staff: 27

- Ministry: Urban Ministry
- Language: Korean, English
- Schools: DTS
- Outreach Locations: C.I.S., Asia, Egypt/Turkey, Tanzania, N.A. Cities, N.A. Indians
- Staff Needs: Administrator, Training Staff, Building Management, Kings Kids (Male), Musician, Carpenter, Receptionist, Evangelist

Quebec, Dunham

Jeunesse En Mission
165 College
Box 280
Dunham, Quebec, JOE 1MO
Canada

Director: Rene Laframboise
Phone: 1-514-295-2744
Fax: 1-514-295-2555 :
BA Dunham
Avg.# Staff: 19

- Ministry: Family Ministry, Counseling
- Language: French
- Schools: DTS, Counseling Training School
- Outreach Locations: Quebec
- Staff Needs: Administrator, DTS Leader (bi), DTS Staff (bi), Counselors (French), Preschool Teacher, Accountant, Evangelists

Quebec, Montreal

Youth With A Mission
C.P. 2194
Succ. Delorimier
Montreal, Quebec, H2H 2R8
Canada

Director: Pierre LeBel
Phone: 1-514-847-0497
Avg.# Staff: 6

- Ministry: AIDS Victims, Street Kids, Campus Evangelism, Homosexual Ministry, Urban Ministry
- Language: French, English
- Outreach Locations: Montreal
- Staff Needs: Secretary, Street Wrker/Evang., Administrator, Campus Workers, Social Worker, Pastor

CENTRAL AMERICA

(Regional Office:USA)

Central America, Mexico, Caribbean
Regional Office
(See USA Florida)

CHILE

Santiago

Juventud Con Una Mision
National & South Hispanic Area Office

Director: Patricio Ibarra
Contact: Ricardo A. Rodriguez

Casilla 10161
Santiago 1
Chile

(S. Hispanic)
National: Ricardo Rodriguez (Chile)
Phone: 56-2-577-9922
Avg.# Staff: 50

- Ministry: Training, Church Planting, Prison Ministry
- Language: Spanish
- Schools: DTS, SBS, SOW, Foundations in Performing Arts
- Outreach Locations: Chile
- Staff Needs: Administrator (bi), Accountant, Bookkeeper, Gardener, Cook

Calbuco

Juventud Con Una Mision
Casilla 67
Calbuco
Chile

Director: Raul Llancabure

Castro

Juventud Con Una Mision
Clasificador #2
Castro
Chile

Director: Ana Maria Garrido Vidal

Puerto Montt

Juventud Con Una Mision
Casilla 760
Puerto Montt, Chile

Phone: 56-65-255215

Punta Arenas

Juventud Con Una Mision
Casilla 1113
Punta Arenas
Chile

Director: Sergio Canales Parra
Phone: 56-61-222786

Temuco

Juventud Con Una Mision
Casilla 1031
Temuco
Chile

Director: Fernando Ossandon
Phone: 56-45-242329

COLOMBIA

Bucaramanga

Juventud Con Una Mision, Bucaramanga
National & North Hispanic Area Office
Apartado Aereo 1624
Bucaramanga
Colombia

Contact: Ricardo Rodriguez (N. Hispanic)
National: Ricardo Ignacio Rodriguez
Phone: 57-76-36-54-85
Fax: 57-76-36-54-85
Avg.# Staff: 12

- Ministry: Frontier Missions, Training, Church Planting, Church Ministries, Youth Ministry, Children's Ministry
- Language: Spanish
- Schools: DTS, SOFM, SBS
- Outreach Locations: Colombian Coast, Peru, Lima, Colombia, Tribes, Ecuador
- Staff Needs: Secretary (bi), Kings Kids Leader, Coord. Church Ministry, Administrator, DTS Director

Bogota

Juventud Con Una Mision
Proyecto Restauracion
A.A. 54141
Bogota 2
Colombia

Director: Miss Venetia Rumbold
Phone: 57-1-255-2536
Fax: 57-1-235-4036
Avg.# Staff: 12

- Ministry: Relief, Community Development, Mercy Ministry
- Language: Spanish, English
- Schools: Kings Kids Health Team
- Outreach Locations: Amazonas Brazil, Bogota, Colombia
- Staff Needs: Accountant, Nurses, Secretaries, Administrators, Receptionist, Carpenter, Clerk/Typist, Hospitality, Housekeeper, Bookkeeper, Researcher/Stat., Doctor

Bogota

Youth With A Mission
Light to the Nations Christian School
A.A. 91558
Santa Fe De Bogota, 8
Colombia

Director: Fernando Hernandez
Phone: 57-1-2-63-29-67
Fax: 57-1-2-50-73-66
Avg.# Staff: 21

- Ministry: Training:Teacher, Kings Kids, Music, Education, Creative Arts, Seminars

- Language: Spanish, English
- Schools: Teacher Training, KK
- Outreach Locations: Peru, Bolivia, Colombia, Brazil, Equador
- Staff Needs: Secretary:School, Administrator, Maintenance, Art Teacher, Math Teacher, English Teacher, Science Teacher, Music Teacher, Computer/Graphics, Physical Ed. Teacher

Bogota

Juventud Con Una Mision
(Bogota DTS)
A.A. 54595
Bogota 2
Colombia

Director: Edilberto Alzate (DTS)
Phone: 57-1-255-2536
Fax: 57-1-235-4036
Avg.# Staff: 9

- Ministry: DTS, training for ministry in Bogota/Latin America.
- Language: Spanish
- Schools: DTS, DTS Phase II
- Outreach Locations: Colombia, South America
- Staff Needs: Administrator, Secretary, DTS Staff, DTS Phase II Staff, Secretary (bi)

Bogota (Street Children)

Juventud Con Una Mision
(Street Children's Ministry)
Apartado Aereo 54141
Bogota 8
Colombia

Director: Steve Bartel
Phone: 57-1-269-8960
Fax: 57-1-285-1725

Cartagena

Juventud Con Una Mision
A.A. 3526
Cartagena, Bolivar
Colombia

Director: Markus Buser
Phone: 57-53-605-748
Fax: 57-53-601-207
Avg.# Staff: 9

- Ministry: Training, Evangelism, Mercy Ministry
- Language: Spanish, English
- Schools: DTS
- Outreach Locations: Colombian Coast, Cuba, Central America, Caribbean
- Staff Needs: DTS Staff, Musician, Translator, Mercy Ministry Wrkr

COOK ISLANDS

Rarotonga

Youth With A Mission
National Office:Cook Islands
PO Box 436
Rarotonga
Cook Islands

National: Pafelio Momoisea
Phone: 682-21185
Fax: 682-24780 Attn:YWAM
Avg.# Staff: 10

- Ministry: Training, Evangelism, Kings Kids, Prison Ministry, Evangelism:Islands
- Language: English
- Schools: DTS
- Outreach Locations: Canada, Samoa, Niue, Tahiti, Australia, New Zealand

- Staff Needs: DTS Staff, Mobile Evangelism, Prison, Bible-In-Schools, Kings Kids Staff, Coffee Bar

CROATIA

Zagreb

Youth With A Mission
c/o YWAM Bishop, CA
Rt 1, Box A-3
Bishop, CA, 93514
USA

Director: Lisa Bell
Phone: 1-619-872-4387 (USA)
Fax: 1-619-872-3271 (USA)
Avg.# Staff: 3

- Ministry: Training, Hosting Teams, Mercy Ministry, Relief
- Language: English, German

CYPRUS

Nicosia

Youth With A Mission
PO Box 5662
Nicosia
Cyprus

Phone: 357-2-347-515
Fax: 357-2-473-138

Nicosia (Wee Care)

Youth With A Mission
(Wee Care)
PO Box 5662
Nicosia
Cyprus

Director: Rawya Boctor

CZECH REPUBLIC

Plzen

Mladez S Misii (YWAM)
Taborska 18
Plzen, 301 45
Czech Republic

Director: Pat Foye
Phone: 42-19-484-45
Fax: 42-19-222-168
Avg.# Staff: 2

- Ministry: Music, Mobilization, Worship/Prayer
- Language: English, Czech
- Staff Needs: Musicians

Prague

Youth With A Mission - Prague
Post Box 32
Praha 54, 150 04
Czech Republic

Director: Joan E. Herwig
Avg.# Staff: 6

- Ministry: Pioneering, Training, Discipleship, Worship/Prayer, Mobilization
- Language: Czech, English
- Staff Needs: Secretarial, Pioneers, School Leaders, Outreach Leaders, Pastoral Gifts

DENMARK

Morke

Ungdom Med Opgave
National Office:Denmark
Randersvej 195

Director: Torben Vestergaard
National: Per Eivind Stig
Phone: 45-86-97-40-55

8544 Morke
Denmark

Fax: 45-86-97-43-85
Avg.# Staff: 30

- Ministry: Training, Evangelism, Youth Ministry
- Language: English, Danish
- Schools: DTS, CDTS
- Outreach Locations: Turkey, Yugoslavia, Bulgaria, Tibet, Albania, Russia
- Staff Needs: Secretarial, Caretakers, Childcare Wrkr, CDTS Staff, DTS Staff, CDTS Director, Graphic Designer, Researcher, Evangelism:Mobile, Youth Workers, Intercession, Bus Drivers

Copenhagen

Ungdom Med Opgave
Knabrostraede 26
1210 Kobenhavn K.
Denmark

Director: Henrik Madsen
Phone: 45-33-12-23-07
Fax: 45-33-12-00-94
Avg.# Staff: 15

- Ministry: Evangelism, Worship/Prayer, Urban Ministry
- Language: Danish, English
- Schools: Principles in Child & Youth Ministry
- Outreach Locations: Balkan, Albania, E. Europe
- Staff Needs: Evangelism:Urban, Church Planting, Intercessors

DJIBOUTI

Djibouti
c/o YWAM Eastern Africa
PO Box 76046
Nairobi, Kenya

Director: Arne Peterson
Phone: 254-2-71-42-46
Fax: 254-2-71-42-45
Avg.# Staff: 3

PLAIN ENVELOPE !!!
- Ministry: Relief, Community Development
- Language: French, English
- Staff Needs: Administrator, Project Director, Team Leader, Nurse, Intercessor, Housekeeper, Bookkeeper/Account, Health Worker, TESOL Teachers

DOMINICAN REPUBLIC

Santo Domingo

YWAM Dominican Republic
National Office:Dominican Republic
Lynx Air - SD/DR
PO Box 5600
Ft. Lauderdale, FL, 33340
USA

Director: Kent Norell
Phone: 1-809-530-2884
Fax: 1-809-531-8754
Avg.# Staff: 21

- Ministry: Church Planting, Short Term, Prison Ministry, Mobilization, Unreached Peoples
- Language: Spanish
- Schools: DTS, KK
- Outreach Locations: Dominican Rep., Cuba, Spain/N.Africa
- Staff Needs: Receptionist, Coord. Hospitality, Secretary, Kitchen Manager, Kings Kids Leader, Mechanic, Church Planters, Accountant, Bible Teachers, DTS Staff, Child Care Worker, Children's Ministry

ECUADOR

Juventud Con Una Mision
Casilla 09-04-219
Guayaquil
Ecuador

Director: David Medina
Phone: 59-34-526-682
Fax: 59-34-526-682

EGYPT

Cairo

Middle East Services Office
Mounir Boctor
13 Highfield Oval, Ambrose Lane
Harpenden, Herts, AL5 4BX
England, U.K.

Director: Mounir Boctor
Phone: 44-582-765-481
Fax: 44-582-768-048
Avg.# Staff: 4

- Ministry: Communication on behalf of Middle East/North Africa region., Coordination of resources for Middle East/North Africa.
- Language: English, Arabic
- Schools: Arabic/English DTS
- Outreach Locations: Cyprus, Lebanon, Egypt, Jordan, Spain
- Staff Needs: Secretarial (U.K.), Preschool Teach (Egy), Secretarial (Egypt), DTS Staff (Egypt)

EQUATORIAL GUINEA

Youth With A Mission
National Office: Equatorial Guinea
Apartado 115
Bata
Equatorial Guinea

Contact: Ceferino Quilapan
Fax: 240-8-2131 c/o Jucum
Avg.# Staff: 9

- Ministry: Mercy Ministry, Church Planting
- Language: Spanish
- Staff Needs: Secretary (bi), Preschool Teacher, Primary Sch. Teacher, Doctor, Nurse, Construction:Housing, Water Resource Eng., Farm Technician, Church Planter

ESTONIA

Tallinn

Noored Missiooniga
Valgevase 3-3 EE0004
Tallinn
Estonia

Director: Peter Vosu
Phone: 372-2-448-212
Fax: 372-2-451-530

ETHIOPIA

Ethiopia
c/o Bernd Frost
Schlossgasse 1
D-8931 Hurlach
Germany

Director: Bernd Frost
Phone: 49-8248-12239
Fax: 49-8248-12241

PLAIN ENVELOPE !!!

- Ministry: Training, Mercy Ministry
- Language: English, Amharic
- Outreach Locations: Addis Ababa, Asmara,
- Staff Needs: DTS Staff, Nurses, Comm. Health Wrkr, Bookkeeper/Account, TESOL Teachers, Housekeeper, Cooks, Team Leader

FIJI

(Administration)

Youth With A Mission
(Administration)
PO Box 9542
Nadi Airport
Fiji

Director: Beryle Wilson
Phone: 679-71035
Fax: 679-780166 Attn:YWAM

(DTS Location)

Youth With A Mission
(DTS Location)
PO Box 9542
Nadi Airport
Fiji

Director: Beryle Wilson
Phone: 679-71035
Fax: 679-780166 Attn:YWAM

(Maranatuna)

Youth With A Mission
(Maranatuna)
PO Box 9542
Nadi Airport
Fiji

Director: Ulu Delailomaloma

(Preschool)

Youth With A Mission
(Preschool)
PO Box 9542

Director: Miriama Koroi

Nadi Airport
Fiji

FINLAND

Kirkkonummi

Lahetysnuoret R.Y.
(Helsinki Christian School)
Bronrinne 1 as 10
Kirkkonummi, 02400
Finland

Director: Seppo Saari
Phone: 358-0-296-28-26
Fax: 358-0-296-28-26

- Ministry: Education
- Language: Finnish, English

Siuntio

Karismakoti
02580
Siuntio
Finland

Director: Jan Nyberg
Phone: 358-0-263-644
Avg.# Staff: 6

- Ministry: Rehab:Drug/Alcohol
- Language: Finish

FRANCE

Paris

Jeunesse En Mission
National Office:France
92, rue Rebeval
Paris, 75019
France

National: Robert Cau
Phone: 33-1-42-02-09-57
Fax: 33-1-42-06-79-21
Avg.# Staff: 30

- Ministry: Evangelism
- Language: French
- Outreach Locations: Marseille, Algeria
- Staff Needs: Urban Evang., Secretarial, Bookstore Mgr., Bookstore Clerks, Administrator, Accountant, Editor:Public.

Chateaux

Jeunesse En Mission
French Ministries Office
3 Place Tour Neuve
St Paul-Trois, Chateaux, 26130
France

Director: Etienne Atger
International: Daniel Schaerer (French Min.)
Phone: 33-75-04-75-51
Fax: 33-75-04-51-30
Avg.# Staff: 25

- Ministry: Evangelism, Training
- Language: French, English
- Schools: DTS, SOFM
- Outreach Locations: France, French Africa, French Asia, Marseille
- Staff Needs: Secretary, Administrator, Accountant, Children Evang., Kings Kids Min., Gardener, Evangelism Team, DTS Staff, Church Planter, Worship Team, Logistical Wrkr

(Le Bookshop)

Jeunesse En Mission
(Le Bookshop)

Director: Gislaine Rochat
Phone: 33-1-42-02-65-68

67 rue de Belleville
75019 Paris
France

Le Gault-Soigny

Jeunesse En Mission
Maison de Blonay
Le Gault-Soigny, 51210
France

Director: Jean Pillonel
Phone: 33-26-81-61-46
Fax: 33-26-81-67-12
Avg.# Staff: 30

- Ministry: Training, Counseling, Communication
- Language: French, English
- Schools: DTS, CDTS, IBC, SBS
- Outreach Locations: Albania, France, Martinique
- Staff Needs: DTS Staff, CDTS Staff, SBS Staff, Construction Wrkr, Pastor Workers, Secretarial, Hospitality

FRENCH POLYNESIA

Jeunesse En Mission
B.P. 4538
Papeete, Tahiti,
French Polynesia

Director: Richard Betts
Phone: 689-41-94-03

GERMANY

Bispingen

YWAM North Germany
National Office:Germany
29646 Bispingen
Germany

National: Steve McPeek
Phone: 49-5194-1493
Fax: 49-5194-7033
Avg.# Staff: 32

- Ministry: Missions for the world!
- Language: English, German
- Schools: DTS, SBS, SOFM
- Outreach Locations: Albania, Siberia
- Staff Needs: DTS Staff, Communication, Maintenance, Bookkeeping, Secretary, Gardener, Cook

Altensteig

Media Plus
Postfach 1333
D-72208 Altensteig
Germany

Director: Joseph Avakian
Phone: 49-7453-4345
Fax: 49-7453-27566
Avg.# Staff: 8

- Ministry: Communication, Research, Training, Media
- Language: English, German, French
- Schools: School of Desktop Communication
- Staff Needs: Designers, Graphic Artists, Videographers, Writers,

Altensteig

Jugend Mit Einer Mission
German Speaking Nations Coordination
Postfach 1154
D-72206 Altensteig
Deutschlang (Germany)

Director: Horst Othmar Koch
Contact: Keith Warrington (German Spkg)
Phone: 49-7453-27542
Fax: 49-7453-27566
Avg.# Staff: 45

- Ministry: Media, Family Ministry, Kings Kids, Training

CANADA NORTHWEST TERRITORIES
Turner Valley, Canada
CROIX CIS RUSSIA
Dear friend,
How about joining us at our Training Centre?
Discipleship Training for '94
▪ 6-month DTS held in April & Oct.
▪ Outreach to Dominica, Caribbean
Outreach Teams for '94
▪ Northern Exposure: Canada's Northwest Territories
▪ Summer of Service: Canada/USA/Mexico
▪ Winter of Service: Mexico/Caribbean
▪ WISE Team: Croatia
For more information, please give me a call:
Tel: (403) 933-3754 or Fax: (403) 933-5080.
Allan Burney, Director
CANADA 43
YWAM
P.O. Box 730
Turner Valley,
Alberta
T0L 2A0
Canada
ONTARIO QUEBEC USA
DOMINICA GRENADA JAMAICA

- Language: German, English
- Schools: DTS, Gifts & Ministry of the Holy Spirit
- Outreach Locations: Philippines, Chile, Macedonia, Albania
- Staff Needs: School Staff, Media People, Kings Kids Staff

Buchholz

JMEM Ostdeutschland
East Germany Regional Office
Dorfstrasse 63
02894 Buckholz,
Germany

Director: Andreas Fresz
Phone: 49-171-5204-104
Avg.# Staff: 8

- Ministry: Family Ministry, Kings Kids
- Language: German, English,
- Schools: Family DTS, King's Kids

Hurlach

Jugend Mit Einer Mission
Schlossgasse 1
Hurlach, 86857
Germany

Director: Norbert Grieswald (KK Nat'l)
Phone: 49-8248-1220
Fax: 49-8248-12241
Avg.# Staff: 60

- Ministry: Young generation. Discipling nations - Albanian project.
- Language: English, German
- Schools: DTS, CDTS, SECE, KK
- Outreach Locations: Albania, Ethiopia
- Staff Needs: Cook, Hospitality, Maintenance, Secretary, CDTS Leader, Computer, Graphics, Communication, Kinder. Teacher, Prayer People

Tuebingen

Jugend Mit Einer Mission
Friedrich-Zundel-Str. 4
72074 Tuebingen,
Germany

Director: John Krabbendam
Phone: 49-7071-818-67

GHANA

Tema

Youth With A Mission
National Office:Ghana
PO Box 8138
Community 7
Tema,
Ghana

National: Faithful Biney
Phone: 233-221-6279
Fax: 233-221-6279
Avg.# Staff: 34

- Ministry: Church Planting, Evangelism, Leadership Training
- Language: English
- Schools: DTS, SBS, PHC, School of Church Planting & Leadership
- Outreach Locations: Central Ghana, Western Ghana
- Staff Needs: Typist, Printer, SBS Staff, SCPL Staff, Kings Kids Staff, Cook, Live Stock Farmer, Hospitality, Auto Mechanics

GREECE

Youth With A Mission
PO Box 11125
Thessaloniki, 541 10
Greece

Director: Sverker Weissglas
Phone: 30-392-26672
Fax: 30-392-26672
Avg.# Staff: 4

- Ministry: Evangelism, Worship/Prayer, Training
- Language: English, Greek
- Outreach Locations: Greece, Albania, Bulgaria, Former Yugoslavic
- Staff Needs: Evangelists, Coord. Intercession, Bible Teacher, Secretary (bi)

GREENLAND

Sisimiut
Box 1005
DK 3911 Sisimiut
Greenland

Director: Errol Martens
Phone: 299-14-114
Fax: 299-14-826
Avg.# Staff: 3

- Ministry: Training, Church Planting
- Language: English, Greenlandic, Danish
- Schools: DTS, Greenlandic Language Culture School
- Outreach Locations: Greenland
- Staff Needs: Cook, Director, Carpenter, Skilled Handy-Man, Secretary, Church Planters

GRENADA

Sauteurs

YWAM Grenada
National Office:Grenada
325 Glebe Street
Sauteurs, St. Patricks
Grenada, West Indies

National: David Harper
Phone: 1-809-442-1225
Fax: 1-809-442-1226
Avg.# Staff: 20

- Ministry: Training, Frontier Missions, Unreached Peoples
- Language: English
- Schools: DTS, School of Missions
- Outreach Locations: Guyana, Brazil, Haiti, Dominican Republic, Albania, West Africa
- Staff Needs: Administrator, Personnel Manager, A/V Production Mgr, SOM Director, Crisis Centre Wrkr, Teacher:Elementary, Maintenance/General, Accounting/Clerk, DTS Staff, Office Manager, Secretary, Youth Worker

GUAM

Agana

Youth With A Mission - Guam
PO Box 1245
Agana, Guam, 96910
USA

Director: Hinrich Kranzlin (Micronesia)
Phone: 1-671-646-7180
Fax: 1-671-477-2446
Avg.# Staff: 9

- Ministry: Discipleship, Training, Evangelism, Rehab:Drug/Alcohol
- Language: English
- Schools: Pacific DTS, King's Kids
- Outreach Locations: Micronesia, Indonesia, Asia
- Staff Needs: Administrator, Secretary, Cook/Food Admin., Gardener, Maintenance, Youth Wrkr:Rehab, Counselors, Social Workers, Kings Kids Staff, DTS Staff

GUATEMALA

Guatemala

Juventud Con Una Mision

Director: Edgard Chavez

Area Office:Central America & Mexico
Apdo Postal 77 "I"
CP 01907
Guatemala
Guatemala, Central America

Area: Edgard Chavez (C. Amer/Mexico)
Phone: 502-295-1023
Phone: 502-295-1024
Fax: 502-295-0862
Avg.# Staff: 20

- Ministry: Training, Mercy Ministry
- Language: Spanish
- Schools: DTS, SBS, PHC
- Outreach Locations: Guatemala, Panama, El Salvador, Honduras, Nicaragua, Costa Rica
- Staff Needs: Kings Kids Leader, DTS Leader, Coord. Short Term, Gov't Relations, Schools Staff, Secretarial (bi), Accountant, Writer (bi), Auto Mechanic, Health Care Wrkr, Hospitality Wrkr, Public Relations

GUINEA BISSAU

Jovens Com Uma Missao
National Office:Guinea Bissau
Cx Postal 326
Bissau,
Guinea Bissau, West Africa

Director: Carlos Roberto Sobreira
Fax: 245-201-465 (post office)
Avg.# Staff: 32

- Ministry: Church Planting, Children's Ministry, Education, Kings Kids
- Language: Portuguese
- Schools: DTS
- Staff Needs: Teachers, Nurses, Doctors, Secretary, Bookkeeper, Accountant, Cooks, Mechanic, Electrician, Brick Layer, DTS Staff, Teacher Trainer

GUYANA

Georgetown

Youth With A Mission
National Office:Guyana
PO Box 101050
Georgetown
Guyana

Director: Jackie Rozier
Phone: 592-2-58760
Fax: 592-2-72411

HAITI

Youth With A Mission - Haiti
National Office:Haiti
c/o LYNX Air/PAP
PO Box 407139
Ft. Lauderdale, FL, 33340
USA

Director: Terry W. Snow
Phone: 509-79-14-20
Avg.# Staff: 11

- Ministry: Training, Evangelism, Youth Ministry
- Language: English
- Schools: DTS
- Outreach Locations: Caribbean
- Staff Needs: Accountant, DTS Staff, Coord. Outreach, Mechanic

HONDURAS

Juventud Con Una Mision

Director: Doug Houston

Apdo 3602
Tegucigalpa, D.C.
Honduras

Phone: 504-35-2317
Fax: 504-37-9715
Avg.# Staff: 3

- Ministry: Mobilizing for missions within Honduras. Short-term outreaches.
- Language: Spanish, English
- Staff Needs: Coord. Medical Team, Coord. Outreach Team, Spanish Material, Translators

HONG KONG

Youth With A Mission - Hong Kong
Reg'l & Nat'l Office:East Asia/Hong Kong
10 Borrett Road
Hong Kong

National: Craig Snow
Regional: Gary Stephens (E. Asia)
Phone: 852-524-6057
Fax: 852-810-5198
Avg.# Staff: 50

- Ministry: Training, Evangelism, Preschool, Sports Ministry, Orphanage
- Language: English, Cantonese
- Schools: DTS, SBS
- Outreach Locations: China, Taiwan, Philippines, Thailand, India, Hong Kong
- Staff Needs: Preschool Teachers, Coord. Visiting Team, Admin. Children's Serv., Basketball Coach

(Chinese Ministries)

Youth With A Mission
(Chinese Ministries)

Director: Rob Penner
Phone: 852-471-1148

Box 161
San Tin
Yuen Long, N.T.
Hong Kong

Fax: 852-471-5262

(Chinese Training)

Youth With A Mission
(Chinese Training)
PO Box 161
San Tin
Yuen Long, N.T.
Hong Kong

Director: John Del-Favero
Phone: 852-471-1148
Fax: 852-471-5262

Kowloon

Youth With A Mission
PO Box 70707
Kowloon, CPO
Hong Kong

Director: Samuel Lai
Phone: 852-3852-396
Fax: 852-7822-691

HUNGARY

Budapest

YWAM Budapest
1425 Budapest Pf. 766
Hungary

Director: Hal Young
Phone: 36-1-163-2773
Fax: 36-1-163-2773
Avg.# Staff: 5

- Ministry: Evangelism, Youth Ministry, Church Planting
- Language: English, Hungarian
- Schools: DTS
- Outreach Locations: Romania, Turkey, Ukraine
- Staff Needs: Accountant/Business, Small Group Leaders, Church Planters, Musicians/Perform, Youth Band:Evang., SBS Leader, KK Pioneer Leader, Coord. Children Min., Youth Worker:Club, Office Help

ICELAND

Reykjavik

Ungt Folk Med Hlutverk
National Office:Iceland
PO Box 5244
125 Reykjavik
Iceland

National: Fridrik Schram (Mr.)
Phone: 354-1-27460
Fax: 354-7-12271
Avg.# Staff: 2

- Ministry: Administration, Seminars, Evangelism, Music, Worship/Prayer
- Language: Icelandic
- Staff Needs: Evangelism, Music, Drama

Egilsstadir

Ungt Folk Med Hlutverk
Eyjolfsstadir
701 Egilsstadir
Iceland

Director: Olaf Engsbraten (Mr.)
Phone: 354-7-12171
Fax: 354-7-12271
Avg.# Staff: 4

- Ministry: Training, Family Ministry, Youth Ministry, Seminars
- Language: Icelandic
- Outreach Locations: Iceland Towns

- Staff Needs: Maintenance Wrkr, Construction, Food Service Staff

INDIA

Madras

Youth With A Mission
National Office:India
PO Box 1301
St. Thomas Mount, Madras
Tamil Nadu, 600 016
India

National: Tim Svoboda
Phone: 91-44-234-5474
Fax: 91-44-568-990
Avg.# Staff: 10

- Ministry: Administration
- Staff Needs: Coord. Nat'l Training, Coord. Nat'l Personnel, Coord. Nat'l Pastoral, Secretary, Office Manager, Graphic Artist, Journalist, Photographer, Human Resource Dev.

Bangalore

Dan Eastep
No. 16 Ashwini Nivas
Kammanaltalli
Bangalore, Karnataka, 560 084
India
PLAIN ENVELOPE !!!

Director: Dan Eastep
Phone: 91-80-578-571
Fax: 91-80-578-571
Avg.# Staff: 35

- Ministry: Unreached Peoples
- Language: English, Kannada
- Schools: DTS, SOE
- Outreach Locations: North Kerala, Karnataka, Kashmir
- Staff Needs: Evangelists, Secretarial, Accountant, Church Planters, Nurses, Orphanage Wrkr

Bhopal

Winston D'Sylva
M-31 Apsara Complex
Indrapuri East
Bhopal 462 022, M.P.
India
PLAIN ENVELOPE !!!

Director: Winston Lloyd D'Sylva
Phone: 91-755-586-454
Phone: 91-755-588-260
Fax: 91-755-510-806
Avg.# Staff: 14

- Ministry: Church Planting
- Language: Hindi, English
- Schools: DTS
- Outreach Locations: Indore, Jhansi, Jabalpur, Ujjain, Sagar, Bhilwara
- Staff Needs: Accountant, Coord. Ministry, Coord. Training, Secretarial, Hospitality, Maintenance Mgr, English Tutor, Governess, Pastoral Care, Ministry Leaders, Coord. Mercy Min, DTS Staff

Bombay

Reinhard Meyer
PO Box 16726
Khar (West) Bombay, 400 052
India
PLAIN ENVELOPE !!!

Contact: Reinhard Meyer
Phone: 91-22-542-242
Fax: 91-22-542-242
Avg.# Staff: 15

- Ministry: Church Planting
- Language: English

- Staff Needs: SOFM Graduates, Mercy Ministry Wrkr, Long-Term Staff

Calcutta

Youth With A Mission
13/1 MG Road
Karunamoyee Market
Tollygange, Calcutta, West Bengal, 700 041
India

Director: Michael Bordon
Phone: 91-33-244-9833
Fax: 91-33-249-7455 Attn:YWAM
Avg.# Staff: 22

- Ministry: Training, Evangelism
- Language: English, Bengali
- Schools: DTS
- Outreach Locations: India
- Staff Needs: Administrator, Hospitality Director, Accountant, Typist, Kitchen

PLAIN ENVELOPE !!!

Dehradun

Cheol Man Choi
c/o David Osmand
14/A Teg Bahadur Road
Dehradun 248 001, Uttar Pradesh
India

Director: Cheol Man Choi
Phone: 91-135-84-2219

PLAIN ENVELOPE !!!

Kalimpong

Ben & Heather Rex
Co Post Master, Kalimpong
Darjeeling Dist., W.B.
India

Director: Ben Rex

PLAIN ENVELOPE !!!

Madras

Youth With A Mission
8/17 GST Road
PO Box 1301
St. Thomas Mount, Madras
Tamil Nadu, 600 016
India

Director: Diane Ressler (Mrs.)
Phone: 91-44-234-4716
Fax: 91-44-568-990 Attn:YWAM
Avg.# Staff: 50

- Ministry: Training, Evangelism
- Language: English, Tamil
- Schools: DTS
- Outreach Locations: South India, India
- Staff Needs: Secretarial, Graphics, Medical Workers, ACE School Staff, Men's Evang. Team, DTS Staff, Maintenance

Manali

Samuel Hoffman
Lady Willingdon Hospital
Manali Dist. Kulu
Himachal Pradesh, 175 131 India

Director: Samuel Hoffman

PLAIN ENVELOPE !!!

New Delhi

Youth With A Mission

Director: David/Wendy Radford

M3 Lajpat Nagar III, 2nd Floor
PO Box 3643
New Delhi, 110024
India

Fax: 91-11-312-515 Attn:YWAM
Avg.# Staff: 8

- Ministry: Training
- Language: English
- Schools: DTS, PCYM, KK
- Outreach Locations: North India, Pune, Madras
- Staff Needs: DTS Leader, DTS Staff, Coord. Pastoral, Accountant, Secretary, Administrator, School Registrar, Coord. Min/Outreach, PCYM & KK Staff

Pratapdighi

Jayanta Kumar Maity
PO Pratapdighi
Midnapore, West Bengal, 721440
India

Director: Jayanta Maity

PLAIN ENVELOPE !!!

Pune

Pune Multiple Training/Ministry Centre
Reg'l Office:South Asia
104 Salisbury Park
GPO Box 127
Pune, Maharashtra, 411 001
India

Director: Elisabeth Cochrane
Regional: Steve/Elisabeth Cochrane (S. Asia)
Phone: 91-212-659-601
Fax: 91-212-659-601
Avg.# Staff: 70

PLAIN ENVELOPE !!!

- Ministry: Church Planting, Literacy, Evangelism, Kings Kids, Children's Ministry
- Language: English, Marathi
- Schools: DTS, IPHC, SOFM, FCD, SCPL, ACE
- Outreach Locations: Bombay, Nepal, Maharastra Village
- Staff Needs: Coord. Church Ministry, Coord. Training, Registrar, Primary School Teacher

Secunderabad

Jim Larson/Francis Kumar
PO Box 2079
Secunderabad 500 003, Andhra Pradesh
India

Director: Jim Larson/Francis Kumar
Phone: 91-842-825-112
Fax: 91-842-844-553

PLAIN ENVELOPE !!!

Shimla

Himalaya Social Service
(A Ministry of YWAM India)
Below B.C.S. Bypass Road
New Shimla
Hamachal Pradesh, 171 009
India

Director: Elisha Tan
Phone: fax: Attn: H.S.S. Elisha Tan
Fax: 91-177-204026
Avg.# Staff: 8

PLAIN ENVELOPE !!!

- Ministry: Church Planting, Children's Ministry, Literacy, Evangelism, Medical Ministry
- Language: Hindi, English

MAUI
On the cutting edge...
HAWAII
Discipleship Training School
School of Evangelism
Summer of Missions
King's Kids
Mission Builders
Missions to Mormons
Surfers for Missions
Youth With A Mission
P.O.Box 237, Paia-Maui,
Hawaii 96779-0237 USA
Ph.(808) 579-8402
Fax (808) 579-8405
WE WELCOME YOU AS GUESTS ON OUR BASE.
For a taste of missions, try our Mission Builders
program for a week to 12 weeks.

- Staff Needs: Health Care Workers, Full-Time Doctor, Kindergarten Wrkr, Secretarial/Computer, Church Planters, Maintenance Wrkr, Graphic Artist, Worship Leader, Support Leader/Base, Family:Staff, Older Couple:Staff, Driver

Varanasi

David Krishnan
PO Box 2126
Varanasi Cantt. H.P.O.
Varanasi, Uttar Pradesh, 221002
India

Director: David Krishnan
Fax: 91-542-320692
Avg.# Staff: 16

PLAIN ENVELOPE !!!

- Ministry: Church Planting, Mercy Ministry, Evangelism
- Language: Hindi, English
- Schools: SOFM
- Staff Needs: Church Planters:Hindi, Envagelists (bi), Accountant, Secretary, Comm. Develop (bi), Worshippers, Intercessors

INDONESIA

Jakarta

Yayasan Wahana Anak Muda
National Office:Indonesia
PO Box 415 JKSMG
Jakarta 12710 A,
Indonesia

Director: Johnny Salindeho
Phone: 62-21-769-4376

Ambon

Yayasan Wahana Anak Muda
PO Box 60
Ambon 97001, Maluku
Indonesia

Director: Paul Tapilatu
Phone: 62-911-41309

Bali

Ventje Tambuwun
PO Box 132
Singaraja 80010, Bali,
Indonesia

Director: Ventje Tambuwun
Phone: 62-362-41078

PLAIN ENVELOPE !!!

Jember

Yayasan Wahana Anak Muda
PO Box 122
Jember, East Java, 68101
Indonesia

Director: Ananta Atmadja
Phone: 62-331-86904
Avg.# Staff: 3

- Ministry: Children's Ministry, Orphanage, Mercy Ministry, Evangelism, Training
- Language: Indonesian, English, Dutch
- Schools: DTS
- Staff Needs: Children's Wrkr, Cooks, Carpenter/Furniture, Maintenance Wrkr, Farmer, Gardener, Children's Teacher, Health Care Wrkr, Hospitality Wrkr, Teacher:Drama

Kuta (Bali)

Yayasan Wahana Anak Muda
PO Box 2015

Director: Joel Nababan
Phone: 62-361-51915

Kuta 80361, Bali
Indonesia

Fax: 62-361-51915

Lombok

Yayasan Wahana Anak Muda (Lombok)
PO Box 1114
Mataram, Lombok, N.T.B., 83011
Indonesia

Director: Mozes Turangan
Phone: (62-361-51915 -urgent)
Avg.# Staff: 10

- Ministry: Medical Ministry, Evangelism
- Language: Indonesian, English
- Staff Needs: Administration, Church Planter, Health Care Wrkr

Manado

Yayasan Wahana Anak Muda
PO Box 1314
Manado 95013, Sulawesi Utara
Indonesia

Director: David Halim
Phone: 62-431-51140

Pontianak

Yayasan Wahana Anak Muda
PO Box 139 PNK
Pontianak 78001, Kalimantan Barat
Indonesia

Director: Franky Tuerah
Phone: 62-561-32-757

Surabaya

Surabaya Youth With A Mission
PO Box 160 SBS
Surabaya, East-Java, 60401
Indonesia

Director: Yulianti Liemarto
Fax: 62-31-716-405
Avg.# Staff: 20

- Ministry: Training, Church Planting, Creative Arts
- Language: Indonesian
- Schools: DTS, SOFM, SBS
- Outreach Locations: Indonesia
- Staff Needs: English Secretary, English Teacher, Maintenance Wrkr, Construction Wrkr, Bookkeeper, Computer Operator, School Staff, Communications Dir., Gardener, Hospitality, Creative Ministry

Ujungpandang

Yayasan Wahana Anak Muda
PO Box 359
Ujungpandang 90001, Sulawesi Selatan
Indonesia

Director: Alberthus Immanuel
Phone: 62-751-22551

Timor, Kupan

Yayasan Wahana Anak Muda
PO Box 1003
Kupang, Timor, 85001
Indonesia

Director: John P. Fanggidae
Phone: 62-391-22186
Fax: 62-391-31001
Avg.# Staff: 18

- Ministry: Training, Church Planting, Evangelism, Campus Evangelism, Youth Ministry
- Language: Indonesian
- Schools: DTS
- Outreach Locations: Timor Province, Indon. Islands

- Staff Needs: Secretarial, Dance/Drama Teacher, Personnel Director, Communications Dir.

IRAQ

Youth With A Mission
(Iraq Contact Office/R. Tulett)
Pr. Hendrikkade 50
1012 AC Amsterdam
Netherlands

Phone: (see Netherlands)

IRELAND

Dublin

Youth With A Mission
National Office:Ireland
High Park, Grace Park Rd.
Drumcondra
Dublin 9
Ireland

National: Rob Clarke
Phone: 353-1-374-676
Fax: 353-1-367-044
Avg.# Staff: 25

- Ministry: Training, Youth Ministry, Youth Ministry, Discipleship
- Language: English,
- Schools: DTS, BLS, Foundations for Leadership, KK
- Outreach Locations: Albania, Poland, Philippines, Africa, Ireland
- Staff Needs: DTS Staff, Evangelism Teams, Secretarial, Kings Kids Staff, Pre-School Staff, Maintenance Wrkr

ISRAEL

(Coordinating Office)

Israel Coordinating Office
Jewish Ministries Office - USA
PO Box 780
Richmond, VA, 23206-0780
USA

Phone: 1-804-648-8821 (USA)
Fax: 1-804-648-6236 (USA)

Jerusalem

Window Ministries
Harm Tees
PO Box 32298
Jerusalem
Israel

Director: Harm Tees
Phone: 972-2-284-018
Fax: 972-2-271-397
Avg.# Staff: 5

PLAIN ENVELOPE !!!

- Ministry: Arab people groups. Apprenticeships in the Middle East.,
- Language: English
- Schools: SOFM

ITALY

Cadegliano (National)

Gioventu In Missione
National Office:Italy
Via Provinciale no. 31
Cadegliano (VA), 21031
Italy

National: Enos Nolli
Phone: 39-332-590209
Fax: 39-332-590154
Avg.# Staff: 20

- Ministry: Training
- Language: Italian, English, French
- Schools: DTS, SBS
- Outreach Locations: Italy, Albania
- Staff Needs: Secretary (bi), Maintenance, Kitchen

Rome

David & Colleen Mayhew
Via dei Pedagogisti 10
00135 Roma
Italy

Director: David Mayhew
Phone: 39-6-337-0739

JAMAICA

Manchester

Youth With A Mission
"Stones Hope", PO Box 7
Newport, Manchester, West Indies
Jamaica

Director: Jannel Small
Phone: 1-809-965-7346 (base)
Phone: 1-809-965-7342 (Training)
Fax: 1-809-965-7344
Avg.# Staff: 15

- Ministry: Training
- Language: English
- Schools: DTS
- Outreach Locations: Cuba
- Staff Needs: Bookkeeper, DTS Staff, DTS Director, SOM Director,

Secretarial, Outreach Director, Maintenance, Coordinator:Farm, Mission Bridge Staff, Mission Bridge Leader, Primary Teacher, Food Service

JAPAN

Takatsuki (National)

Youth With A Mission
National Office:Japan
2-15-3 Kanmaki-cho
Takatsuki-shi,, Osaka-fu, 569
Japan

National: Lawrence Nicholas
Phone: 81-726-69-0555
Fax: 81-726-69-0566
Avg.# Staff: 20

- Ministry: Training, Campus Evangelism, Coffee House
- Language: English, Japanese
- Schools: DTS, SOI
- Outreach Locations: Thailand, Japan, SE Asia
- Staff Needs: DTS Staff, Maintenance, Secretary, Accountants, Coord. Evangelism

Akashi

Sheila and Kim Sonder
Higashi-Futami 302, Futami-cho
Akashi-shi, Hyogo Ken, 674
Japan

Director: Kim Sonder
Phone: 81-78-943-4113
Phone: 81-78-943-4318
Avg.# Staff: 2

- Ministry: Church Planting
- Language: English, Japanese
- Outreach Locations: Kobe City
- Staff Needs: Co-Workers, DTS/GO Teams...

Chiba

Chiba Prefecture, Chiba City
PO Box 121
Chiba City, Wakaba, 264
Japan

Director: Tone Faialaga
Phone: 81-43-227-9588
Fax: 81-43-227-5495
Avg.# Staff: 7

- Ministry: Youth Ministry, Church Planting, Children's Ministry, Church Ministries, Women's Ministry
- Language: English
- Staff Needs: Church Planters, Secretarial, Youth Workers, Businessmen Wrkr, Housewives Wrkr, Children's Wrkr

Itabashi

Youth With A Mission
(Discipleship House Ministry)
38-5A Minami-cho
Itabashi-Ku
Tokyo 173,
Japan

Director: Kathy Newton
Phone: 81-3-5995-2693

Kobe

Youth With A Mission
5-106 Koryo-cho
Kita-Ku
Kobe-Shi 651-12,
Japan

Director: Warren Okerman
Phone: 81-78-583-3202

Maebashi

Youth With A Mission
Aoyagi-cho 436-49
Maebashi-shi
Gunma-ken 371
Japan

Director: Trevor Majoinen
Phone: 81-272-34-2237

Narita

Youth With A Mission
Crown Child Placement
Tamatsukuri 1-43-5
Narita-shi, Chiba-Ken, 286
Japan

Director: Bill Stapleton
Phone: 81-476-28-4436
Fax: 81-476-28-4437
Avg.# Staff: 8

- Ministry: Church Planting, Adoption Ministry
- Language: English, Japanese
- Staff Needs: Church Staff, Translators, Counselors, Secretarial, Desk Top Publ.

Noda

Youth With A Mission
Futatsuzuka 547-6
Noda-Shi
Chiba-Ken 278,
Japan

Director: John Somers-Harris
Phone: 81-471-38-2903
Fax: 81-471-38-3423

Okinawa City

Youth With A Mission
371 Ozato
PO Box 156
Okinawa City, Okinawa, 904-21
Japan

Director: Topi Kivimaki
Phone: 81-98-937-9027
Fax: 81-98-937-9047
Avg.# Staff: 30

- Ministry: Training, Church Ministries
- Language: Japanese, English
- Schools: DTS, SOE
- Outreach Locations: Tokyo, Japan, Taiwan, China, Micronesia
- Staff Needs: Secretarial, Word Processors, Accountant, Kitchen, Hospitality

Osaka

Osaka City Team
Awaji 3-12-18
Higashi Yodogawagu
Osaka, 533
Japan

Director: Jung Hwan Kim
Phone: 81-6-325-1614
Phone: 81-6-322-5250
Fax: 81-6-325-1614
Avg.# Staff: 11

- Ministry: Youth Ministry, Bible Study, Evangelism, Mercy Ministry, Worship/Prayer
- Language: Japanese, Korean, English
- Outreach Locations: Kuushu, Japan, Hong Kong, Philippines, China, Taiwan
- Staff Needs: Translator (Eng/Jap), Teacher (English)

Osaka

Impact Japan
(Church Construction Program)
2-2-6 Showa-cho
Tondabayashi-City, Osaka, 584
Japan

Director: Don Jackson
Phone: 81-721-24-7031
Fax: 81-721-25-0896
Avg.# Staff: 4

- Ministry: Construction
- Language: Japanese, English,
- Outreach Locations: Japan,
- Staff Needs: Long Term Supervisor,

Shinano

Youth With A Mission
#36 Kamiyama, Aza Nojiriko
Shinano-machi, Kami Minochi-gun
Nagano-ken 389-13
Japan

Director: Jon Benedict
Phone: 81-262-55-6088

Tokyo

YWAM Greater Tokyo Area
Communications Center
PO Box 149 Shinjuku-ku
Tokyo, 163
Japan

Director: John H. LaDue
Phone: 81-3-5995-2693
Fax: 81-3-5995-2684
Avg.# Staff: 20

- Ministry: Urban Ministry, Coffee House, Church Ministries, Mercy Ministry
- Language: Japanese, English
- Staff Needs: Evangelists, English Teachers

Toyoshina

Matsumoto Church Planting Work
462 Mitake-cho Nariai Toyoshina-machi
Minamiazumi-gun
Nagano-ken, 399-82
Japan

Contact: Glynis Osborne
Phone: 81-263-72-9923
Avg.# Staff: 3

- Ministry: Church Planting, Olympic Outreach
- Language: Japanese, English
- Staff Needs: Intercession Team, Drama/Sing Team (Jul)

Yachiyo

Youth With A Mission
Oowada Shinden 59-98
Yachiyo-Shi
Chiba-Ken 276
Japan

Director: Stefan Emilsson
Phone: 81-474-50-9165
Fax: 81-474-50-9165

Yokohama

Youth With A Mission
1218 Tsurugamine-Honcho
Asahi-ku
Yokohama 241
Japan

Director: Juha Mikkonen
Phone: 81-45-951-8665
Fax: 81-45-955-5446

Tokyo, (King's Kids)

Kings Kids Japan

Director: Brent Droullard

National Coordinating KK Office
Ark Village, B1
4-41-5 Akazutsumi
Setagaya-ku, Tokyo, 156
Japan

Phone: 81-3-5300-0872
Fax: 81-3-5300-0872
Avg.# Staff: 5

- Ministry: Kings Kids, Youth Ministry, Family Ministry
- Language: English, Japanese
- Schools: KK
- Outreach Locations: Japan, China, East Asia, Far East Russia
- Staff Needs: Youth Workers, Youth Teachers, Office Manager, Writer, Curriculum, Family Ministry Wrkr

Tokyo, Kodaira

Space Needle Coffee House
1-23-20 Gakuen Nishi Machi
Kodaira-shi, Tokyo, 187
Japan

Director: Terry Giles (Mr.)
Phone: 81-423-41-0576
Fax: 81-423-41-0576
Avg.# Staff: 3

- Ministry: Community friendship evangelism.
- Language: English
- Staff Needs: English Teachers

KENYA

Nairobi

Youth With A Mission
East Africa Area Office
PO Box 76046
Nairobi
Kenya

Director: Arne Peterson
Area: Arne Peterson (East Africa)
Phone: 254-2-71-42-46
Fax: 254-2-71-42-45

- Ministry: Pioneering, Coordinating, Relief
- Outreach Locations: East Africa

Nairobi (National)

Youth With A Mission
National Office:Kenya
PO Box 59443
Nairobi
Kenya

Director: John Kisamwa
Phone: 254-2-726-258
Phone: 254-2-891-112 (Training)
Fax: 254-2-714-245

Likoni-Mombasa

Youth With A Mission
PO Box 96063
Likoni, Mombasa
Kenya

Director: Ezekiel/Debbie Charo
Phone: 254-11-451-100 (office)
Phone: 254-11-451-331 (base)
Avg.# Staff: 15

- Ministry: Training, Preschool
- Language: English, Swahili
- Schools: DTS
- Outreach Locations: Kenyan Coast, Parts of Kenya
- Staff Needs: Kitchen Staff, Administrator, Accountant, Housekeeping Mgr, Evangelists, Driver, Mechanic, Poultry Farm Mgr, Preschool Teacher, Maintenance Wrkr, DTS Staff

Mombasa

Youth With A Mission

Director: Charles Babler

fon: 305/895-4744 ◇ fax: 305/895-6573

Box 611480 Miami, FL 33261

Dear Friend,

After ten years the MIAMI Base is going strong. As an Extension School of the University of the Nations, we offer courses in Discipleship Training, Basic Leadership, Evangelism, Kings Kids, and Urban Missions. We need mechanics, secretaries, bookkeepers, childcare, hospitality, cooks, and more. Every gifting can be used in the ministry. It takes a lot of tender loving care to provide a homey atmosphere for our students. For that special time in their life when they want to lay aside everything so they can focus on the Lord, His Character, and His Call on their Life, we offer an intense 3 months of study, prayer, worship, intercession, and spartan living with likeminded people, hungry for fellowship and a change of lifestyle. Then, off to a foreign land to share the Lord and His love!

Sincerely, Walden Owen

MIAMI

FLORIDA

ORLANDO

Are you a pioneer? Then come to ORLANDO where we do more than mickey mouse around. This new base is also an Extension School of the University of the Nations, and our first class will be held in April of 1994 for older people at a CROSSROADS in their life. When you do not have anything, you need everything! So come join us as we press into the Lord for His anointing of love and mercy upon us. Regardless of your experience, you can serve the Lord in many different ways. Plus, we are recruiting musicians, dancers, artists, computer graphics, etc; to establish a touring team. If you have a ministry idea, tell us about it. We are open to new ideas, and new methods. Come join us!

Greenwich Ministries

ORLANDO

Box 621057 Orlando, FL 32862

fon: 407/273-1667 ◇ fax: 407/273-3243

(Shimba Hills)
PO Box 96600
Mombasa
Kenya

Phone: 254-11-451-110
Fax: 254-11-315-557 Attn:YWAM
Avg.# Staff: 25

- Ministry: Training, Community Development, Relief
- Language: English, Swahili
- Schools: DTS, Intro to Primary Health Care
- Outreach Locations: Local Villages, Maasai Land
- Staff Needs: Secretaries, Accountant, Asst. Farm Manager, Agriculture Wrkr, Kitchen Manager, IPHC School Staff, DTS Staff, Maintenance Person, Nurses, Pastoral Care Staff, Base Leaders

KOREA, SOUTH

Seoul (National)

YWAM Korea
National Office:Korea
Kwanak PO Box 131
Kwanak-gu
Seoul, 151-600
Korea

National: Sung-Gun Hong
Phone: 82-2-871-7351
Phone: 82-2-871-7352/3
Fax: 82-2-871-7354
Avg.# Staff: 26

- Ministry: Administration
- Language: Korean
- Staff Needs: English Teacher

Chunchon

Youth With A Mission
Goomwha-Dong, 743-1
Chunchon-Si, Kwangwon-Do
Korea, South

Director: Kwangim Lee
Phone: 82-361-52-1128
Fax: 82-361-241-5599

(Farm for the Nations)

YWAM (Farm for the Nations)
Jawoon 2 Ri, 2-Ban, Naemyun
Hongcheon-Gun, Kangwon-Do
Korea, South

Director: Sunshin Kang
Phone: 82-366-32-5613
Fax: 82-361-241-559

Kwangju

Youth With A Mission
Kwangju PO Box 84
Choong-Gu, Kwangju 530-600
Korea, South

Director: Hyungsup Jung
Phone: 82-62-527-1452
Fax: 82-62-941-1455

Mokpo

Youth With A Mission
Mokpo PO Box 117
Mokpo City, 530-600, Chullanam-Do
Korea, South

Director: Joseph Kim
Phone: 82-631-2-4072

Pusan

Youth With A Mission - Pusan
PO Box 820
Choong Gu
Pusan, 600-608
Korea

Director: Rea Won Choi
Phone: 82-51-626-1005
Phone: 82-51-626-1006
Fax: 82-51-626-9507
Avg.# Staff: 35

- Language: Korean
- Schools: DTS, CDTS, Business DTS
- Outreach Locations: Nepal, Japan, Egypt, Bangladesh, Ethiopia, Senegal
- Staff Needs: Business DTS Staff, Campus Ministry, Frontier Mission Staff

Seoul
Youth With A Mission
872-20 Bongcheon 10 Dong
Kwanak-Gu, Seoul 151-060
Korea, South

Director: Kiho Kwun
Phone: 82-2-872-8057/8
Phone: 82-872-4650 (College M)
Fax: 82-2-872-7735

Seoul
Youth With A Mission
(Praise & Worship Team of Seoul)
Bange-Dong 115-7
Songpa-Gu, Seoul 138-170
Korea, South

Director: Haesoo Chang
Phone: 82-2-417-3021

Seoul (King's Kids)
YWAM King's Kids Korea
J Building 4 Fl.
Dogok-2-Dong, 414-12
Kangnam-Gu, Seoul, 135-272, Korea, South

Director: Benedict Won
Phone: 82-2-574-1630
Phone: 82-2-573-1489
Fax: 82-2-572-1011

Seoul (Training)
Youth With A Mission
(Training Office)
Kuian-Dong, 185-35
Sosa-Gu, Buchoo-Si, 422-103
Korea, South

Director: Yongjoo Lee
Phone: 82-2-686-2649
Phone: 82-2-344-9519
Fax: 82-32-343-7890

LATVIA

Talsi
J.A.M. (YWAM Latvia)
(or c/o Slavic Ministry - Salem, OR USA)
P.K. No 172
LV-3200 Talsi,
Latvia

Phone: 371-88-28-337
Fax: 371-88-28-337
Avg.# Staff: 6

- Ministry: Training, Evangelism, Discipleship, Mercy Ministry
- Language: Latvian, English
- Schools: DTS, Mini-DTS
- Outreach Locations: Latvia, Former Soviet
- Staff Needs: DTS Director, DTS Staff, Secretarial, Kitchen/Hospitality, Maintenance/Grounds, Coord:Outreach, Translators, Bookkeepers, Construction Wrkr, Bible Teachers, Church Planters, Evangelism:Children

LESOTHO
Youth With A Mission
PO Box 183
Ketane 774
Lesotho

Director: George Sander

LIBERIA
Youth With A Mission

Director: Sue Pratt

PO Box 32298
1000 Monrovia 10
Liberia

MACAU

Jovens Com Uma Missao
PO Box 1801
Macau (via Hong Kong)

Director: Jorge Luiz Vendramini
Phone: 853-831-1443
Fax: 853-831-1443

MALAWI

Elisabeth Schassberger
PO Box 2389
Blantyre
Malawi
PLAIN ENVELOPE !!!

Director: Elisabeth Schassberger
Phone: 265-630-938

MALAYSIA

Ipoh

Seng Hock Teh
National Office:Malaysia
1, Jalan Cantik
Taman Canning
31400 Ipoh, Perak
Malaysia
PLAIN ENVELOPE !!!

Director: Seng Hock Teh
Phone: 60-5-553-236
Fax: 60-5-523-980

Penang

YWAM (M) Sdn. Bhd.
PO Box 451
10750 Penang
Malaysia
PLAIN ENVELOPE !!!

Director: Thomas Davidson
Phone: 60-4-890-22-14
Fax: 60-4-890-22-14
Avg.# Staff: 13

- Ministry: TrainingTraining, mission camps, social ministry, coordination, YWAM alumni, resources.
- Language: English, Bahasa Malaysia, Tamil
- Schools: DTS, Basic Leadership Course
- Outreach Locations: India, Philippines, Thailand, Indonesia, Malaysia
- Staff Needs: Coord. Social Min., Accountant, Secretary, DTS Staff, CDTS Prep Staff, SBS Director, SBS Staff, Coord. Kitchen, Church Ministry, Coord. Teams, Special Projects, Coord. YWAM Alumni

MALI

Jeunesse En Mission
National Office:Mali
Boite Postale 83
Kouhala
Mali

National: Jean Patrick Perrin
Phone: 223-64-00-55
Fax: 223-64-00-49 (evenings)
Avg.# Staff: 18

- Ministry: Evangelism, Training, Church Planting, Kings Kids, Medical Ministry
- Language: French, Bambara
- Schools: DTS, PCYM, IPHC
- Outreach Locations: Mali, Guinea, Senegal, Burkina Faso
- Staff Needs: Secretary, Accountant, Maintenance Worker, Car Mechanic,

Construction Wrkr, DTS Staff, Evangelism Leader, Church Planters, Nurse, School Teachers, Children Workers, Worship Leader

MEXICO

Juarez

Youth With A Mission
(El Paso USA/Juarez Mexico)
4444 Edgar Park
El Paso, TX, 79904
USA

Director: Leo Prieto
Phone: 1-915-757-33-87 (USA)
Fax: 1-915-755-57-27
Avg.# Staff: 13

- Ministry: Training:Church, Training, Short Term, Children's Home, Mercy Ministry
- Language: Spanish
- Schools: DTS, Intensive Bible School
- Outreach Locations: Mexico, USA, Cuba, Guatemala
- Staff Needs: Spanish Secretarial, Teacher (bi), Eng/Span Translator

Mexico City

Juventud Con Una Mision
Ap. Post. 71
Camp. GPNA 57120
Edo. de Mexico
Mexico

Director: Sergio Jimenez
Phone: 52-5-780-8503
Fax: 52-5-577-11-06
Avg.# Staff: 6

PLAIN ENVELOPE !!!

- Ministry: Urban Ministry
- Language: Spanish, English
- Schools: DTS, KK
- Outreach Locations: Brasil, Mexico, Central America
- Staff Needs: Cook, Secretarial, DTS Staff, Kings Kids Staff, Drama Teacher

Oaxaca

Juventud Con Una Mision
Apdo Postal 1352
Oaxaca, Oaxaca, 68000
Mexico

Director: Mark Fadely
Phone: 52-951-57-927
Fax: 52-951-57-927
Avg.# Staff: 6

- Ministry: Reaching unreached ethnic groups in Oaxaca and the world.
- Language: Spanish
- Schools: DTS, SOFM
- Outreach Locations: Oaxaca
- Staff Needs: Church Planters, DTS Staff, SOFM Staff, Librarian, Prayer Coordinator, Translator, Print Shop Mgr, Pressman, Elementary Teacher, High School Teacher, Computer

(Rancho Los Amigos)

Juventud Con Una Mision
(Rancho Los Amigos)
c/o 4406 Edgar Park
El Paso, TX, 79904
USA

Director: Arvid Avery
Phone: 1-915-757-3387 (USA)

Tijuana

Youth With A Mission

Director: Sean Lambert

(San Diego USA/Tijuana Mexico)
PO Box 8873
Chula Vista, CA, 91912
USA

Phone: 52-66-30-18-69
Fax: 52-66-30-18-69
Avg.# Staff: 18

- Ministry: Medical Ministry, Construction, Short Term, Training
- Language: Spanish, English
- Schools: DTS
- Outreach Locations: Tijuana, Hermosillo, Baja, Mexico
- Staff Needs: Secretarial, DTS Staff, Medical Personnel, Administration, Accounting, Auto Repair, Evangelism, Kitchen, Hospitality, Creative Arts

Jalisco, Guadalajara

Juventud Con Una Mision - Guadalajara
Apartado Postal #1-1314
Guadalajara, Jalisco, 44100
Mexico

Director: Jose Curiel
Phone: 1-305-895-4744 (USA)
Fax: 1-305-895-6573 US
Avg.# Staff: 2

- Ministry: Evangelism, Hosting Teams
- Language: Spanish
- Schools: DTS
- Outreach Locations: Mexico
- Staff Needs: Secretarial, Training, Evangelism, Drama

Nayarit, Tepic

Juventud Con Una Mision
Apdo 39-A

Director: Bruce Stefanik
Phone: 52-321-43283

Tepic, Nayarit, 63085
Mexico

Phone: 52-321-39145
Fax: 52-321-43283
Avg.# Staff: 10

- Ministry: Training, Medical Ministry, Mercy Ministry, Evangelism, Indigenous Groups
- Language: Spanish, English
- Schools: DTS, KK
- Outreach Locations: Mexico, Central America, Muslim World, South America, Russia
- Staff Needs: Bookkeeper, Financial Administrator, Secretarial, DTS Leader, DTS Staff, Communications Dir., Kings Kids Staff, Construction Supervisor

Sinaloa, Mazatlan

YWAM Mazatlan Mexico
PO Box 562
Mazatlan, Sinaloa, 82000
Mexico

Director: Tom Hackett
Phone: 52-69-853166
Fax: 52-69-850767
Avg.# Staff: 18

- Ministry: Short Term, Surfers, Medical Ministry, Construction, Church Planting
- Language: Spanish, English
- Schools: DTS
- Outreach Locations: Mexico tour, Central America
- Staff Needs: Surfers, Church Planters, Kings Kids Staff

MICRONESIA

Yap

Youth With A Mission - Yap
PO Box 727
Colonia, Yap-State, 96943
Federated States of Micronesia

Director: Annet Geerlof
Phone: 691-350-3719
Avg.# Staff: 1

- Ministry: Church Planting
- Language: English,
- Staff Needs: Church Planters

MONGOLIA

Ulaanbaatar

YWAM - Mongolia
c/o Youth With A Mission Korea
PO Box 84
Kwang-Ju-Ciey
Kwang Ju, 501-600
South Korea

Contact: Lee Hae Sik
Phone: 82-62-527-1452
Fax: 82-62-941-1455

- Ministry: Church Planting, Hosting Teams
- Language: English, Korean
- Staff Needs: Agricultural Wrkr, Baker, Bookkeeper, Bricklayer, Carpenter, Church Planter, Engineer/Agricult., Farm Manager, Farm Worker, Farmer:Vegetable, Cook, Carpenter

MOROCCO

Morocco
c/o Safari Trips

Phone: 34-9-52-382-233
Fax: 34-9-52-382-233

Apdo. 109
Torremolinos, Malaga, E-29620
Spain

PLAIN ENVELOPE !!!

- Ministry: Tentmaking
- Outreach Locations: Morocco
- Staff Needs: Tentmakers

MOZAMBIQUE

Jovens Com Uma Missao
C.P. 1329
Beira
Mozambique

Director: Anneke Douma
Phone: 258-3-327-621

NAMIBIA

Uis

YWAM Damaraland
PO Box 43
Uis 9000
Namibia

Director: Koos Basson
Phone: 264-62262-282
Avg.# Staff: 2

- Ministry: Church Planting, Evangelism, Discipleship
- Language: English, Afrikaans, Damara
- Outreach Locations: Damaraland
- Staff Needs: Secretary, Workers (2 years)

Windhoek

YWAM Windhoek
National Office:Namibia
PO Box 11574
Win Klein Windhoek, 9000
Namibia

Director: Brian Kinghorn
Phone: 264-61-32774
Fax: 264-61-38989
Avg.# Staff: 20

- Ministry: Mobilization, Pioneering
- Language: English, Afrikaans
- Schools: DTS
- Outreach Locations: Namibia, Botswana, Angola
- Staff Needs: Cook, Bricklayer, Evangelism/Frontiers, Primary Health Care, Community Develop., Church Planting, DTS Staff, Maintenance Worker, Secretary, Mechanic, Coord. Kings Kids

NEPAL

Kathmandu

John Handcock
PO Box 1119
Kathmandu
Nepal

Director: Paul Heiligenberg
National: Dan Bushy
Phone: 977-1-525-980
Phone: ph/fax c/o P. Heiligenberg
Fax: 977-1-525-980
Avg.# Staff: 36

PLAIN ENVELOPE !!!

- Ministry: Evangelism, Training, Church Planting, Church Ministries
- Language: Nepali, English
- Schools: DTS, SOFM
- Outreach Locations: Nepal

- Staff Needs: Secretary, Bookkeeper, Coord. Foreign Teams, Worship Leaders

Pokhara

Mick & Mary Haegeland
PO Box 5
Pokhara
Nepal
PLAIN ENVELOPE !!!

Director: Mick Haegeland
Phone: 977-61-21191
Fax: 977-61-21859 M. Haegeland
Avg.# Staff: 16

- Ministry: Training
- Language: Nepali, English
- Schools: DTS, FSBS
- Outreach Locations: Nepal
- Staff Needs: School Teachers, Health Care Wrkr, Accountant, Computer Operators, English Teachers

NETHERLANDS

Amsterdam

Jeugd Met Een Opdracht
National Office:Netherlands
Prins Hendrikkade 50
1012 AC Amsterdam
Netherlands

Director: Jon Petersen
National: Warren Lancaster
Phone: 31-20-696-23-97
Fax: 31-20-620-18-23
Avg.# Staff: 135

- Ministry: Urban Ministry, Mercy Ministry, Church Planting, Relief, Community Development
- Language: Dutch, English
- Schools: DTS, IBC, SOFM, Addictive Behaviors Counseling
- Outreach Locations: Siberia, India, Israel, Balkans, Hungary, Czech Republic
- Staff Needs: Building Mgr., Financial Dir., Bookkeepers, Administrative, Secretaries, Computer Programmer, Pastoral Director, Building Maint., Evangelists, Church Planters, Educator:Urban Trng, Coord. Health Care

Heidebeek

Jeugd Met Een Opdracht (Heidebeek)
Regional Office:Europe
Mussenkampseweg 32
8181 PK Heerde
Netherlands

Director: Bill Hoopes
Regional: Jeff Fountain (Europe)
Phone: 31-5782-1534
Phone: 31-5780-16755
Fax: 31-5782-4276/5780-15399
Avg.# Staff: 80

- Ministry: Mobilization, Unreached Peoples, Training
- Language: English, Dutch
- Schools: DTS, SOFM, PCYM, Hospitality School
- Outreach Locations: India, Indonesia, Niger, Albania
- Staff Needs: Accountant, Secretarial/Admin., Maintenance/Const., Garden Workers, Children's Wrkr, Hospitality, Receptionists, Field Ministry Mgr., Evangelism/Drama, Food Service Staff, Housekeeping, Training Ministries

Amsterdam

Siloam
Weteringschans 261
Amsterdam, 1017 XJ

Director: Bert Kwakkel
Phone: 31-20-626-5493
Avg.# Staff: 9

TACKLE THE URBAN FRONTIERS!

Whatever your gift or skill is:

Evangelism

Pastor or Teacher

Relief & Development

Church Planting

Support Work—

WE NEED YOU!!

Millions of people live in the cities. And God cares for each city dweller! Come. Join us in **Amsterdam!** We'll train and prepare you to work in major cities from Europe to the Far East.

For information write: Youth With A Mission, Registrar's Office, Kadijksplein 18, 1018 AC Amsterdam, The Netherlands or Phone: 31 (20) 6279536, Fax: 31 (20) 6221451

Netherlands

- Ministry: Rehab:Drug/Alcohol
- Language: Dutch, English
- Staff Needs: Counsellor/male, Social Worker, Construction Wrkr, Maintenance Wrkr, Counsellor:Female

Amsterdam (De Poort)

Youth With A Mission
(De Poort)
Kadijksplein 18
1018 AC Amsterdam
Netherlands

Director: Pete Thompson
Phone: 31-20-627-95-36
Phone: 31-20-625-98-58
Fax: 31-20-622-1451

Amsterdam (The Cleft)

Jeugd Met Een Opdracht
(The Cleft)
O.Z. Voorburgwal 63
1012 EK Amsterdam
Netherlands

Director: Lynette Kong
Phone: 31-20-622-76-46

Arnhem

Jeugd Met Een Opdracht
Arnhem/Nijmegen
Amsterdamseweg 98
6814 GG Arnhem
Netherlands

Director: Floor Vogelaar
Phone: 31-85-45-93-09
Fax: 31-85-45-93-09
Avg.# Staff: 2

- Ministry: Working with local churches in training and evangelism.
- Language: Dutch
- Outreach Locations: Romania
- Staff Needs: Secretarial

Rotterdam

Mercy Ships Holland
Strevelsweg 700/317
3083 AS Rotterdam
Netherlands

Director: Menno Gort
Phone: 31-10-410-28-77
Fax: 31-10-410-13-80
Avg.# Staff: 9

- Ministry: Mercy ministries through Mercy Ships., Technical & administrative support.
- Language: English, Dutch
- Staff Needs: Accountant, Receptionist, Communication/P.R., Procurement Wrkr

Westervoort

Jeugd Met Een Opdracht
(Intermedia)
Mollevite 24
6931 KG Westervoort
Netherlands

Director: Theo Aerts
Phone: 31-8303-13-700
Fax: 31-8303-18-044

NEW CALEDONIA

Noumea

Jeunesse En Mission
National Office:New Caledonia
B.P. 4426

National: David King
Phone: 687-43-40-00
Fax: 687-43-40-00

Noumea
New Caledonia
Avg.# Staff: 5

- Ministry: Training, Youth Ministry, Church Ministries
- Language: French
- Schools: DTS
- Staff Needs: Construction Wrkr, Church Renewal, Kings Kids, DTS Staff, Evangelism, Administration, Secretarial

NEW ZEALAND

Auckland

Youth With A Mission
National Office:New Zealand
PO Box 13-580
Onehunga, Auckland, 1132
New Zealand

National: Frank Naea
Phone: 64-9-636-7209
Fax: 64-9-634-1817National Office
Avg.# Staff: 2

- Language: English
- Staff Needs: Secretarial, Communications

Amberley

YWAM Associates (Int'l)
(New Zealand Branch)
Beach Road
No. 1 R.D.
Amberley, North Canterbury, 8251
New Zealand

Director: Jim/Allison Wescombe
Phone: 64-3-3148-750
Fax: 64-3-3148-751
Avg.# Staff: 3

- Ministry: Ministry to former YWAMers and friends of YWAM.
- Language: English

Auckland

Early Childhood Education Centre
PO Box 33-222
Auckland
New Zealand

Director: Christine Barrow
Phone: 64-9-4895-548
Fax: 64-9-4880-453
Avg.# Staff: 10

- Ministry: Children's Ministry, Education, Training:Teacher
- Language: English
- Schools: Early Childhood Teacher Training
- Outreach Locations: Pacific
- Staff Needs: Early Child. Teacher, Secretarial

Auckland

Steiger N.Z.
31 Barry's Point Road
Takapuna, Auckland
New Zealand

Director: Ken Green
Phone: 64-9-4864-782
Fax: 64-9-6341-817
Avg.# Staff: 12

- Ministry: Evangelism:Night Club, Music
- Language: English
- Outreach Locations: New Zealand

Auckland

YWAM Family Minstries
28 Court Crescent
Panmure, Auckland
New Zealand

Director: Albert Jupe
Phone: 64-9-5272-055
Fax: 64-9-5272-055
Avg.# Staff: 15

- Ministry: Family Ministry
- Language: English
- Schools: Family DTS, Family Ministries Course
- Outreach Locations: New Zealand, Fiji, Australia, Pacific
- Staff Needs: Office Manager, Accountant, Cook, Counsellers, Mission Builders, Preschool Wrkr, Nursery Wrkr

Auckland

Polynesian Ministries
74 Kirkbride Road
Mangere, Manukau City
Auckland
New Zealand

Director: Sio Leo
Phone: 64-9-275-2435
Fax: 64-9-275-2435
Avg.# Staff: 6

- Ministry: Evangelism, Training
- Language: English, Samoan, Maori
- Schools: Cross-Cultural DTS
- Outreach Locations: Pacific Islands, India, Indonesia, Canada, Philippines
- Staff Needs: Secretarial, Evangelists, School Staff

Auckland

Heine Bay Evangelism Centre
PO Box 47229
Ponsonby, Auckland
New Zealand

Director: Craig Allan
Phone: 64-9-378-8901
Fax: 64-9-378-8907
Avg.# Staff: 7

- Ministry: Urban Ministry, Evangelism, Training

- Language: English
- Schools: DTS, Children In Need
- Outreach Locations: India, Braz/Argen/Chile, Mexico
- Staff Needs: Administrator, Coord. Hospitality, Kitchen Staff, DTS Director, Evangelists, Coordinator SOS, Maintenance Wrkr

Auckland

Island Breeze New Zealand
PO Box 13-580
Onehunga, Auckland
New Zealand

Director: John Nu'ualiitia
Phone: 64-9-262-0162
Fax: 64-9-262-0162

- Ministry: Redemption of the cultures of the nations to fulfill the Great Commission., International: reaching indigenous people of the land.
- Language: English
- Staff Needs: Secretary, Accountant, Musicians (Islands), Dancers (Polynesian)

Auckland

King's Kids New Zealand
Reg'l & Nat'l Kings Kids:S.Pacific/N.Z.
PO Box 13-301
Auckland, 1132
New Zealand

Director: Kevin Stitt
Phone: 64-9-636-9333
Fax: 64-9-636-9333
Avg.# Staff: 4

- Ministry: Kings Kids
- Language: English
- Schools: King's Kids
- Outreach Locations: New Zealand, Pacific Islands
- Staff Needs: Street Kid Evangelism, Children's Wrkr/Teach, Secretarial

Auckland (Media Plus)

Youth With A Mission
(Media Plus)
PO Box 41-120
St. Lukes
Auckland 1030,
New Zealand

Director: Patrick Dodson
Phone: 64-9-846-6205
Fax: 64-9-846-7216

Christchurch

Youth With A Mission
(SBS Base)
1 R.D. Lyttelton
Christchurch
New Zealand

Director: Alistair Donaldson
Phone: 64-3-3299-784
Fax: 64-3-3299-649
Avg.# Staff: 3

- Ministry: Training - Inductive Bible Study
- Language: English
- Schools: School of Biblical Studies
- Staff Needs: Administrator, SBS Staff Lecturers, Cook

Christchurch

Youth With A Mission - Christchurch
South Island of N.Z. Regional Office
PO Box 47
Oxford, 8253

Director: Bob Scroggins
Phone: 64-3-3124-955
Fax: 64-3-3124-955
Avg.# Staff: 12

New Zealand

- Ministry: Frontier Missions, Training, Church Planting
- Language: English
- Schools: DTS, School of Evangelism & Church Planting
- Outreach Locations: India, Russia, New Zealand
- Staff Needs: SECP Leaders, SECP Staff, DTS Staff, DTS Director, Secretarial, Builder

Dunedin

Youth With A Mission
PO Box 1048
Dunedin
New Zealand

Director: Sandy Kimpton
Phone: 64-3-477-5533
Fax: 64-3-477-5533

Hastings

Youth With A Mission
(Hawkes Bay)
PO Box 595
Hastings
New Zealand

Director: Hank Overeem
Phone: 64-6-877-4595

Tauranga

Mercy Ships - M/V Pacific Ruby
Regional Mercy Ships Office: S. Pacific
PO Box 1028
Tauranga
New Zealand

Director: David Cowie
Phone: 64-7-571-0407
Fax: 64-7-571-0411
Avg.# Staff: 40

- Ministry: Mercy Ministry, Evangelism:Islands
- Language: English
- Schools: Discipleship Training Course
- Outreach Locations: S. Pacific Islands
- Staff Needs: Marine Engineers, Deck Officers, Admin. Secretary, Receptionist, Photographer, Videographer

Te Puke

Youth With A Mission
(Whaia Te Matauranga)
PO Box 20
Te Puke 3071,
New Zealand

Director: David Moko
Phone: 64-7-573-4700
Fax: 64-7-573-4700

"Crystal Springs", Matamata

Crossroads DTS Office
111 Pill Hercock Street
Napier, Hawkes Bay, 4001
New Zealaand

Director: George Dingle
Phone: 64-7-888-5827 (Feb-May)
Phone: 64-6-843-5750 (Jun-Jan)
Fax: same as phone
Avg.# Staff: 8

- Ministry: Training
- Language: English
- Schools: Crossroads Discipleship Training School
- Outreach Locations: Philippines, Pacific Islands, New Zealand, Australia
- Staff Needs: CDTS Staff

Northland, Paparoa

YWAM Oak Ridge
(Formerly Pahi)
Wairere Road
R.D. 1
Paparoa, Northland
New Zealand

Director: Mark Parker
Phone: 64-9-4317-311
Fax: 64-9-4317-532
Avg.# Staff: 25

- Ministry: Training, Discipleship, Leadership Training
- Language: English
- Schools: DTS, BLS, Cross-Cultural DTS
- Outreach Locations: Indonesia, India, Pacific Islands, Australia, Malaysia, Olympics, etc.
- Staff Needs: Accounts Clerk, DTS Registrar, Secretary, Cook, Gardener, Maintenance, Mission Builders, Mobile Evangelism, DTS Staff, Communication/P.R.

NICARAGUA

Managua

Juventud Con Una Mision
National Office:Nicaragua
Apartado 2213
Managua 5,
Nicaragua

National: Don Johnson
Phone: 505-2-65-12-11
Avg.# Staff: 5

- Ministry: Community Development, Evangelism, Children's Ministry, Training
- Language: Spanish, English

- Schools: DTS
- Outreach Locations: Nicaragua, Central America, Arab World, Cuba, Russia
- Staff Needs: Administrative, Health Care Wrkr, Children's Wrkr, Teachers, Kings Kids Leaders, Coord. Short Term, Comm. Develop. Wrkr, Communications, Worship Leaders, Construction Leader, Office Development, P.R./Hospitality

NIGER

Jeunesse En Mission
National Office:Niger
B.P. 10469
Niamey
Niger

Director: Jeff Woodke
Phone: 227-73-35-15
Fax: 227-73-35-15
Avg.# Staff: 11

- Ministry: Church Planting, Mercy Ministry, Relief, Community Development, Pioneering
- Language: French, English
- Outreach Locations: North Niger, East Niger, Niamey
- Staff Needs: Secretarial, Church Planters, Coord. Teams, Livestock Specialist, Women's Evangelist, Evangelists, Pastor

NORTHERN MARIANAS

Saipan

Youth With A Mission - Saipan
PO Box 5230
Saipan, MP, 96950 via Guam
Northern Mariana Islands

Director: Donatina Osima
Phone: 670-322-9891
Fax: 670-322-5208
Avg.# Staff: 10

- Ministry: Preschool, Evangelism:Islands, Battered Women
- Language: English
- Schools: DTS
- Outreach Locations: Indonesia, Micronesia, Pacific Islands, South Asia
- Staff Needs: Preschool Staff, Maintenance Wrkr, Evangelists, Accountants, English Teachers

NORWAY

Hamar

Ungdom I Oppdrag
National & Nordic Lands Office
Grimerud Gard
2312 Ottestad, (Hamar)
Norway

Director: Ola Simon Osttveit
Contact: Alv J. Magnus (Nordic Lands)
Phone: 47-625-72-333
Fax: 47-625-72-972
Avg.# Staff: 60

- Ministry: Youth Ministry, Family Ministry, Communication, Publishing, Missions Service Center
- Language: Norwegian, English
- Schools: SOFM, SOE, DTS
- Outreach Locations: Turkey, Russia, The Baltic, India, Mongolia, Philippines
- Staff Needs: Kitchen, Maintenance, Pre-School Teacher, Secretarial, Kings Kids Staff, Music/Drama, SBS Leader/Staff, SBCW Leader/Staff, Computer Technician, Intercession/Worship

Halden

Ungdom I Oppdrag
(Andrew's House)
Festningsgt. 24
1750 Halden,
NORWAY

Director: Oyvind Haereid
Phone: 47-9-17-15-40

Kristiansand

Skottevig
PO Box 4692 Grim
Kristiansand, 4616
Norway

Director: Elin/Geir Fagerbakke
Phone: 47-38-15-43-18
Avg.# Staff: 12

- Ministry: Recruiting for missions in Southern Norway. Mission in Ghana, India and Mexico.
- Language: Norwegian
- Schools: DTS
- Outreach Locations: Ghana, Mexico, India
- Staff Needs: Cook, DTS Staff

Lensvik

Uio Eintroa
Lensvik, 7136
Norway

Director: Lars Stian Tveit
Phone: 47-72-49-1820
Fax: 47-72-49-1861
Avg.# Staff: 12

- Ministry: Evangelism, Worship/Prayer, Training
- Language: Norwegian, English
- Schools: DTS, School of Intercession, Worship & Spiritual Warfare
- Outreach Locations: The Baltics, Albania, Khazakstan, Russia, Bello Russia
- Staff Needs: Kitchen, DTS Staff, School Secretary, School Leader

Oteren

Ungdom I Oppdrag
(Borgen)
9046, Oteren
Norway

Director: Terje Konradsen
Phone: 47-89-14-562
Phone: 47-89-14-829
Fax: 47-89-14-886

Tonsberg

Ungdom I Oppdrag
(Matthew's House)
Nedre Langate 39
3100 Tonsberg
Norway

Director: Ragnar Aamli
Phone: 47-33-10-449
Phone: 47-33-10-695
Fax: 47-33-12-681

PAKISTAN

Von & Isabelle Heckman
PO Box 10109
Ferozepur Road
Lahore
PAKISTAN
PLAIN ENVELOPE !!!

Director: Von Heckman
Phone: 92-42-445-249
Fax: 92-42-445-249

PANAMA

Panama City

Juventud Con Una Mision
Apartado #16
Correo de Penonome
Rep. de Panama

Director: Ruth Lockhart
Phone: 507-93-35-92
Fax: 507-93-35-91
Avg.# Staff: 4

- Ministry: Chruch Planting, Mercy Ministry
- Language: Spanish
- Outreach Locations: Oajaca, Panama, El Retiro, Pan., Farallon, Pan., Panama City
- Staff Needs: Accountant, Secretary, Carpenter, Plumber, Grounds Maint., Cook, Health Care Wrkr

PAPUA NEW GUINEA

Lae

Youth With A Mission
National Office:Papua New Guinea
PO Box 1913
Lae
Papua New Guinea

National: David Tabor
Phone: 675-42-2829
Fax: 675-42-2829
Avg.# Staff: 15

- Ministry: Evangelism, Kings Kids, Medical Ministry
- Language: English
- Staff Needs: Accountant, Health Care Wrkr, Electronic Tech., English/2nd Lang., Prmy School Teacher, Secretarial, Puppeteer

Boroko

Youth With A Mission
PO Box 5635
Boroko, N.C.D., 675
Papua New Guinea

Contact: Wakanesi Toronibau (Miss)
Phone: 675-21-4970
Fax: 675-25-1277 Attn:YWAM
Avg.# Staff: 7

- Ministry: Mobilization, Children's Ministry, Kings Kids, Preschool, Youth Ministry
- Language: English, PNG Pidgin
- Schools: KK, School of Missions and Evangelism
- Outreach Locations: Papua New Guinea, Irian Jaya, Australia, Indonesia, India, Japan
- Staff Needs: S.O.M.E. Staff, S.O.M.E. Director, Kings Kids Staff, Preschool Teacher, Construction Wrkr, Personnel Director, Kings Kids Director, Secretarial, 2 Married Couples

Mt. Hagen

Kamp Kalina
Youth With A Mission
PO Box 1171
Mt. Hagen, Western Highlands
Papua New Guinea

Director: Paul Fuglestead
Phone: 675-52-1943
Fax: 675-52-1112
Avg.# Staff: 15

- Ministry: Training, Evangelism
- Language: English, PNG Pidgin
- Schools: DTS
- Outreach Locations: Irian Jaya, Australia, Solomon Island, Papua New Guinea

- Staff Needs: DTS Staff, Mechanic, Cook, Secretarial, Accounts Clerk, Registrar, Administrator, Child Care, Electrician, Carpenter, Plumber

PARAGUAY

Asuncion

Juventud Con Una Mision
Regional Communications & Kings Kids
Casilla de Correo 1961
Asuncion,
Paraguay

Director: Pablo Sanchez
Phone: 595-21-26940
Avg.# Staff: 24

- Ministry: Communication, Kings Kids, Mercy Ministry, Church Planting
- Language: Spanish
- Schools: Spanish DTS, Print Production School
- Outreach Locations: Paraguay
- Staff Needs: Secretarial, Administrator, Offset Printer, Kings Kids Wrkr, Illustrator, Church Planter, Mercy Ministry, Video Technician, Mobile Team Wrkr, Nurse, Agriculture Spec., Spanish Editor

PERU

Juventud Con Una Mision
Casilla 909
Cuzco
Peru

Director: John Alberto Campos
Phone: 51-84-224-892
Fax: 51-84-240-378

PHILIPPINES

Manila

Youth With A Mission
National Office:Philippines
PO Box 1195
Ortigas Center
Pasig, Metro Manila, 1651
Philippines

Director: Allan Balbuena
National: Larry Baldock
Phone: 63-2-631-1681
Fax: 63-2-631-7660
Avg.# Staff: 10

- Ministry: National Administration
- Language: English, Tagalog
- Staff Needs: Accountants, Secretaries, Receptionist, Computer Programmer, Writer, Personnel Manager

Antipolo

Youth With A Mission
Antipolo Training Centre
PO Box 1195
Ortigas Center
Pasig, Metro Manila, 1651
Philippines

Director: David Stevens
Phone: 63-2-631-1681
Fax: 63-2-631-7660
Avg.# Staff: 20

- Ministry: Training
- Language: Tagalog, English
- Schools: DTS, Intro to Biblical Counseling
- Outreach Locations: Philippines, Hong Kong
- Staff Needs: Kitchen Manager, Computer, Accountant, Carpenter, Electrician, Plumber, Driver, DTS Staff, Evangelist, Secretary:IBC, Public Relations

Baguio City

Youth With A Mission
PO Box 252
Baguio City, 2600
Philippines

Director: Chuck Hamm
Phone: 63-74-442-2218
Fax: 63-74-442-3638 Attn:YWAM

Balut

Youth With A Mission - Balut
C.P.O. Box 771
Metro Manila, 1099
Philippines

Director: Ruddy A. Ancheta
Phone: 63-2-200-170
Phone: 63-2-204-282
Avg.# Staff: 16

- Ministry: Mercy Ministry, Youth Ministry, Medical Ministry
- Language: English, Tagalog
- Staff Needs: Accountant, Secretary, Maintenance Wrkr, Children's Wrkr, Medical Workers

Banaue

Youth With A Mission
Banaue, 3601 Ifugao
Philippines

Director: Julius Angawa
Phone: 63-73-386-4019

Bangued

Youth With A Mission
PO Box 3
Bangued, Abra, 2800
Philippines

Director: Santi S. Tabilla
Avg.# Staff: 7

- Ministry: Church Planting, Church Ministries, Relief, Community Development
- Language: English, Ilocano
- Staff Needs: Comm. Development, Church Ministries, Evangelists, Church Planters, Health Care Staff, Communication, Bookkeeping

Batangas City

Youth With A Mission
c/o Jesus is Lord Fellowship
Kumitang Ibaba
Batangas City
Philippines

Director: Mel Hilario

Bontoc

Youth With A Mission
Bontoc, Mountain Province, 2616
Philippines

Director: Jacinto Banosan

Cebu City

YWAM Cebu Badjao Ministry
PO Box 335
Cebu City, 6000
Philippines

Director: Petrus Vercueil
Phone: 63-32-21-3486
Fax: 63-32-22-1830
Avg.# Staff: 6

- Ministry: Church Planting, Children's Ministry, Unreached Peoples
- Language: English, Cebuano
- Staff Needs: Teachers, Preschool Wrkr, Church Planters, Accountant, Bible Study Leader, Construction, Driver, Literacy Teacher, Children's Teacher

Davao City

Youth With A Mission
Mindanao Region Office
PO Box 80531
Davao City, 8000
Philippines

Director: Victor C. Roca
Contact: Graeme Jones (Mindanao)
Phone: 63-82-76348
Fax: 63-82-221-0423
Avg.# Staff: 28

- Ministry: Training, Street Kids, Kings Kids, Mercy Ministry, Discipleship
- Language: English, Cebuano, Tagalog
- Schools: DTS, School of Frontier Missions
- Outreach Locations: Indonesia, G.Santos City, Zamboanga City, Bukidnon, Cagayao De Oro
- Staff Needs: Primary Health Wrkr, Coord. Discipleship, Graphic Artist, Discipleship:Mobile, Trained Medical Wrkr, Kings Kids Staff, Base Administrator, DTS Staff, Project Manager, KK Logistical Staff, Maintenance/Mechanic, DTS Logistical Staff

Manila

New Manila
PO Box 1195
Ortigas Center
Pasig, Metro Manila
Philippines

Director: Allan Balbuena
Phone: 63-2-721-7873
Phone: 63-2-702-174
Fax: 63-2-631-7660
Avg.# Staff: 20

- Ministry: Hospitality, Hosting Teams
- Language: English, Tagalog
- Outreach Locations: Metro Manila

- Staff Needs: Cook, Driver, Hospitality Wrkr, Maintenance/Repair

Manila (King's Kids)

King's Kids Philippines
(National King's Kids Office)
PO Box 1195
Ortigas Center
1651 Pasig, Metro Manila,
Philippines

Contact: David Gunn (Nat'l KK)
Phone: 63-2-631-1682
Fax: 63-2-631-7660
Avg.# Staff: 7

- Ministry: Evangelism, Children's Ministry, Family Ministry, Kings Kids, Youth Ministry
- Language: Tagalog, English
- Outreach Locations: Europe, Asia, Philippines
- Staff Needs: Youth Workers, Children's Wrkrs, Choreographer, Administrator

Olongapo

Youth With A Mission - Olongapo
18 - 20th St. East
Bajac Bajac
Olongapo, 2200
Philippines

Director: Asmund Orjasaeter
Phone: 63-47-222-4948
Avg.# Staff: 11

- Ministry: Prostitution Recovery, AIDS Victims
- Language: English, Tagolog
- Staff Needs: Discipleship Wrkr, Evangelism Wrkr, Staff:Aids Ministry, Business Management

Palawan

Youth With A Mission - Palawan
PO Box 35
Puerto Princesa City, Palawan, 5300
Philippines

Director: Felix Dexel
Avg.# Staff: 10

- Mobile tribes team, guesthouse conference center., Vietnamese asylum seeker training. Prison colony evangelism.
- Language: English
- Schools: DTS
- Outreach Locations: Veit. Refugees, Tribal Comm., Prison Colony, Rural Churches, Poor Fishermen
- Staff Needs: Secretary, Hospitality, Bookstore Manager, Maintenance, Farm Manager

Rizal

Pastoral Care House
PO Box 249, Q-Plaza P.O.
Cainta, Rizal, 1900
Philippines

Director: Margaretha Pretorius
Phone: 63-2-631-1681
Fax: 63-2-631-7660
Avg.# Staff: 3

- Ministry: Pastoral Care:YWAM
- Language: English
- Staff Needs: Coord. Pastoral Care

Surigao City

Youth With A Mission
Ensomo Building

Director: Evangeline B. Fuentes
Phone: 63-8661-873-46

Corner Borromeo - Amat Street
Surigao City, Surigao del Norte, 8400
Philippines

Avg.# Staff: 9

- Ministry: Church Planting, Preschool, Training:Church, Hospitality, Evangelism, Children's Ministry
- Language: English, Cebuano, Tagalog
- Staff Needs: Accountant, Secretary, Youth Workers, Preschool Teacher, Church Planters, Worship Leader, Kings Kids Staff, Pastor Care Staff, Church Workers

Zamboanga

Youth With A Mission
PO Box 155
Zamboanga City, 7000
Philippines

Director: Rheo Loseo
Phone: 63-62-6381

Cebu, Talisay

Youth With A Mission
(Mobile Discipleship Ministry)
3rd Street Carmen Village
Talisay, Cebu,
Philippines

Director: Douglas G. Sharpe
Avg.# Staff: 12

- Ministry: Training, Discipleship, Evangelism, Church Planting, Worship/Prayer
- Language: English, Filipino, Visaya
- Outreach Locations: Cebu, Visayas
- Staff Needs: Evangelists, Teachers, Worship Leaders, Administrator, Accountant, Campus Workers

POLAND

Krakow

Youth With A Mission
National Office:Poland
Skr. Poczt 35
30-093 Krakow 23
Poland

Director: John Hess
Phone: 48-12-21-11-53
Fax: 48-12-22-36-06 Attn:YWAM
Avg.# Staff: 12

- Ministry: Church Ministries, Training, Evangelism, Leadership Training
- Language: English, Polish
- Schools: DTS, KK
- Outreach Locations: Russia, Poland, Ukraine
- Staff Needs: Bible Study Leader, Evangelism:Church, Evangelism:Mobile, Kings Kids, Youth Ministry, Secretarial

PORTUGAL

Sintra

Jovens Com Uma Missao
National Office:Portugal
Apartado 6
2711 Sintra
Portugal

Director: Rachel Lovell
Phone: 351-1-923-5186
Fax: 351-1-924-0104
Avg.# Staff: 6

- Ministry: Kings Kids, Training, Short Term
- Language: Portuguese, English
- Schools: Kings Kids

- Outreach Locations: Spain, England, Portugal
- Staff Needs: Secretarial, Bookkeeper, Kitchen, Hospitality, Kings Kids Staff

PUERTO RICO

Juncos

Juventud Con Una Mision
PO Box 116
Juncos
Puerto Rico 00777

Director: Yarley Nino
Phone: 809-734-4788
Fax: 1-809-792-8528
Avg.# Staff: 4

- Ministry: Kings Kids, Training, Youth Ministry
- Language: Spanish
- Schools: DTS, KK
- Outreach Locations: Latin America, Dominican Rep.
- Staff Needs: DTS Director, Small Group Leaders, Secretary, Bookkeeper, Chef/Cook, Computer Programmer, Computer Data Entry, Construction/Builder, Handyman, Housekeeper, DTS Staff, Maintenance Workers

REUNION ISLAND

St. Pierre

Jeunesse En Mission
B.P. 241
97456 St. Pierre, Cedex
Reunion Island, France

Director: Tim Bauer
Phone: 262-26-06-87

RWANDA

Rwanda
c/o YWAM Eastern Africa
PO box 76046
Nairobi
Kenya
PLAIN ENVELOPE !!!

Director: Method Kamanzi
Phone: 254-2-71-42-46
Fax: 254-2-71-42-45

- Ministry: Training, Evangelism, Seminars, Ministry to Pastors
- Language: French, English
- Outreach Locations: Eastern Zaire, Burundi, Southern Uganda
- Staff Needs: DTS Staff, Team Leader, TESOL Teacher, Administrator, Accountant, Secretary (bi)

SAO TOME & PRINCIPE

Jovens Com Uma Missao
Cx. Postale 362
RDSTP
Sao Tome

Director: Robson Soares Oliveira
Phone: 239-12-22011
Phone: 239-12-22649

SENEGAL

Dakar-Fann

Jeunesse En Mission
National Office:Senegal
B.P. 5738
Dakar-Fann
Senegal

National: Jean-Marc Fritsch
Phone: 221-25-50-67
Fax: 221-25-50-67
Avg.# Staff: 6

- Ministry: Evangelism, Mercy Ministry, Church Planting, Training
- Language: French
- Schools: DTS
- Outreach Locations: Dakou, Senegal
- Staff Needs: Evangelist, Secretarial, Nurse, Physician, Midwife, Lab Technician, Dentist

SIERRA LEONE

Freetown

Youth With A Mission - Sierra Leone
National Office:Sierra Leone
P.M.B.978
90 Pademba Road
Freetown
Sierra Leone

Director: Moses T. Sesay
Phone: 232-22-223-809
Fax: 232-22-229-040
Avg.# Staff: 11

- Ministry: Relief, Community Development, Church Ministries
- Language: English, Creole
- Schools: Evening Discipleship Program
- Outreach Locations: Freetown Area
- Staff Needs: Health Care Wrkr, Water/Sanitation Eng., Civil Engineer, Architect, Statistician, Coord. Staff Devel.

SINGAPORE

Singapore

Youth With A Mission
National Office:Singapore
Balestier Estate
PO Box 0475
Singapore, 9132
Singapore

National: Alan Lim
Phone: 65-251-0166
Fax: 65-253-3962

- Schools: DTS, SOFM, CDTS, SBS, Principles of Small Groups

(CREATE Int'l)

CREATE International
Balestier Estate
PO Box 410
Singapore, 9132
Singapore

Contact: Calvin/Carol Conkey
Phone: 65-282-4862
Fax: 65-382-5631
Avg.# Staff: 5

- Ministry: Producing mobilization and evangelisitc audio-visuals for frontier missions., Training and internships available.
- Language: English
- Outreach Locations: Indonesia, India, China
- Staff Needs: Marketing/Distrib., Graphic/Desktop Pub., Photographer, Videographer, Studio/Field Recordist, Creative Arts/Drama, Script Writer, Multi-Media Specialist, Secretary, Computer Data Entry, Translators (Indon.), Video Producers

SOMALIA

Somalia
c/o YWAM Eastern Africa
PO Box 76046

Director: Nick Archer
Phone: 254-2-71-42-46
Fax: 254-2-71-42-45

Nairobi
Kenya
PLAIN ENVELOPE !!!

Avg.# Staff: 3

- Ministry: Relief, Community Development
- Language: English
- Staff Needs: Administrative, Nurses, Secretary, Comm. Health Wrkr, TESOL Teachers, Intercessors, Project Director, Team Leader, Housekeeper, Bookkeeper/Account

SOUTH AFRICA

Muizenberg

Youth With A Mission
National Office:South Africa
PO Box 129
Muizenberg, Cape Town, 7950
South Africa

National: Murray Kilgour
Phone: 27-21-788-7322
Fax: 27-21-788-1247
Avg.# Staff: 85

- Ministry: Training for the frontiers.
- Language: English
- Schools: DTS, SOE, CDTS, IBC, IPHC, SBS
- Outreach Locations: Namibia, Malawi, Zambia, Madagascar, Kyrgyzotan
- Staff Needs: Catering Manager, Housing Manager, Maintenance Manager, Hospitality, Graphic Designers, Writers, Evang/Drama:Mobile, Foster Home Min., Community Develop., IBC Staff, Secretarial/Computer, Outreach Team Leader

Stilfontein

Youth With A Mission
South Africa Area Office
PO Box 932
Stilfontein, 2550
South Africa

Area: Don Price (Southern Africa)
Phone: 27-18-482-1382
Fax: 27-18-482-1370
Avg.# Staff: 30

- Ministry: Discipleship training of 2/3 world missionaries combined with vocational skills.
- Language: English
- Schools: DTS, CDTS, School of Church Planting & Leadership
- Outreach Locations: South Africa, Lesotho, Mozambique, Botswana, Swaziland, 10/40 Window
- Staff Needs: Vocational Teachers, Secretarial, Hospitality/Catering, Kings Kids Staff, Maintenance, Pioneer Missionaries, Preschool Teachers, DTS/CDTS Staff, SCPL School Staff, Coord. Outreach/Evang.

Boland

Youth With A Mission - Boland
PO Box 926
Worcester, 6849
South Africa

Director: Brian Reed
Phone: 27-231-94022
Fax: 27-231-20378
Avg.# Staff: 55

- Ministry: Frontier Missions, Training, Preschool, Kings Kids
- Language: English, Afrikaans
- Schools: DTS, SOE
- Outreach Locations: Usbekistan, Mozambique, India, Indian Ocean Island, South Africa

- Staff Needs: Building Contractor, SBS Leader, Maintenance Manager, Transport Manager

Hammanskraal

Youth With A Mission
(Sunshine Preschool)
PO Box 74
Hammanskraal 0400
South Africa

Director: Peter Kinahan
Phone: 27-12012 (operator 123)

Jozini

Jeug Met N Sending
(Zulu Ivangeli)
PO Box 20
Jozini 3969
South Africa

Director: Kobus Van Niekerk
Phone: 27-35672 (ask for 30)

Kuils River

Youth With A Mission
8 Kamp Street
Mabille Park
Kuils River, 7580
South Africa

Director: Samuel Jacobsen
Phone: 27-21-903-7356

Stellenbosch

Jeug Net 'N Sending
PO Box 145
Stellenbosch, 7600
South Africa

Director: Eric Boshoff
Phone: 27-2231-74873
Fax: 27-2231-98722

SOUTH AMERICA

(Regional Office:USA)

South America
Regional Office
(See USA Florida)

SPAIN

Madrid

Juventud Con Una Mision
National Office:Spain
Apdo. 133
Torrejon de Ardoz, 28850 (Madrid)
Spain

Director: Gary McKinney
Phone: 34-1-676-4371
Fax: 34-1-675-6130

Torremolinos

Safari Trips
North Africa Area Office
Apdo. 109
Torremolinos, Malaga, E-29620
Spain

Area: Garry Tissingh (N. Africa)
Phone: 34-9-52-382-233
Fax: 34-9-52-382-233
Avg.# Staff: 6

- Ministry: Reaching peoples of North Africa
- Language: English, Spanish, French
- Schools: SOFM (North Africa Focus)
- Outreach Locations: Morocco, Algeria, Tunisia, Niger, Chad, Mauritania

- Staff Needs: Church Planter, Community Devel. Wrkr, Cook, Development Work, Evangelism:Mobile, Handy Person, Hospitality Wrkr, Market Research, Pastoral Care Work, Public Relations, Tentmaker:Various, Teachers

Barcelona

Hospitality Center
Espanya Industrial, 22, Pral
08018 Barcelona
Spain

Phone: 343-245-3467
Fax: 343-265-7821

- Ministry: Lo-cost accomodation for missionaries passing through.
- Language: Spanish, English

Barcelona

Juventud Con Una Mision
Espana Industrial 22
Principal
08014 Barcelona
Spain

Phone: 34-3-296-43-77

Las Palmas

Bryan Thompson
(Church Planting Team)
Apartado 2284
E-35007 Las Palmas, De Gran Canaria
Spain

Contact: Bryan Thompson
Phone: 34-28-46-83-64
Avg.# Staff: 2

- Ministry: Church Planting
- Language: Spanish
- Staff Needs: DTS Leader, Mobiliser:Church, Coord.-Short Term

Sevilla

Juventud Con Una Mision
Apdo. 4042
41080 Sevilla
Spain

Director: Hans Bernreuther
Phone: 34-5-442-19-04
Fax: 34-5-453-84-19

SRI LANKA

Kandy

Jung Ha Yang
43 Louis Peiris Mawatha
Kandy
Sri Lanka

PLAIN ENVELOPE !!!

Director: Jung Ha Yang
Phone: 94-9-482-5446

SUDAN

Sudan
c/o YWAM Eastern Africa
PO Box 76046
Nairobi
Kenya

PLAIN ENVELOPE !!!

Director: Arne Peterson
Phone: 254-2-71-42-46
Fax: 254-2-71-42-45
Avg.# Staff: 3

- Ministry: Relief, Community Development
- Language: English

Northwoods

- Impact World Tour
- DTS
- School of CSE
- Music Ministry
- King's Kids
- YWAM
- Mission Builders

School of Crusade-Style Evangelism (CSE)

This school will train you in innovative methods of evangelism and how to work within interdenominational and cross-cultural settings. Topics will include campaign organizational structure, mobilizing the church and business community, marketing and advertising strategies and follow-up. This course will work in conjunction with the Impact World Tour '95.

Youth With A Mission - Northwoods
2824 - 130 th St.
Frederic, Wisconsin 54837
Phone 715-327-8147
Fax 715-327-8146

Impact World Tour '95

Join Loren and Darlene Cunningham, along with King's Kids, Island Breeze, a Mobile DTS and other YWAM teams on a tour through the U.S. to challenge rural America to missions. Contact YWAM Northwoods to find out how you can be involved.

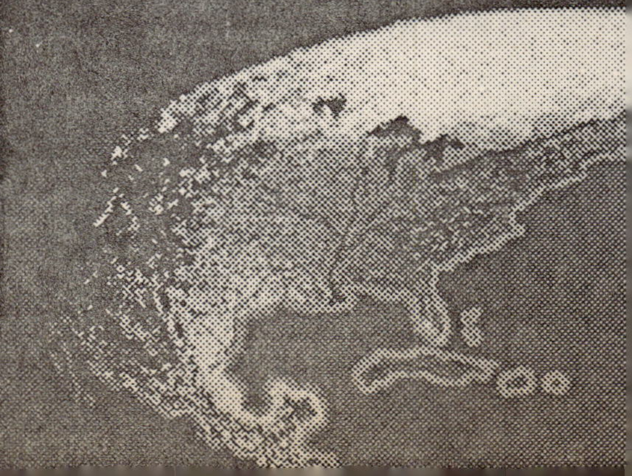

- Staff Needs: Administrator, Project Director, Team Leader, Nurses, Intercessors, Housekeeper, Bookkeeper/Account, Comm. Health Wrkr, TESOL Teacher, Water Engineer

SWEDEN

Stockholm

Ungdom Med Uppgift
National Office:Sweden
Birger Jarlsgatan 66, 3tr
11429 Stockholm
Sweden

National: Tjebbo v.d. Eykhof
Phone: 46-8-20-61-64
Fax: 46-8-20-61-77

- Ministry: National Office
- Language: English, Swedish
- Outreach Locations: Sweden, Turkey, Estonia, Li Touwen
- Staff Needs: Secretary, Communications, Translator (Eng/Swe)

Laxa

Ungdom Med Uppgift
(Mercy Ships Sweden)
Rattarstigen 18
695 32 Laxa
Sweden

Director: Bo Rudolfsson
Phone: 46-584-12200
Fax: 46-584-12211

Ljungskile

Ungdom Med Uppgift
Restenas P.L. 32200
Ljungskile, 45993
Sweden

Director: Eric Spady
Phone: 46-522-210-20
Fax: 46-522-202-45
Avg.# Staff: 37

- Ministry: Training, Short Term
- Language: English, Swedish
- Schools: DTS, CDTS, CTC, SOFM, SOMM, SBS, IBC
- Outreach Locations: Baltic States, SE Asia, India
- Staff Needs: Secretarial, Kitchen Cook, DTS Staff, School Staff, Maintenance Wrkr, Database Manager, Hospitality Leader, Hospitality Wrkr

Stockholm

Youth With A Mission - Stockholm
Birger Jarlsgatan 66, 3tr
11429 Stockholm
Sweden

Director: Tamme De Leur
Phone: 46-8-10-26-18
Fax: 46-8-20-61-77
Avg.# Staff: 5

- Ministry: Urban Ministry, Training, Evangelism
- Language: Swedish, English
- Schools: Operation Year, Community Counseling School
- Outreach Locations: Stockholm, The World
- Staff Needs: Secretaries, Accountant, Training:Secretary, Operation Yr Leader, CHC Leader/Staff, Evangelists, Intercessors, Coord.:Mission, Mercy Ministry Devel., Trng Devel. Leader, Trng Devel. Worker

Stockholm

King's Kids Sweden
Birger Jarlsgatan 66, III
11429 Stockholm
Sweden

Phone: 46-8-24-70-67
Fax: 46-8-20-61-77
Avg.# Staff: 11

- Language: Swedish, English
- Schools: King's Kids
- Outreach Locations: Sweden, Baltic States
- Staff Needs: KK Perf. Arts Leader, KK HANDS Leader, Sports Leader, Youth Counselor, Administrator

(STORM)
Ungdom Med Uppgift - STORM
(Short Term Outreach Ministries)
Restenas 32200
Ljungskile, 45993
Sweden

Director: Samuel Yeboah
Phone: 46-522-210-20
Fax: 46-522-202-45
Avg.# Staff: 17

- Ministry: Evangelism, Discipleship, Training, Short Term
- Language: English, Swedish
- Staff Needs: Urban Evangelists, Teachers, Financial Manager, Auto Mechanic, Computer/Graphics, Pastoral Care, Performing Arts, Cook

SWITZERLAND

Einigen
Jugend Mit Einer Mission
National Office:Switzerland
3646 Einigen
Switzerland

Director: Markus Steffen
National: Eliane Lack
Phone: 41-33-54-81-81
Fax: 41-33-54-82-55

Biel
Jugend Mit Einer Mission

Director: Peter Liechti

Calvinweg 15
2504 Biel
Switzerland

Phone: 41-32-41-09-70
Fax: 41-32-41-09-20
Avg.# Staff: 14

- Ministry: Training
- Language: German, English
- Schools: Basic Leadership Training, DTS
- Outreach Locations: Albania, Philippines, Switzerland, Germany, South America
- Staff Needs: Kitchen Staff, Maintenance, Receptionist, DTS Staff, DTS Leaders, Hospitality

Biel

Jugend Mit Einer Mission
German Speaking Switz. & KK Europe
Poststrasse 16
2504 Biel
Switzerland

Director: Markus Steffen
Contact: Walter Durr (Swiss-German)
Phone: 41-32-41-09-60
Fax: 41-32-41-09-20
Avg.# Staff: 35

- Ministry: Kings Kids, Creative Arts, Communication, Publishing
- Language: German, English
- Schools: King's Kids
- Outreach Locations: Albania, South America
- Staff Needs: Receptionist, Administrator, Bookkeeper, Professional Dancer, Worship Team Leader, Kings Kids Staff, Graphics

Burtigny (U of N)

Jeunesse En Mission
(U of N Regional Academic Affairs)
La Maison
1261 Burtigny
Switzerland

Director: Mark Stettler
Contact: Tom Bloomer (Reg'l Acad. Affairs)
Phone: 41-22-366-3915
Fax: 41-22-366-41-16

Chatel

Jeunesse En Mission
Chatel
1186 Essertines, Sur Rolle,
Switzerland

Director: Bernhard Langer
Phone: 41-21-825-1244

Lausanne

Mercy Ships Europe
Rue de Geneve 77B
1004 Lausanne
Switzerland

Director: Robert Ole Berg Jr.
Phone: 41-21-624-55-33
Fax: 41-21-625-25-60

- Ministry: Communications, promotions, personnel, finances, material/resources
- Language: English, French, German
- Schools: DTS on board 3 ships: M/V Good Samaritan, M/V Pacific Ruby, M/V Anastasis
- Outreach Locations: Europe, Middle East, Africa
- Staff Needs: Graphic Artist, Administrators, Secretaries, Database Manager, Accountant, P.R. Officer, Home School Teacher, Construction Wrkr, Maintenance Wrkr, Cook/Hospitality

Lausanne
Jeunesse En Mission
Ch. en Praz-d'Eau, 1
1000 Lausanne, 25
Switzerland
Phone: 41-21-784-23-23
Fax: 41-21-784-23-20

Lausanne (MEDAIR)
MED AIR
Rue De Geneve 77B
Lausanne, CH-1004
Switzerland
Contact: Dr. Erik Volkmar
Phone: 41-21-624-55-33
Fax: 41-21-625-25-60
Avg.# Staff: 30

- Ministry: Emergency relief work in crisis situations.
- Language: English, French, German
- Outreach Locations: Uganda North, South Sudan, Iraq, Liberia, Somalia, Armenia
- Staff Needs: Project Dir/Mgr, Procurement Officer, Short Term Medical, Short Term Constr., Short Term Water/San., Short Term Logistics, Short Term Admin.

Wiler
Jugend Mit Einer Mission
(Haus Jeruel)
3226 Wiler, bei Seedorf
SWITZERLAND
Director: Christoph Leu
Phone: 41-32-82-50-51
Fax: 41-32-82-45-72
Avg.# Staff: 25

- Ministry: Training, Kings Kids, Counseling
- Language: German, English
- Schools: IBC, SBS, PCYM, SBCW, CDTS, MMBC
- Outreach Locations: Germany, Albania, Philippines, Kenya
- Staff Needs: Receptionist, Hostess, Graphic Designer, Cook, School Staff

Yverdon
Jeunesse En Mission
Departement Musique
Aveune Haldiman, 13
1400 Yverdon
Switzerland
Director: Rolf Schneider
Phone: 41-24-22-31-60
Fax: 41-24-22-31-44

TAIWAN

Taipei
Youth With A Mission
National Office:Taiwan
PO Box 73-264
Taipei, 111
Taiwan, R.O.C.
Director: Jo van Bakel
Phone: 886-2-872-1684
Fax: 886-2-875-2237
Avg.# Staff: 50

- Ministry: Training, Urban Ministry
- Language: English, Mandarin
- Schools: DTS, SBS, SOI, SOFM
- Outreach Locations: China, Hong Kong, Macau, Japan, Canada
- Staff Needs: Bookkeeper, Administrator, English Teachers, Kings Kids Staff

Miaoli
Hakka Chinese Ministries
PO Box 40
Director: Fono Fepuleai
Phone: 886-37-660-513

Toufen, Miaoli, 351
Taiwan, R.O.C.

Fax: 886-37-660-513
Avg.# Staff: 12

- Ministry: Church Planting, Evangelism
- Language: English, Mandarin
- Schools: School of Frontier Missions
- Outreach Locations: Taiwan
- Staff Needs: Church Planters, Children's Ministry, Children's Teacher

Taichung City

Taichung
PO Box 27-102
Taichung City
Taiwan, R.O.C.

Director: Mr. Myung-Kook Kim
Phone: 886-4-276-1266
Fax: 886-4-276-1266
Avg.# Staff: 7

- Ministry: Church Planting, Discipleship, Campus Evangelism
- Language: Chinese
- Schools: Mini-DTS
- Outreach Locations: China, Mongolia, Hong Kong, Taiwan, Inner Mongolia, Macau

Tainan

YWAM Tainan, Taiwan
c/o Taipei National Office
PO Box 73-264
Taipei, 111
Taiwan, R.O.C.

Director: Dick/Carolyn Ardron
Phone: 886-2-872-1684
Fax: 886-2-875-2237
Avg.# Staff: 8

- Ministry: Training, Mercy Ministry
- Language: English, Madarin
- Schools: Bi-Lingual DTS

TANZANIA

Dar-es-Salaam

YWAM Tanzania
National Office:Tanzania
PO Box 72100
Dar-es-Salaam,
Tanzania

National: Jeremiah Kiwinda
Phone: 255-51-21147 (messages)
Fax: 255-51-24513 Attn:YWAM
Avg.# Staff: 8

- Ministry: Evangelism, Training, Farming
- Language: Kiswahili, English
- Schools: DTS
- Outreach Locations: Tanz. Coast
- Staff Needs: Preschool Teacher, Bookkeeper/Account, Administrator, DTS Staff, Comm. Development, Agriculturalist, Team Leader, Cook, Housekeeper

THAILAND

Bangkok

YWAM - Relief Services Thailand
National Office:Thailand/Cambodia
G.P.O. Box 177
Bangkok, 10501
Thailand

Contact: Roslyn Jackson (Relief Services)
National: G. Stephen Goode
Phone: 66-2-212-6060
Phone: 66-2-212-6061
Fax: 66-2-212-6062

Avg.# Staff: 25

- Ministry: Relief, Community Development
- Language: English, Thai
- Staff Needs: Administrator, Bookkeepers, Secretarial, Primary Teacher, Preschool Teachers, Postal Supervisors, Sewing Supervisors, Knitting Supervisors, Maintenance, Hospitality, Project Supervisors

Bangkok

Project L.I.F.E. Foundation
Youth With A Mission - Thailand
G.P.O. Box 177
Bangkok, 10501
Thailand

Director: Anita D. Horton
Phone: 66-2-212-6060
Phone: 66-2-212-6061
Fax: 66-2-212-6062
Avg.# Staff: 25

- Ministry: Relief, Community Development, Children's Ministry, Women's Ministry, Medical Ministry, AIDS Victims
- Language: Thai, English
- Outreach Locations: Thai Villages, Children's Homes, Slum Clinic/Poor
- Staff Needs: Admin./Secretarial, Healthcare Workers, Therapists, Drivers/Ordering, Coord. Outreach, Rural Development, Teachers, Vocational Teacher, Counselors, Slum Ministries, Writers:Publications, Children's Ministry

Bangkok

YWAM Thai Ministries
G.P.O. Box 177
Bangkok, 10501
Thailand

Director: Steve Garlington
Phone: 66-2-212-6060
Fax: 66-2-212-6062
Avg.# Staff: 45

- Ministry: Church Planting, Unreached Peoples, Training
- Language: English, Thai
- Schools: School of Frontier Missions
- Outreach Locations: Universities, Slum Dwellers, Rural Areas, Thai Muslims, Provincial Towns
- Staff Needs: Church Planters, DTS Staff, Administrator, Secretary, Linguist, Maintenance Staff, Aqua Cultural Farmer, Builder/Carpenter

(Christjak Ramkhamhaeng)

Youth With A Mission
(Christjak Ramkhamhaeng)
GPO Box 177
Bangkok, 10501
Thailand

Director: Phillip Anderson
Phone: 66-2-314-7455-7 (Rm. 121)
Fax: 66-2-212-6062

(House of Refuge)

Youth With A Mission
(House of Refuge)
GPO Box 177
Bangkok, 10501
Thailand

Director: Christine Overeem
Phone: 66-2-468-0849

Nakhon Si Thammarat

Jesse Ylauan
PO Box 52
Nakhon Si Thammarat, 80000, Thailand

Director: Jesse Ylauan

PLAIN ENVELOPE !!!

Phanat Nikhom

Youth With A Mission
(Relief Services)
PO Box 18
Phanat Nikhom, Chonburi, 20140
Thailand

Director: Elaine Holwell
Phone: 66-38-461-275
Fax: (see Nat'l Office)

(Site 2)

Youth With A Mission
(Site 2)
GPO Box 177
Bangkok, 10501
Thailand

Director: Patty Timbrell
Phone: 66-37-269-011
Fax: (See Nat'l Office)

(Slum Ministry)

Youth With A Mission
(Slum Ministry)
GPO Box 177
Bangkok, 10501
Thailand

Director: Samuel Sarvis
Phone: 66-2-212-6060
Fax: 66-2-212-6062

Taphraya

Youth With A Mission
(Taphraya Church Planting)
GPO Box 177
Bangkok, 10501
Thailand

Director: Rob Vander Feen

TOGO

Lome

Jeunesse En Mission
National Office:Togo
B.P. 80210
Lome
Togo

Director: Raymond Serex
Phone: 228-21-81-38
Fax: 228-21-81-38

Aneho

Jeunesse En Mission
B.P. 60
Aneho
Togo

Director: Paul Dangtoumda

Ketao

Jeunesse En Mission
B.P. 45
Ketao
Togo

Director: Palakiem Tcheckpassi
Phone: 228-21-81-38
Fax: 228-21-81-38

Kpalime

Jeunesse En Mission
B.P. 40
Kpalime
Togo

Director: Salomon Hadzi
Phone: 228-21-81-38
Fax: 228-21-81-38

TONGA, KINGDOM OF

(U of N South Pacific)

YWAM - U of N South Pacific
Private Bag 62
Nuku'alofa
Kingdom of Tonga

Director: Nu'u La'apui
Phone: 676-32340
Fax: 676-32234

TURKEY

Youth With A Mission
(Turkey Contact Office)
Prins Hendrikkade 50
1012 AC Amsterdam
Netherlands

Director: Rosemary Tulett
Phone: 31-20-626-92-33
Fax: 31-20-620-18-23

UGANDA

Wairaka

Youth With A Mission - Uganda
National Office:Uganda (Wairaka)
PO Box 9245
Kampala, Jinja District
Uganda

Director: Harry Mwebesa
Phone: 256-43-21740
Fax: 256-43-22050
Avg.# Staff: 20

- Ministry: Training, Education
- Language: English
- Schools: DTS, BLS, ECES, Community Development School
- Staff Needs: DTS Staff, Secretarial, Builder/Maintenance, Driver, Base Administrator

(Hope House)

Youth With A Mission
(Hope House)
PO Box 9245
Kampala
Uganda

Director: Leopold Kiwanuka
Phone: 256-43-22219
Fax: 256-43-22050

(Jinja)

Youth With A Mission
(Jinja)
PO Box 9245
Kampala
Uganda

Director: Nigel Marsh
Phone: 256-43-22219
Fax: 256-43-22219

Soroti

Youth With A Mission - Soroti
PO Box 792
Soroti
Uganda

Director: Jon Armstrong (Mr.)
Phone: Soroti 359 (via operator)
Avg.# Staff: 8

- Ministry: Relief, Community Development, Mercy Ministry, AIDS Victims, Medical Ministry
- Language: English
- Staff Needs: Admin/Accounting
-

UNITED KINGDOM

England, Harpenden

Youth With A Mission - Harpenden
Nat'l:England, Field:Europe/Mid-East/Afr
Highfield Oval
Harpenden, Herts, AL5 4BX
England, United Kingdom

Director: John Peachey
Contact: Mounir Boctor
(Mid-East/N Africa)
International: Pari Rikard
(Target 2000)
National: Laurence Singlehurst
Regional: Iain Muir (Africa)
Field: Lynn Green (EMA Field)
Phone: 44-582-765-481
Fax: 44-582-768-048
Avg.# Staff: 80

- Ministry: Training, Evangelism, Mercy Ministry, Coordinating
- Language: English
- Schools: DTS, BLS, KK, Orientation to Medical Missions, SOFM
- Outreach Locations: Africa, Asia, Europe, South America, Central America
- Staff Needs: Secretarial, Catering, Hospitality, Maintenance, Journalist, Graphic Artist, Bookkeeper, Gardener, Cook, Mail Manager

England, Acacia

Youth With A Mission - Acacia

Director: David Portway

PO Box 8
Manchester, M60 1RA
England, United Kingdom
Phone: 44-61-273-2335
Avg.# Staff: 8

- Ministry: AIDS Victims, Urban Ministry, Mercy Ministry, Rehab:Drug/Alcohol, Homosexual Ministry
- Language: English
- Staff Needs: Women's Refuge Leader, Base Administrator, Secretary, Nurse - Trainer, Outreach Workers, Outreach Counselors, Personnel/Pastor, Church Planter:Urban, Aids Home Care Staff, Journalist/Designer, Procurement/Fundraise, Coord. Outreach

England, Birmingham

Youth With A Mission
719 Stratford Road
Sparkhill, Birmingham, B11 4DN
England, United Kingdom
Director: Else Tarbitt
Phone: 44-21-778-6478
Avg.# Staff: 4

- Ministry: Mercy Ministry, Urban Ministry
- Language: English
- Staff Needs: Manager:Living Altern., Secretarial

England, Bristol

Youth With A Mission - Bristol England
Elmgrove Centre, Redland Road
Bristol, BS6 6AG
England, United Kingdom
Director: Andy Irwin
Phone: 44-272-421-966
Fax: 44-272-421-966
Avg.# Staff: 11

- Ministry: Evangelism
- Language: English
- Schools: Operation Year
- Outreach Locations: Ghana, Portugal, Albania, France
- Staff Needs: Evangelists, Accountant, Homeless Workers, Teacher:Church Min., Actors:Drama, Counsellors, Musicians, Youth/School Wrkr

England, Croydon

Youth With A Mission
(Dar Al Aman)
13 Highfield Oval
Ambrose Lane
Harpenden, Herts, AL5 4BX
England, United Kingdom
Phone: 44-81-654-1309

England, Cuckfield

Holmsted Manor
Staplefield Road
Cuckfield, West Sussex, RH17 5JF
England, United Kindgom
Director: Peter Bunton
Phone: 44-444-440-229
Fax: 44-444-450-770
Avg.# Staff: 30

- Ministry: Discipleship, Evangelism, Frontier Missions, Church Planting
- Language: English
- Schools: DTS, BLS, SOFM
- Outreach Locations: Albania, India, Spain, Denmark
- Staff Needs: Maintenance, Construction Wrkr, Gardener, Housekeeper, Cooks, SOFM Staff

England, Derby
Youth With A Mission
(Third Wave Centre)
Bakewell Street
Derby, Derbyshire, DE22 3SB
England, United Kingdom

Phone: 44-332-29-96-58
Fax: 44-332-29-96-58

Derby
Derby
Midlands Regional Office
Overdale, 96 Whitaker Road
Derby, DE23 6AP
United Kingdom

Director: Ian White (Midlands Region)
Phone: 44-332-299-658
Fax: 44-332-299-658

- Ministry: Church Ministries, Evangelism, Mobilization
- Language: English
- Schools: Operation Year, TESOL, SOE, School of Creative Ministries
- Outreach Locations: Venezuela, India, United Kingdom, Portugal, Slovenia
- Staff Needs: Evangelism Team, TESOL Staff, SOE Staff, Creative Min. Staff, SOCM Staff, Painter/Decorator, Joiner, Maintenance, Housekeeper

England, (Dunamis Team)
YWAM (Dunamis Team)
76 Bolten Crescent
Camberwell New Road
London, SE5 0SE
England, United Kingdom

Director: John Bedingfield
Phone: 44-71-820-1508

England, Liverpool
Youth With A Mission
"Spekelands"
Oakhill Park, Broadgreen
Liverpool, L13 4BP
England, United Kingdom

Director: David Leage
Phone: 44-051-228-1013
Fax: 44-51-259-7162
Avg.# Staff: 20

- Ministry: Training, Evangelism, Creative Arts, Kings Kids, Campus Evangelism
- Language: English
- Schools: Operation Year
- Outreach Locations: Sierra Leone, N. Ireland, United Kingdom
- Staff Needs: Base Leaders, Operation Yr Leaders, Cook, Maintenance, Housekeeping, Schools Wrkr

England, London
Beth Shalom Rehabilitation Centre
16 The Chase
Clapham, London, SW11 5TU
England, United Kingdom

Director: Warwick Murphy
Phone: 44-71-498-2423
Avg.# Staff: 4

- Ministry: Rehab:Drug/Alcohol
- Language: English
- Staff Needs: Secretarial, Discipleship:Couple, Discipleship:Male, Discipleship:Female

England, London
Earl's Court Project

Director: Richard Lahey-James

24 Collingham Road
Earl's Court, London, SW5 OLX
England, United Kingdom
Phone: 44-71-370-4424
Avg.# Staff: 15

- Ministry: Rehab:Drug/Alcohol, Urban Ministry, Mercy Ministry, AIDS Victims, Homeless
- Language: English
- Staff Needs: Evangelism, Counselling, Coffee Bar Wrkr, Musician:Worship, Rehab House Staff

England, London

East London Base
YWAM London Office & South England Off.
3 Bromley Street
London, E1 ONB
England, United Kingdom
Director: John Taylor (South England)
Phone: 44-71-702-8707
Fax: 44-71-702-8684
Avg.# Staff: 30

- Ministry: Urban Ministry, Training
- Language: English
- Schools: Operation Year, SBS, DTS
- Outreach Locations: Albania, Bulgaria, India, Turkey, France
- Staff Needs: Cook, Hospitality, Housekeeping, Receptionist, Evangelists, Musicians, Maintenance, DTS Staff, Accountant, Administrator, Communications, TESOL Staff

England, London

The Shepherd's Community Team
71 Tressillian Road
Brockley, London, SE4 1YA
England, United Kingdom
Director: David Pott
Phone: 44-81-692-5015
Avg.# Staff: 13

- Ministry: Training:Teacher, Children's Ministry
- Language: English,
- Schools: (DTS) Diploma in Christian Community Education
- Outreach Locations: Slovakia, Czech Republic,
- Staff Needs: Teachers, Kings Kids Staff, Secretarial, Maintenance, Intercessor, Staff:DECE, Hospitality,

England, Nuneaton

YWAM - The King's Lodge
Personnel/Pastoral Care:Europe
Watling Street
Nuneaton, Warwickshire, CV10 0T2
England, United Kingdom
Director: Iain McAuliffe
Contact: Barry Austin (Pastoral)
Phone: 44-203-348-128
Fax: 44-203-344-464
Avg.# Staff: 43

- Ministry: Training, Evangelism:Mobile, Family Ministry, Prison Ministry
- Language: English
- Schools: CDTS, SBS, DTS
- Outreach Locations: India, Egypt, Poland, Ghana, Albania, Uganda
- Staff Needs: Accounts, Secretarial, CDTS Staff, DTS Staff, SBS Staff, Maintenance, Kitchen, Housekeeping, Evangelism, Family Ministries, Graphics/Communic.

England, St. Helens

Youth With A Mission
Parr Mount School
Parr Mount
Director: Phil Pawley
Phone: 44-744-24786
Fax: 44-744-23433

St. Helens, Merseyside, WA9 1AX — Avg.# Staff: 23
England, United Kingdom

- Ministry: Urban Ministry, Training
- Language: English
- Schools: DTS, Community Counselling School, BLS
- Outreach Locations: Poland, N. Ireland, Uganda, England
- Staff Needs: Counselling Staff, DTS Staff, DTS Leaders, Secretarial, Bookkeeper, Hospitality, Housekeeping, Maintenance

England, Torquay

Youth With A Mission, Torquay-England
South West England Regional Office
6/7 Factory Row
Torquay, Devon, TQ2 5QQ
England, United Kingdom

Director: Steve Jones (SW England)
Phone: 44-803-296-863
Fax: 44-803-299-532
Avg.# Staff: 12

- Ministry: Urban Ministry, Evangelism, Kings Kids, Training
- Language: English
- Schools: Christian Character Development Program, KK
- Outreach Locations: Ghana, Portugal
- Staff Needs: Communications Mgr., Secretary/Admin., Evangelism Team Wrkr, Community Team Wrkr, Pastoral Support, King's Kids Wrkr, Oper/Year Leader, Oper/Year Staff, First Fruits Leader, First Fruits Staff

England, Torquay

Youth With A Mission
(The Orchard)
69 Abbey Road
Torquay, Devon, TQ2 5NN
England, United Kingdom

Director: Richard Konrad
Phone: 44-803-294-756
Fax: 44-803-299-532

Scotland, Paisley

Youth With A Mission Scotland Ltd
National & UK/Ireland Area Office
11 Fulbar Road
Paisley, Renfrewshire, PA2 9AW
Scotland, United Kingdom

Contact: Jez Simpson
National: Stephe Mayers
(UK/Ireland Area)
Phone: 44-41-887-8584
Fax: 44-41-848-1519
Avg.# Staff: 15

- Ministry: Administration for YWAM Scotland and Evangelism into Paisley.
- Language: English
- Staff Needs: Personnel Asst., Personnel Asst., Receptionist, Personnel Staff, Bookkeeper, Bookkeeper, Secretary, Secretary, Communications, Church Contacts, Project Team Member, Administrator

Scotland, Catrine

Lighthouse
Daldorch Estate, Sorn Rd
Catrine, Mauchline, Ayrshire, KA5 6NA
Scotland, United Kingdom

Director: Richard Mayers
Phone: 44-290-551-205
Phone: 44-290-552-085
Avg.# Staff: 6

- Ministry: Mercy Ministry, Discipleship
- Language: English
- Staff Needs: Gardener, Cook, Fundraiser, Maintenance, Builder, Plumber, Electrician, Housekeeper, Hospitality, Discipleship:Couple, Discipleship:Men, Discipleship:Women

Scotland, Dumbarton

Youth With A Mission
(Overtoun House)
Milton Brae
Dumbarton, G82 2SH
Scotland, United Kingdom

Director: Wade Robertson
Phone: 44-389-63005
Fax: 44-389-31054

Scotland, Edinburgh

Youth With A Mission
53 Bernard Street
(2nd Floor) Leith
Edinburgh, EH6 65L
Scotland, United Kingdom

Director: Mark Pecqueur
Phone: 44-31-554-5701
Avg.# Staff: 10

- Ministry: Operation Year, Urban evangelism - reaching out to people with drug problems and HIV.
- Language: English
- Schools: Operation Year
- Outreach Locations: France
- Staff Needs: Females:EvangelismScotland, Glasgow

Youth With A Mission
(Possil Park Team)
124 Allander St.

Director: Andy Glover
Phone: 44-41-840-2824

Possil Park
Glasgow, G22 5JH
Scotland, United Kingdom

Scotland, (Operation Year)
Youth With A Mission
(Operation Year)
53 Bernard Street
(2nd Floor)
Leith, Edinburgh, EH6 65L
Scotland, United Kingdom
Director: Stephen Nunn

Scotland, Paisley
Ferguslie Park Evangelism Team
26 Banfoot Road
Paisley
Scotland, United Kingdom
Contact: Mark Fairweather
Phone: 44-41-889-5217
Avg.# Staff: 6
- Ministry: Friendship evangelism in surrounding locality
- Language: English
- Staff Needs: Male Evangelist, Male Evangelist, Female Evangelist

Scotland, Paisley
King's Kids
EMA and Scotland/Ireland Kings Kids Off.
Stanely House, 14, Stanely Crescent
Paisley, PA2 9LF
Scotland, United Kingdom
Director: Wynne Stearns
Phone: 44-41-884-3338
Fax: 44-41-884-3868
Avg.# Staff: 15
- Ministry: Training in child and youth ministries.
- Language: English,
- Schools: Principles in Child and Youth Ministry & Internship
- Outreach Locations: North Africa, Middle East, U.K. & Ireland, Europe
- Staff Needs: House Manager, House Manager, Bookkeeper, Housekeeper, Maintenance, Cook, Hospitality

Scotland, Paisley
Wee Friends Pre-School
12 William Street
Paisley, PA1 2L2
Scotland, United Kindgom
Contact: Rite Mayers
Phone: 44-41-840-2824
Fax: 44-41-840-2824
Avg.# Staff: 8
- Ministry: Discipling pre-school children and training pre-school staff.
- Language: English
- Schools: Principles in Early Childhood Education
- Staff Needs: Floor Workers, Floor Workers, Floor Workers, Officer Worker, Team Leader

Wales, Pontyclun
YWAM South Wales
PO Box 37
Pontyclun, Mid-Glam, CF7 9XX
Wales, United Kingdom
Director: Martin Abel
Phone: 44-443-229-963
Fax: 44-443-229-963
Avg.# Staff: 8
- Ministry: Youth Ministry, Kings Kids, Children's Ministry
- Language: English, Welsh
- Schools: PCYM, Operation Year

- Outreach Locations: Wales, Middle East, North Africa
- Staff Needs: Operation Year Leader, KK Team Leaders, Pastor Care Worker

Wales, Porth

Youth With A Mission
c/o Y.M.C.A. Eirw Road
Brittania, PORTH
Mid Glamorgan, CF39 9LT
Wales, United Kingdom

Director: Dave Davis
Phone: 44-443-68-69-64
Fax: 44-443-68-64-00

URUGUAY

Montevideo

Juventud Con Una Mision - Uruguay
National Office:Uruguay
Lima 1338
Casilla de Correo 6765
Correo Central, Montevideo
Uruguay

Director: Cleire Suarez
Phone: 598-2-94-80-24
Fax: 598-2-71-14-04
Avg.# Staff: 5

- Ministry: Training
- Language: Spanish
- Schools: SOFM
- Outreach Locations: India, Uruguay, Argentina, Chile
- Staff Needs: Kitchen, Secretarial, School Staff, Ministry Prostitutes, Administration

USA

AR, Elm Springs

Youth With A Mission
(Mission Network Center)
PO Box 7
Elm Springs, AR, 72728
USA

Director: Oren Paris
Phone: 1-501-248-7229
Phone: 1-501-248-7236
Fax: 1-501-248-1455

CA, Los Angeles

Youth With A Mission - Los Angeles
District Office:Southwest USA
PO Box 296
Sunland, CA, 91041
USA

Director: Dave Meissner
Contact: John Bills
(Southwest District)
Phone: 1-818-896-2755
Fax: 1-818-897-6738
Avg.# Staff: 53

- Ministry: Training, Worship/Prayer, Short Term, Creative Arts, Leadership Training
- Language: English
- Schools: DTS, Leadership & Ministry Skills School
- Outreach Locations: Mexico, France, Brazil, Eastern Europe, Russia
- Staff Needs: Accounting Clerk, Computer Specialist, Receptionist, Bookstore Manager, Graphic Design, Church Mobil. Dir., Video Prod. Tech., Maintenance/Landscape

CA, Bishop

Youth With A Mission
Rt 1, Box A-3
Bishop, CA, 93514
USA

Contact: Ken Cluff
Phone: 619-872-4387
Fax: 619-872-3271
Avg.# Staff: 12

- Ministry: Training, Short Term
- Language: English
- Schools: DTS, CDTS
- Outreach Locations: Croatia, Mexico
- Staff Needs: Graphic Artist, Store Clerk, Auto Mechanic, Cook

CA, Chula Vista

Youth With A Mission
(San Diego USA/Tijuana Mexico)
PO Box 8873
Chula Vista, CA, 91912
USA

Director: Sean Lambert
Phone: 1-619-425-5304
Fax: 1-619-425-5314
Avg.# Staff: 18

- Ministry: Medical Ministry, Construction, Short Term, Training
- Language: English, Spanish
- Schools: DTS
- Outreach Locations: Tijuana, Hermosillo, Baja, Mexico
- Staff Needs: Secretarial, DTS Staff, Medical Personnel, Administration, Accounting, Auto Repair, Evangelism, Kitchen, Hospitality, Creative Arts

CA, (Gleanings)

Gleanings for the Hungry
PO Box 309
Sultana, CA, 93666

Director: Wally Wenge
Phone: 1-209-591-5009
Fax: 1-209-591-5036

USA Avg.# Staff: 11

- Ministry: Processing food for the needy
- Language: English
- Outreach Locations: Russia, Philippines, Mexico, Bosnia, Arizona Indians
- Staff Needs: Secretary, Landscaper, General Maintenance, Auto Mechanic, Electrician, Cook, Constructions Wrkr

CA, Hollywood

Youth With A Mission - Hollywood
Box 1110
Hollywood, CA, 90078
USA

Director: Nick Schreifels
Phone: 1-213-660-6040
Fax: 1-213-662-2018
Avg.# Staff: 3

- Ministry: Kings Kids
- Language: English
- Staff Needs: Secretarial

CA, Idyllwild

Youth With A Mission
PO Box 3432
Mountain Center, CA, 92561
USA

Director: David Hewitt
Phone: 1-909-659-7070
Fax: 1-909-659-7074

CA, (Int'l Staff Pastor)

Youth With A Mission
(International Staff Pastor)
PO Box 591
Tujunga, CA, 91043
USA

Director: Jim Dawson
Phone: 1-818-352-3070
Fax: 1-818-352-0990

CA, Richardson Springs

Youth With A Mission
Springs of Living Water
15850 Richardson Springs Rd.
Richardson Springs, CA, 95973
USA

Contact: Lori Matthias
Phone: 1-916-893-6750
Fax: 1-916-893-6752
Avg.# Staff: 50

- Ministry: Training campus, youth camps, Christian conferences
- Language: English
- Schools: DTS, CDTS, Community Health Care Internship
- Outreach Locations: San Francisco, Mexico, Brazil, SE Asia
- Staff Needs: Youth Department, DTS Staff, Printer, Writer (P.R.), Secretarial, Bookkeeper Asst., Communications Dir., Children's Wrkr/Teach, Maintenance Wrkr, Food Service, Landscaper, Housekeeping

CA, San Francisco

Youth With A Mission
501 Cambridge Street
San Francisco, CA, 94134
USA

Director: Paul Wood
Phone: 1-415-587-5028
Fax: 1-415-587-5040

CA, Santa Barbara

Youth With A Mission - Santa Barbara
(Recovery House)
421 Bath Street
Santa Barbara, CA, 93101, USA

Contact: Michael Dye
Phone: 1-805-966-4353
Avg.# Staff: 4

- Ministry: Rehab:Drug/Alcohol, Counseling, Training
- Language: English
- Staff Needs: Counselor:Subst. Abuse, Counselor:Clinic, Director:Clinic, Rehab Worker, Manger:Coffehouse

CA, Santa Barbara

Youth With A Mission - Santa Barbara
Sea & Summit Expeditions
PO Box 387
Santa Barbara, CA, 93102
USA

Contact: Will Toms
Phone: 1-805-962-6314
Fax: 1-805-569-1050
Avg.# Staff: 5

- Ministry: Outdoor Adventure, Youth Ministry, Family Ministry, Teambuilding
- Language: English, Korean
- Outreach Locations: Mountains of CA, Dominican Repub., Pacific Coast, CA
- Staff Needs: Administrator, Mtn Adventure Leaders, Sea Adventure Leaders, Teambuilding Leaders, School Program Leader, Logistics Leaders

CO, Cimarron

Youth With A Mission
PO Box YWAM
Cimarron, CO, 81220
USA

Director: Charlie Green
Phone: 1-303-249-7004
Phone: 1-303-249-5774
Fax: 1-303-249-9164

CO, Denver

Youth With A Mission - Denver
12750 West 63rd Ave
Arvada, CO, 80004
USA

Director: Peter Warren
Phone: 1-303-424-1144
Fax: 1-303-424-5121
Avg.# Staff: 60

- Ministry: A training and equipping base focused on sending to the nations., Strongly emphasize praise and worship.
- Language: English
- Schools: DTS, Phase II, SOFM, KK, School of Intercession
- Outreach Locations: Mexico - Indians, USA, Russia/Europe, Nepal/India, Central America, Chad (N. Africa)
- Staff Needs: Accountant, Bookkeeper, Carpenter/Mechanic, Child Care Worker, Secretary, Evangelism, Electrician, Evangelism:Mobile, Graphic Designer, House Parents, Kitchen Worker, Musician

CO, (Int'l Communications)

International Communications (YWAM)
PO Box 26479
Colorado Springs, CO, 80936
USA

Director: Paul Filidis
Phone: 1-719-380-0505
Fax: 1-719-380-0936
Avg.# Staff: 15

- Ministry: Communication
- Language: English
- Staff Needs: Executive Secretary, Journalist/Writer, Research Assistant, Research Assistant

CO, (Strategic Frontiers)

Strategic Frontiers
N. American Reg'l Off. Frontier Missions
PO Box 25490
Colorado Springs, CO, 80936, USA

Director: Fred Markert
Phone: 1-719-495-8748
Fax: 1-719-528-1703
Avg.# Staff: 25

BISHOP
CALIFORNIA

In 1906, Cardinal Village housed one of the most successful gold mining operations in eastern California.

During the 1990s, gold of a different kind will be mined here -- spiritual gold, of eternal value. Cardinal Village is now the home of YWAM/Bishop.

A Discipleship Training School in the Eastern Sierra mountains is an experience which will change a person's life forever.

Call today for information -- 619-872-4DTS (4387)...or write us at Route 1, Box A-3, Bishop, CA, 93514.

A fully accredited U of N course ... other schools to be added.

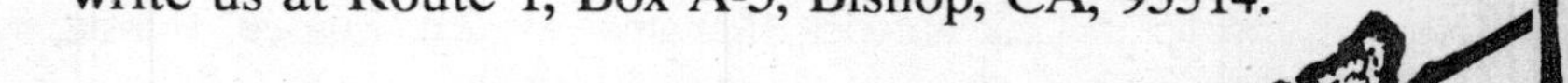

Youth With A Mission

Rt. 1, Box A-3
Bishop, CA 93514
619-872-4387

- Ministry: Frontier Missions, Worship/Prayer, Mobilization
- Language: English
- Schools: DTS, CDTS, SOI, SOSM, Mission Bridge
- Outreach Locations: Nepal, Azerbaijan, Mongolia, India, C.I.S. Nations
- Staff Needs: Graphic Artists, Secretarial, Accountant, Coord. Summer Outreach, Book Dist. Mgr, Worship Leader, School Staff, Computer Programmer, Coord. Adopt-A-People, TESOL:Azerb/Mongolia, Coord. Church Missions, Church Relations Dir.

CO, Trinidad

Youth With A Mission
Mission Village
PO Box 5
Trinidad, CO, 81082 USA

Director: Floyd McClung
Phone: 1-719-846-4555
Fax: 1-719-846-4363
Avg.# Staff: 20

- Ministry: Leadership Development
- Language: English
- Schools: Leadership Development Internship
- Outreach Locations: Mexico, USA, Africa
- Staff Needs: Construction, Secretarial, Bookkeeping, Youth Evangelism, Marketing, Well Drilling, Road Construction

FL, Miami

Youth With A Mission
Greater Miami Area Office
PO Box 611480
Miami, FL, 33261-1480
USA

Director: Walden Owen
Phone: 1-305-895-4744
Fax: 1-305-895-6573
Avg.# Staff: 24

- Ministry: Training, Leadership Training, Creative Arts
- Language: English, Spanish
- Schools: DTS, Basic Leadership School, KK
- Outreach Locations: Latin America, Panama, Mexico, Europe, Russia, Caribbean
- Staff Needs: DTS Leaders, School Staff, Evangelism:Urban, Food Service Mgr., Secretary/Bookkeep., Grounds Maintenance, Auto Mechanics, Building Maint., Computer/Data Entry, Cooks, Hospitality Superv., Outreach Leader

FL, (Central America Office)

Youth With A Mission
Reg'l Off:C. America, Caribbean, Mexico
PO Box 970471
Miami, FL, 33197-0471
USA

Regional: Rick Allegretto (C.Amer/Carib)
Phone: 1-305-388-2589
Phone: 1-305-388-5187
Fax: 1-305-388-0903
Avg.# Staff: 13

- Ministry: Go Teams, Leadership Training, Pastoral Care:YWAM, Training
- Language: English
- Schools: DTS
- Outreach Locations: Cuba, Panama, Nicaragua, Mexico City, Guyana, Haiti
- Staff Needs: DTS Staff, Procurement, Special Projects, Horticulturist, Secretarial, Administrative, Go Team Staff, Music/Drama, Construction/Carp., Graphic Artist, Children's Wrkr/Teach

FL, Orlando

Youth With A Mission
Greater Orlando Area Office
PO Box 621057
Orlando, FL, 32862-1057
USA

Director: Walden Owen
Phone: 1-407-273-1667
Fax: 1-407-273-3243
Avg.# Staff: 5

- Ministry: Creative Arts, Music, Kings Kids, Seminars, Training, Retirees
- Language: English, Spanish
- Schools: CDTS, DTS, KK
- Outreach Locations: Panama, Mexico, Philippines, Eastern Europe
- Staff Needs: CDTS Staff, DTS Staff, Kings Kids Staff, Kitchen Staff, Hospitality Staff, Drama, Graphics, Musicians

FL, (South American Office)

Youth With A Mission
Reg'l Office:South America
PO Box 832555
Miami, FL, 33283
USA

Regional: Gerson Ribeiro (S. America)
Phone: 1-305-892-1346
Fax: 1-305-892-1346
Avg.# Staff: 3

- Ministry: Training and evangelism with Latin-Americans.
- Language: Spanish, English, Portuguese
- Schools: DTS
- Staff Needs: Secretarial, Evangelism Teams, School Staff

FL, (Waves)

WAVES Campus Ministries
Youth With A Mission
15806 SW 97 Ave
Miami, FL, 33157
USA

Director: Richard Felder
Phone: 1-305-252-8483
Fax: 1-305-251-0341
Avg.# Staff: 5

- Ministry: Campus Evangelism
- Language: English
- Schools: College Ministries School
- Outreach Locations: Colleges, Universities
- Staff Needs: Coord. Campus Outreach, Child Care, Counselor - College, Desk Top Publ. Dir., Evangelism:College, Evangelism:High School, Maintenance:General, House Parents, Musician:Guitarist, School Staff, Secretary, Worship Leader

GA, Atlanta

Youth With A Mission - Atlanta
Disctrict Office:Southeast USA
PO Box 81204
Atlanta, GA, 30366
USA

Director: Greg Musch
Contact: Greg/Ramona Musch (S.East District)
Phone: 1-404-458-8678
Fax: 1-404-458-8699
Avg.# Staff: 17

- Ministry: Kings Kids, Urban Ministry, Training
- Language: English
- Schools: PCYM, King's Kids
- Outreach Locations: Eastern Europe, South America, Atlanta
- Staff Needs: Urban Evang. Leader, Urban Evang. Staff, P.R.

Leader:Olympics, PCYM School Staff, Kings Kids Staff, DTS Leader, House Ministry Leader, Administrator, Secretarial

HI, (Pacific Regional Office)

Youth With A Mission
Regional Office:Pacific
74-5606 Pawai Pl. Suite #201
Kailua-Kona, HI, 96740-2199
USA

Director: Sosene Le'au
Phone: 1-808-329-0588
Fax: 1-808-329-0580

HI, (University of the Nations)

University of the Nations
Pacific & Asia Academic Affairs Office
75-5851 Kuakini Hwy
Kailua-Kona, HI, 96740
USA

Director: David Boyd
Phone: 1-808-326-7228
Fax: 1-808-329-2387
Avg.# Staff: 300

- Ministry: Training, Mercy Ministry, Evangelism
- Language: English, Japanese
- Schools: See "Schools" Section or request U of N catalog.
- Outreach Locations: Pacific, Asia, Africa, S & C America, Eastern Europe, Middle East
- Staff Needs: Coord. Transport., Mechanic, Food Purchasing Agent, Coord. Food Services, Head Cook, Maintenance Dept., Grounds Dept., Int'l Student Advisor, Secretaries, Accounting Supervisor, Vendor Accounts, Campus Services Mgr.

HI, Honolulu

Youth With A Mission - Honolulu
PO Box 61700
Honolulu, HI, 96839
USA

Director: Danny Lehmann
Phone: 1-808-988-7015
Fax: 1-808-988-5618
Avg.# Staff: 35

- Ministry: Training, Pioneering, Frontier Missions, Evangelism, Urban Ministry
- Language: English
- Schools: DTS, SOME, SBS, KK
- Outreach Locations: India, Himalayan Region, South Pacific, S.E. Asia, Far East, Russia
- Staff Needs: Accounting, Hospitality, Maintenance Wrkr, Mechanic, Food Service Admin., Cook, DTS Staff, Office Staff, Surf Camp Staff, Summer/Missions Staff, Evangelists, Registrar

HI, (King's Kids Int'l)

Youth With A Mission
(King's Kids International)
PO Box 117
Kailua-Kona, HI, 96745-0117
USA

Director: Dale Kauffman
Phone: 1-808-329-5745
Fax: 1-808-329-6323

HI, Maui

Youth With A Mission - Maui
PO Box 237
Paia-Maui, HI, 96779-0237
USA

Director: Tom Bauer
Phone: 1-808-579-8402
Phone: 1-808-579-8403/4
Fax: 1-808-579-8405
Avg.# Staff: 40

- Ministry: Training, Cult Evangelism, Surfers
- Language: English
- Schools: DTS, SOE, KK, Surfers DTS
- Outreach Locations: India, Indonesia, Thailand, Japan, Philippines, South Pacific
- Staff Needs: Food Service Staff, Construction/Maint., Hospitality, Secretaries, Bookkeeper/Account., Data Entry/Programmer, Automotive Mechanic, Desktop Publ., Childcare Wrkr, School Staff, Graphic Designer, Resource Devel.

HI, (President's Office)

Youth With A Mission President's Office
75-5851 Kuakini Hwy
Kailua-Kona, HI, 96740
USA

International: Loren Cunningham
Phone: 1-808-326-7228
Fax: 1-808-326-4453
Avg.# Staff: 11

- Ministry: Administrative support for YWAM President.
- Language: English
- Outreach Locations: The World

IA, (Spanish Ministries)

Youth With A Mission
(Spanish Ministries Coordinating Office)
1303 Grandview Ave
Waterloo, IA, 50703
USA

Director: Wedge Alman
Phone: 1-319-233-0708
Fax: 1-319-235-1808

ID, Kamiah

Youth With A Mission
Native Ministries
PO Box 1391
Kamiah, ID, 83536-1391
USA

Director: Volkhard Graf
Phone: 1-208-935-0499
Fax: 1-208-935-0594
Avg.# Staff: 6

- Ministry: Mercy Ministry, Training, Indigenous Groups
- Language: English
- Outreach Locations: Nez Peru Reserv., Navajo Reserv.

ID, Riggins

Youth With A Mission - Idaho
Box YWAM
Riggins, ID, 83549
USA

Director: LeRoy Shaw
Phone: 1-208-628-3663
Fax: 1-208-628-3202
Avg.# Staff: 25

- Ministry: Family Ministry, Retreats, Youth Ministry, Kings Kids
- Language: English
- Schools: Family DTS, KK, Primary Health Care
- Outreach Locations: USA, Mexico, South America
- Staff Needs: Food Services, Children's Wrkr/Teach, Communications, Maintenance, Gardener/Grounds, Retreat Worker

IL, Chicago

Youth With A Mission - Chicago
PO Box 268408

Director: Brad Stanley
Phone: 1-312-743-7181

Chicago, IL, 60626
USA

Phone: 1-312-743-6712
Fax: 1-312-764-5991
Avg.# Staff: 7

- Ministry: Urban Ministry, Campus Evangelism, International Students
- Language: English
- Staff Needs: Staff (bi), Campus Ministry Help, Computer Operator, Mechanic, Building Maintenance, Construction Wrkr

IL, Urbana

Youth With A Mission
(University of Illinois)
PO Box 381
Urbana, IL, 61801
USA

Director: Bill Burtness
Phone: 1-217-367-1226
Fax: 1-217-351-1558
Avg.# Staff: 6

- Ministry: Campus Evangelism, Short Term
- Language: English
- Outreach Locations: Mexico, Int'l Sports Events
- Staff Needs: Outreach Leader, Worship Leader, Evangelist, Administrator, Development Asst., Secretarial

LA, (Living Alternatives)

Youth With A Mission
(Living Alternatives)
PO Box 2787
New Orleans, LA, 70176
USA

Director: Monica Schumann
Phone: 1-504-821-5118
Phone: 1-504-837-2579

LA, (New Hope Ministries)

Youth With A Mission
(New Hope Ministries)
PO Box 6787
New Orleans, LA, 70174
USA

Director: Steve Niles
Phone: 1-504-368-4808

LA, New Orleans

Youth With A Mission
PO Box 6787
New Orleans, LA, 70174
USA

Director: Michael K. Price
Phone: 1-504-367-6000
Fax: 1-504-368-2026
Avg.# Staff: 26

- Ministry: Urban Ministry, Unwed Mothers, Youth Ministry, Rehab:Drug/Alcohol
- Language: English
- Staff Needs: Maintenance Wrkr, Communications Dir., Mobile Team Staff, Rehab Center Staff, Child Evangelism, Construction Wrkr, Worship Leader, Computer Support, Counselors:Pregnancy, Chastity Team Wrkr, Street Evangelism, Researchers

LA, (Target New Orleans)

Youth With A Mission
(Target New Orleans)
PO Box 740607
New Orleans, LA, 70174
USA

Director: Chuck Morris
Phone: 1-504-522-3843

MA, Boston

Youth With A Mission - Greater Boston
21 Minnesota Ave
Somerville, MA, 02145
USA

Director: Jeff Gilbertson
Phone: 1-617-623-9926
Avg.# Staff: 4

- Ministry: Youth Ministry, Training, Campus Evangelism, Men's Ministry
- Language: English
- Schools: DTS
- Outreach Locations: USA, Europe, 10/40 Window
- Staff Needs: DTS Staff, DTS Leaders, Kings Kids Staff, Kings Kids Leaders, Urban Min. Staff, Urban Min. Leaders, Men's Min. Leader, Men's Min. Staff, Campus Min. Leader, Campus Min. Staff

ME, Camden

Youth With A Mission
PO Box 528
Camden, ME, 04843 USA

Director: Adra Lovley, Jr.
Phone: 1-207-236-6229

MT, Lakeside

Youth With A Mission
District Office:Northwest USA
PO Box 3000
Lakeside, MT, 59922
USA

Director: Gordy McDonald
Contact: Gordy McDonald (Northwest District)
Phone: 1-406-844-2221
Fax: 1-406-844-3730
Avg.# Staff: 105

- Ministry: Training, Music, Creative Arts, Kings Kids, Short Term
- Language: English
- Schools: DTS, CDTS, SBS, SOW, KK
- Outreach Locations: Thailand, Czech Republic, Greece, Ukraine
- Staff Needs: Food Service Staff, Graphic Artist, Secretarial, Children's Wrkr/Teach, Communications Dir., Maintenance Workers, Construction Wrkr, DTS Staff, Personnel Director, KK Staff:Couple

MT, Crow Agency

Youth With A Mission
(Crow Nation)
PO Box 760
Crow Agency, MT, 59022
USA

Director: David Pearson
Phone: 1-406-638-2296

MT, (King's Kids)

King's Kids
North American Strategic Outreach Off.
PO Box 3000
Lakeside, MT, 59922
USA

Contact: Bill Lanterman
Phone: 1-406-844-3072
Fax: 1-406-844-3730
Avg.# Staff: 3

- Ministry: Communications for North America King's Kids Outreaches & Teams., KK Impact World Tour and Atlanta '96 King's Kids Communications.
- Language: English
- Outreach Locations: Impact World Tour, Atlanta '96, Canada Torch Run

MT, (SBS Int'l)

School of Biblical Studies International

International: Ron/Judy Smith

PO Box 3000
Lakeside, MT, 59922
USA

(SBS)
Phone: 1-406-844-3525
Phone: 1-800-484-9715 ext. 7540
Fax: 1-406-844-3548
Avg.# Staff: 3

- Ministry: Oversight of growth and communications for School of Biblical Studies worldwide.
- Language: English
- Schools: SBS Worldwide

NC, Charlotte

Youth With A Mission - Charlotte
PO Box 25087
Charlotte, NC, 28229-5087
USA

Director: Todd A. Hedgepeth
Phone: 1-704-625-2583
Fax: 1-704-568-7704
Avg.# Staff: 8

- Ministry: Mobilization, Short Term, Pioneering, Frontier Missions, Training
- Language: English
- Schools: DTS, SOE
- Outreach Locations: Bulgaria, Romania, Ukraine, Central America, Caribbean
- Staff Needs: Worship Leader, SOS Team Leaders, Accountant, School Staff, Secretary, Recruiters, Youth Camp Staff

NC, (Charlotte Training Outpost)

Youth With A Mission - Charlotte
(Training Outpost)
PO Box 400
Lake Lure, NC, 28746
USA

Director: (See Charlotte NC)
Phone: 1-704-625-4673
Fax: 1-704-625-8044

(Address/phone for Charlotte YWAM - April through November)

NY, New York City

Youth With A Mission - Greater New York
District Office:East Coast, NE USA
PO Box YWAM 422
Islip Terrace, NY, 11752-0422
USA

Director: Nick Savoca
(East Coast Dir.)
Contact: Dave Adams
(Northeast District)
Phone: 1-516-224-4004
Phone: 1-516-737-5042 (District)
Fax: 1-516-224-1115
Avg.# Staff: 8

- Ministry: Urban Ministry, Kings Kids, Missions Service Center, Go Teams, Training
- Language: English
- Schools: DTS
- Outreach Locations: New York City, Ukraine
- Staff Needs: Secretarial, Communications, DTS Staff, Kings Kids Staff, Urban Missions Staff, Musicians/Singers

NY, Ithaca

Youth With A Mission, Ithaca
201 Stewart Ave.
Ithaca, NY, 14850
USA

Director: Edith Johnson
Phone: 1-607-256-2328
Fax: 1-607-256-2328
Avg.# Staff: 2

- Ministry: Campus Evangelism, Discipleship, International Students, Prayer Networking
- Language: English
- Outreach Locations: Ukraine
- Staff Needs: Campus Evangelism, Youth Evangelism, Kings Kids, Int's Student Min., Office Manager, Hospitality

NY, Long Island City

Little Sisters Project
PO Box 6209
Long Island City, NY, 11106
USA

Contact: Shirley Martin
Phone: 1-718-728-3506
Avg.# Staff: 2

- Ministry: Women's Ministry, Mercy Ministry, Prostitution Recovery, Prison Ministry, Education
- Language: English
- Outreach Locations: New York City
- Staff Needs: Women's Outreach Wrkr, Counselors, Women's Recovery Staff, Legal Advocates

NY, New York

Youth With A Mission - Greater New York
The Antioch Connection:
YWAM Korean Min.
35-11150th Street
Flushing, NY, 11354 USA

Director: Donggu Lee
National: David E. Ross (Antioch)
Phone: 1-718-539-1611
Fax: 1-718-539-1613
Avg.# Staff: 8

- Ministry: Recruiting, training Korean-American college youth for cross-cultural missions.
- Language: English, Korean
- Schools: DTS
- Outreach Locations: Russia, Ukraine, Native Americans, Canada
- Staff Needs: Graphic Artist, Campus Worker, Young Adult Urban Min.

NY, Riverhead

Youth With A Mission
(Ukraine Coordination Office)
PO Box 933
Riverhead, NY, 11901
USA

Director: Bill Blatz
Phone: 1-516-727-7878
Fax: 1-516-727-4912

OR, Salem

Youth With A Mission
District Office:West Coast USA
7085 Battlecreek Rd SE
Salem, OR, 97301
USA

Director: Peter Iliyn
Contact: Peter Iliyn (West Coast District)
Phone: 1-503-364-3837
Fax: 1-503-378-7026
Avg.# Staff: 90

- Ministry: To train and send missionaries to bless and disciple the nations.
- Language: English
- Schools: SOI, DTS, CDTS, KK, Impact World Tour DTS
- Outreach Locations: Russia, Latvia, Ukraine, Mexico, USA, Tanzania
- Staff Needs: Kitchen Staff, Communications, Secretarial, Administrative, Children's Workers, Mechanic:Auto, Maintenance, Bookkeeping Staff, Hospitality Wrkr, School Staff, Kings Kids, Mobile Team Staff

OR, Portland

Youth With A Mission
Portland Urban Ministries
PO Box 11601
Portland, OR, 97211
USA

Director: Kelly Cohoe
Phone: 1-503-285-6909
Avg.# Staff: 15

- Ministry: Urban Ministry, Evangelism, Discipleship
- Language: English
- Outreach Locations: Portland
- Staff Needs: Admin/Secretary, Counselor, Crisic Center Dir., Crisis Center Wrkr, Evangelism:Urban, Handy Person, Discipleship, Resource Development, Learning Center Wrkr, Community Center, Church Ministries, Juvenile Girls Home

OR, (Slavic Ministries Int'l)

Slavic Ministries International
(Reg'l Office:Former Soviet Union CIS)
PO Box 4213
Salem, OR, 97302
USA

Director: Shane Murray (Operations)
International: Al Akimoff (Slavic Ministry)
Phone: 1-503-363-1571
Fax: 1-503-363-2417
Avg.# Staff: 50

- Ministry: Facilitating, training, evangelism, pioneering and establishing permanent work -, throughout the former Soviet Empire.

- Language: English, Slavic, Baltic
- Staff Needs: Secretarial, Coord. Outreach, Graphic Artist, Maintenance Wrkr, Translators, Hospitality/Kitchen, DTS Staff, Audio Visual Staff, Youth Workers, Researcher, Research Development, Fundraiser/Donor Mgr

PA, Philadelphia

Youth With A Mission - Philadelphia
Box 31938
Philadelphia, PA, 19104
USA

Director: Kevin King
Phone: 1-215-521-6013
Fax: 1-215-543-6115
Avg.# Staff: 3

- Ministry: Urban Ministry, Training, Tutoring
- Language: English
- Schools: DTS, KK
- Outreach Locations: Philadelphia, Brazil, Ukraine, Europe
- Staff Needs: DTS Staff, Spanish Spkg Staff, Neighborhood Evang., Maintenance, Kings Kids Staff, University Ministry, Tutors (Child/Adult), Medical Staff, Communications, Accounting

PA, Roaring Branch

YWAM - Roaring Branch, PA
RR 1, Box 133R
Roaring Branch, PA, 17765
USA

Director: David Bauman
Phone: 1-717-673-3338
Fax: 1-717-673-3338
Avg.# Staff: 5

- Ministry: Training
- Language: English

- Schools: CDTS
- Outreach Locations: Ukraine, Eastern Europe
- Staff Needs: Food Service Staff, Children's Wrkr/Teach, Maintenance Wrkr, Grounds Keepers, CDTS Staff

PA, Titusville

Pennsylvania Training & Outreach Center
PO Box 264
Titusville, PA, 16354
USA

Director: Ron Southwick
Phone: 1-814-827-2653 Voice/TDD
Fax: 1-814-827-3045
Avg.# Staff: 15

- Ministry: Kings Kids, Campus Evangelism, Deaf Ministry, Training
- Language: English, Sign Language
- Schools: DTS, SOE, KK
- Outreach Locations: USA, Latvia, Mexico, Latin America, Central America
- Staff Needs: Administrative Asst., Secretarial, Interpreters:Deaf, Cook, Housekeeper, DTS & SOE Staff, Kings Kids Staff, Deaf Ministries Wrkr, Maintenance:General, Bookkeeper, DTP Personnel

SD, Spearfish

Youth With A Mission - South Dakota
431 State Street
Spearfish, SD, 57783
USA

Director: David A. McPherson
Phone: 1-605-642-8409
Avg.# Staff: 2

- Ministry: Indigenous Groups, Campus Evangelism, Training:Church, Ministry to Pastors
- Language: English
- Staff Needs: College Campus Min., Kings Kids, Elderly/Retire Min., Native American Min., Worship Leader

TN, Nashville

Youth With A Mission - Nashville
PO Box 681147
Franklin, TN, 37068
USA

Director: Steve Tackett
Phone: 1-615-333-0273
Fax: 1-615-333-0287
Avg.# Staff: 14

- Ministry: Training, Music, Worship/Prayer
- Language: English
- Schools: DTS, SOE, SBS, SOW
- Outreach Locations: Hungary, Mexico, Caribbean, Central America, Eastern Europe, Inner Cities:USA
- Staff Needs: Kings Kids Staff, DTS/SOE Staff, Computer Operators, Graphic Artist, Musicians, Secretarial, Mobile Teams, Public Relations, Administration, Children's Wrkr/Teach, SBS Leaders/Staff, SOW Leaders/Staff

TX, Tyler

Youth With A Mission (Twin Oaks Ranch)
Field Office for the Americas
Tyler, TX, 75712
USA

Director: D. Leland Paris
PO Box 4600
Phone: 1-903-882-5591
Fax: 1-903-882-7673
Avg.# Staff: 220

- Ministry: Training, Evangelism, Frontier Missions, Urban Ministry, Pro-Life, Medical Ministry
  Language: English

- Schools: DTS, SOE, CDTS, SOSM, SOTB, Teacher Training, KK
- Outreach Locations: Romania, Russia, Bulgaria, Peru, Brazil, Nepal
- Staff Needs: Accounting, Secretarial, Building Maintenance, Kitchen Workers, Child Care Leaders, Graphic Artists, Writers/Editors, Hospitality, Medical Professional, Landscapers, Carpenters, Vehicle Maint.

TX, (Building Ministry)

YWAM Building Ministries
4444 Edgar Park
El Paso, TX, 79904
USA

Contact: Charlie Hendrickson
Phone: 1-915-757-3387

- Ministry: Building for YWAM., Training YWAMer's in the construction trades.
- Language: English
- Staff Needs: Architects, Contractors, Construction Wrkrs

TX, Dallas

Youth With A Mission
202 N. Orient St.
Dallas, TX, 75214
USA

Director: David Funke
Phone: 1-214-828-0977
Avg.# Staff: 4

- Ministry: Evangelism, Hosting Teams
- Language: English
- Outreach Locations: Dallas Inner City
- Staff Needs: Evangelism, Evang:Children, Logistical

TX, (Editorial)

YWAM Publishing - Editorial
PO Box 1380
Lindale, TX, 75771
USA

Director: Jim Rogers
Phone: 1-903-882-5591 ext. 288
Fax: 1-903-882-5710
Avg.# Staff: 7

- Ministry: Training for writers in ministry. Preparing manuscripts for publication.
- Language: English
- Schools: Authors School, School of Writing
- Staff Needs: Editors, Secretarial, Desktop Publishing

TX, El Paso

Youth With A Mission
(El Paso USA/Juarez Mexico)
4444/4406 Edgar Park
El Paso, TX, 79904
USA

Director: Jeff Peters
Phone: 1-915-757-3387
Fax: 1-915-755-5727
Avg.# Staff: 50

- Ministry: Training, Short Term, Mercy Ministry
- Language: Spanish, English
- Schools: DTS, School of Bible
- Outreach Locations: Sierra Madre Area, Interior Mexico, Central America, USA, Arizona Navajo
- Staff Needs: Childcare Wrkr, Secretarial, DTS Staff (Eng), DTS Staff (Span), Mercy Ministry, Military Evangelism, Maintenance, Construction, Fundraiser, Lang. School Dir., Lang. School Staff, Accounting

TX, (Last Days Ministries)

Last Days Ministries
PO Box 40

Director: Melody Green Sievright
Phone: 1-903-963-8671

Lindale, TX, 75771
USA

Fax: 1-903-882-7709
Avg.# Staff: 100

- Ministry: Training, Communication, Publishing, Music, Media
- Language: English
- Schools: DTS, Desktop Publishing, Print Production, Culinary School
- Outreach Locations: Russia, Eastern Europe, Israel, South America, Central America
- Staff Needs: Printers/Binding, Writers, Graph. Design/Illust., Data Entry/Clerks, Shipping Manager, Order Fulfillment, Public Relations Mgr., Donor Development

TX, Mercy Ships

Mercy Ships
International Office for Mercy Ships
PO Box 2020
Lindale, TX, 75771-2020
USA

Director: Jack Minton
International: Don Stephens (Mercy Ships)
Phone: 1-903-963-8341
Fax: 1-903-963-7300
Avg.# Staff: 450

- Ministry: Training, Evangelism, Mercy Ministry, Medical Ministry, Relief, Community Development
- Language: English
- Schools: DTS, CDTS, Foundations in Community Development
- Outreach Locations: Africa, Caribbean, S. Pacific, USA, Europe, E. Europe
- Staff Needs: Bookkeeper/Account, Engineer, Welder, Chief Cook, Seamen (Able Bodied), Receptionist, Secretarial, Medical Professionals, Carpenters, Computer Specialists, Evangelism:Drama/Act, Communications

UT, Ogden

Youth With A Mission - Utah
PO Box 6270
Ogden, UT, 84403
USA

Director: Jim Pitts
Phone: 1-801-355-9926
Fax: 1-801-355-9926
Avg.# Staff: 5

- Ministry: Cult Evangelism
- Language: English
- Schools: Mini-DTS
- Outreach Locations: Utah, Israel/Egypt
- Staff Needs: Administrator, School Staff, Secretarial, Counsel/Pregnant Teen, Accountant

VA, Richmond (U of N)

University of the Nations - Richmond
Reg'l Academic Affairs/Israel Coord. Off
PO Box 780
Richmond, VA, 23206-0780
USA

Director: David Swarr
Contact: David Hamilton (Acad. Affairs)
Phone: 1-804-648-8821
Fax: 1-804-648-6236
Avg.# Staff: 40

- Ministry: Urban community development, U of N training campus, Jewish ministries, youth/family.
- Language: English
- Schools: School of Jewish Studies, DTS, SBS, SCPL, SOI

- Outreach Locations: Israel, Africa, Urban/Inner City, College/University, Latin America
- Staff Needs: Bookkeeping, Maintenance, Secretary/Reception, Administrator & Asst., Worship Leader, Intercessors, Inner City Staff, Literacy Training, U of N Records, Communications, Children's Wrkr/Teach, SBS Staff

VA, Richmond

Field Ministry Internships
University of the Nations
YWAM PO Box 780
Richmond, VA, 23231
USA

Director: David Swarr
Contact: John Henry
Phone: 1-804-222-4013
Fax: 1-804-648-6236

- Ministry: Internships:College, International Students
- Language: English
- Schools: DTS
- Outreach Locations: Brazil, Africa, Chile, Richmond, VA, Campus
- Staff Needs: Social Worker, Primary Health Care, Evangelist, Desktop Publishing, Admin. Secretary, Journalist, Nurse, Physician's Asst., Educator/Teacher, DTS Staff, SOE Staff, Administrator

VA, Richmond (ARM)

American Resources For Missions (ARM)
PO Box 23024
Richmond, VA, 23223-0324
USA

Director: Gerrit J. Wolfaardt
Phone: 1-804-788-4995
Fax: 1-804-648-6236/222-4726

- Ministry: Economic development. Gift In Kind.
- Language: English
- Staff Needs: Computer Skills, Resource Development, Business Admin., Accounting, Accountant, Communication, Graphics, Legal, Secretarial, Marketing

Virgin Islands, St. Croix

Youth With A Mission - St. Croix
PO Box 5280
Christiansted, V.I., 00823
U.S. Virgin Islands

Director: Steve Hisey
Phone: 1-809-778-7373
Fax: 1-809-778-7373
Avg.# Staff: 15

- Ministry: Training, Youth Ministry, Children's Ministry, Short Term, Discipleship
- Language: English
- Schools: DTS
- Outreach Locations: Haiti, Jamaica, Guyana, Cuba, Dominican Rep., Caribbean Islands
- Staff Needs: Bookkeeper, Business Admin., DTS Staff, Cook, Kitchen Manager, Mobile Team Staff, Basketball Ministry, Youth Ministry Wrkr, Children's Min. Wrkr, Summer of Serv. Leader, Maintenance Workers, Gardener/Grounds

WA, Seattle

Youth With A Mission
North American Office/
YWAM Washington
PO Box 55309
Seattle, WA, 98155, USA

Regional: Denny Gunderson (N. America)
Phone: 1-206-363-9844
Fax: 1-206-363-9845
Avg.# Staff: 40

- Ministry: Urban Missions, Mission Builders, Mercy Media, Career Counseling, Kings Kids, New Beginnings, Revive America.
- Language: English
- Staff Needs: Secretary/Reception, Secretary:Miss Bldrs, Bookkeeper, Accountant

WA, (King's Kids USA)

King's Kids USA
USA Communication Center - KK
PO Box 64375
Tacoma, WA, 98464-0375
USA

Director: Lee/Libby Goehner
Phone: 1-206-584-9435
Avg.# Staff: 10

- Ministry: Kings Kids
- Language: English
- Outreach Locations: 40 KK Teams
- Staff Needs: Secretarial, Graphic Artist

WA, (Mission Builders)

YWAM Mission Builders
PO Box 55309
Seattle, WA, 98155
USA

Director: Troy Stremler
Phone: 1-206-363-9844
Fax: 1-206-363-9845
Avg.# Staff: 2

- Ministry: Recruiting short-term volunteers to assist YWAM bases with building projects and, practical needs.
- Staff Needs: Promotions, Writer, Fundraiser, Secretarial

WA, Port Orchard

YWAM Revive America Project
PO Box 1634
Port Orchard, WA, 98366
USA

Director: Ron Boehme
Phone: 1-206-876-3432
Fax: 1-206-876-1332
Avg.# Staff: 5

- Ministry: Church Ministries, National Revival, Counseling, Kings Kids
- Language: English
- Outreach Locations: Eastern Europe, Asia, Northwest USA, Latin America
- Staff Needs: Secretarial, Counselors, Project Workers

WA, (Publishing)

YWAM Publishing
PO Box 55787
Seattle, WA, 98155
USA

Director: Tom Bragg
Phone: 1-206-771-1153
Fax: 1-206-775-2383
Avg.# Staff: 7

- Ministry: Publishing
- Language: English

WA, Seattle

Youth With A Mission
Urban Ministries Seattle
PO Box 75145
Seattle, WA, 98125-0145
USA

Contact: Doug Birkebak
Phone: 1-206-323-8222
Fax: 1-206-363-9845
Avg.# Staff: 7

- Ministry: Youth Ministry, Street Kids, Homeless, Rehab:Drug/Alcohol, Urban Ministry
- Language: English

- Outreach Locations: Downtown Seattle
- Staff Needs: Outreach Workers, Accounting, Medical Staff, Fundraiser, Men:Work With Kids

WA, Tacoma

Youth With A Mission
(New Beginnings Home)
PO Box 8303
Tacoma, WA, 98404
USA

Director: Miles Musick
Phone: 1-206-473-4477

WI, Madison

Youth With A Mission - Madison
PO Box 8503
Madison, WI, 53708
USA

Director: Warren Keapproth
Phone: 1-608-233-4125
Fax: 1-608-221-4934
Avg.# Staff: 6

- Ministry: Campus Evangelism, International Students, Discipleship, Coffee House
- Language: English
- Schools: Mission Bridge
- Outreach Locations: Grenada, Belize, Mexico, Latvia, Univ. Campus
- Staff Needs: Secretarial, TESL Instructors, University Evangelism, School Staff (SOE), Mission Bridge Staff, Coffehouse Workers, Musician

WI, Northwoods

Youth With A Mission - Northwoods
Impact World Tour Office
2824 - 130th Street
Frederic, WI, 54837
USA

Director: Mark Anderson
Phone: 1-715-327-8147
Fax: 1-715-327-8146
Avg.# Staff: 15

- Ministry: Crusade-style evangelism. Impact World Tour.
- Language: English
- Schools: School of Crusade-Style Evangelism, Impact World Tour, DTS
- Outreach Locations: Impact World Tour, India
- Staff Needs: Maintenance, Food Service, Computer, Admin/Bookkeeping, DTS/CDTS Staff/Dir., Publications/Graphic, Office/Secretarial, Hospitality, Daycare/Preschool, Construction, Elem/H.S. Teachers, Musicians

WI, Weyerhaeuser

Eden/Youth With A Mission
(International Family Ministry Schools)
W14580 County Rd D
Weyerhaeuser, WI, 54895
USA

Director: Larry Ballard
Phone: 1-715-353-2280
Fax: 1-715-353-2935
Avg.# Staff: 32

- Ministry: Training, Family Ministry
- Language: English
- Schools: Family Ministry School, DTS
- Outreach Locations: Jamaica, Mexico, Romania, Cuba, El Salvador, Nicaragua
- Staff Needs: Kitchen Manager, Secretary/Reception., Accounting/ Bookkeeper, Short Term Director, Auto/Diesel Mechanic, DTS Staff, Maintenance Superv., Childcare Workers, Housekeepers, FMS Staff

VENEZUELA

Caracas

Juventud Con Una Mision
National Office:Venezuela
Apartado 88070
Caracas 1080
Venezuela

National: Miguel Quintana
Phone: 58-2-931-775
Phone: 58-2-711-947
Fax: 58-2-931-775
Avg.# Staff: 12

- Ministry: Training, Evangelism
- Language: Spanish
- Schools: DTS, SOFM, KK, School of Pioneer Ministry
- Staff Needs: Accounting, Secretary (bi), Counselor, Dir. Creative Arts, Kitchen

Estado Guarico

Casa Hogar, San Sebastian
Apartado 137
2301 San Juan de los Morros
Estado Guarico
Venezuala

Director: Alonso Guanita
Phone: 58-46-51768
Phone: 58-46-51016
Fax: 58-46-51016
Avg.# Staff: 10

- Providing home and education for abandoned children (special need).
- Language: Spanish
- Staff Needs: Speech Therapist, Physiotherapist, Occupational Therap., Special Needs Teach., Cook, Maintenance Wrkr, Construction Wrkr, House Parents, Administration, Accounts, General Assistants

Merida

Juventud Con Una Mision
Attn: Chris Donaldson
Apdo. 850
Merida 5101-A
Venezuela

Director: Chris Donaldson
Phone: 58-74-52-91-20
Fax: 58-74-52-91-20

WESTERN SAMOA

Apia

Youth With A Mission - Western Samoa
Pioneer Ministry Centre/Nat'l Office
PO Box 3322
Apia, Upolu Island
Western Samoa

Contact: Pastor Angus Macdonald
National: George E. Betham
Phone: 685-25107
Phone: 685-26525 (Angus Macdonald)
Fax: 685-20912
Avg.# Staff: 3

- Ministry: Evangelism, Preschool, Church Ministries
- Language: Samoan, English
- Schools: DTS
- Outreach Locations: Western Samoa, American Samoa, Tonga, Pacific Islands
- Staff Needs: Preschool Teacher, Preschool Director, DTS Director/Staff, Food Service Staff, Maintenance Wrkr, Gardener, Secretarial, Carpenters/Constr., Electrician, Painters, Plumber, Church Ministry Wrkr

(Christian Preschool)

Youth With A Mission
(Apia Christian Preschool)
PO Box 9255
Apia
Western Samoa

Director: Ruta Manuleleua
Fax: 685-20912

Savaii Island

Youth With A Mission
PO Box 5006
Salelologa (Sapapalii)
Savai
Western Samoa

National: George Betham
Phone: 685-51337 (messages)
Fax: 685-51337
Avg.# Staff: 8

- Ministry: Campus Evangelism, Bible Study, Youth Ministry, Community Development
- Language: Samoan, English
- Schools: DTS
- Outreach Locations: Western Samoa, American Samoa, Pacific Islands
- Staff Needs: Children's Wrkr/Teach, Communications Dir., Maintenance Wrkr, Construction Wrkr, DTS Staff, Secretarial, Church Min. Wrkr, Youth Wrkr/Teach, Campus Wrkr/Teacher, Campus Evangelism

ZAIRE

Zaire
c/o YWAM Eastern Africa
PO Box 76046
Nairobi, Kenya

Director: Method Kamanzi
Phone: 254-2-71-42-46
Fax: 254-2-71-42-45
Avg.# Staff: 2

PLAIN ENVELOPE !!!

- Ministry: Evangelism, Training, Church Planting
- Language: French, English
- Outreach Locations: Eastern Zaire, Rwanda, Burundi, Congo
- Staff Needs: Accountant, Secretary (bi), DTS Staff, Administrator, Team Leader, Nurse, Comm. Devel. Wrkr, TESOL Teachers

ZAMBIA

Youth With A Mission
PO Box 32145
Lusaka, Zambia

Director: Randy Rhoades
Phone: 260-1-210260

ZIMBABWE

Bulawayo

Youth With A Mission
Nat'l Office:Zimbabwe, SC Africa Area
PO Box 2323
Bulawayo
Zimbabwe

National: Don Heyns
(S.Central Africa)
Phone: 263-9-43565
Fax: 263-9-49468
Avg.# Staff: 6

- Ministry: Training, Evangelism, Church Planting
- Language: English
- Schools: DTS, IBC, SBS
- Outreach Locations: Zimbabwe, Mozambique, Malawi
- Staff Needs: DTS Staff, Food Service Staff, Children's Worker, Communications, Maintenance Wrkr, Construction Wrkr, Secretarial, Agrigulture Wrkr, Teaching Ministry, Church Discipleship

Harare

Youth With A Mission
PO Box A420
Avondale, Harare
Zimbabwe

Director: Cornelius Heyns
Phone: 263-4-32435
Phone: 263-4-34880

Section III

YWAM Training Schools

Most YWAM schools offer the following basic programs which consist of two parts: 1) a lecture phase lasting three months, and 2) a field assignment or outreach phase usually lasting 8 - 12 weeks, involving the practical application of principles learned in the first phase. Classes can be taken anywhere in YWAM world wide to complete a degree program.

The Basic Program

Discipleship Training School (DTS)

An intensive training program designed to establish the Christian in his faith and to prepare him for Christian service. Its emphasis is upon the "messenger" of evangelism. Topics covered include: relationship with God and others, humility and openness, intercessory prayer, and principles of Christian living. A period of outreach or field trip follows in which students put into practice the principles learned in the classroom. Students should be High School graduates (or equivalent) to attend a DTS. The DTS is the prerequisite to all other training courses and programs.

Crossroads Discipleship Training School (CDTS)

This course is a special discipleship training program for men and women from all walks of life - those who are at a crossroads in life and are seeking new direction, new vision, and renewal in the Lord. Most Students are over 35 years of age, and the program is suited to their particular needs.

Specialized Training Programs

New schools are constantly coming into existence. Most of these specialized schools require a completed DTS or CDTS. Contact the YWAM operating location(s) where the school is held for requirement information and application. Some of the present schools are:

Addictive Behavior Counseling School

This advanced course is for those who want to pursue a ministry in understanding compulsive lifestyles of individuals and families. It is designed to help develop skills in diagnosis, treatment and recovery. Lectures, personal in-depth study, group work and experiential therapies will be utilized.

Aqua Culture Technology School

The goal of this course is to apply aqua culture development technologies together with biblical principles to meet the physical and spiritual needs of various nations of the world. Students learn to open doors of evangelism and discipleship into unreachable communities by implementing the ancient art of fish farming along with modern technology.

Arts in Ministry

This course provides a challenging and stimulating environment in which students learn to explore and develop their creative potential through seminars and practical workshops on dance, drama, dramatic dance, mime, song writing, theater arts and communication theory.

Author's Training School

This course is for those who already have some skill in writing. The student is trained to write narrative or thematic books and magazine articles. As a result of the course, the sharing of personal experiences or those of others in a logical and interesting way will help multiply missions and the application of biblical principles dramatically.

Basic Construction Technology School

This course can provide great help for those planning and launching new building projects. Students will learn construction from the very beginning stages to completion in a step-by-step method of instruction.

Basic Leadership Course

This school is for people who show leadership potential. Participants are trained in leadership and counseling by being practically involved in the day to day running of a DTS, and by then leading small evangelistic outreach teams either at home or abroad.

Bible, School of the

Intensive study in the Bible, Greek, presupposition analysis, ministry analysis from Kingdom of God principles and historical perspective, ministry principles, public speaking development; evangelism and leadership field trips.

Biblical Christian World View School

This school seeks to equip students with an understanding of prevailing world views and the tools to reinterpret their particular disciplines from a biblical perspective. It is for those called to disciple nations through professional callings, those called to be 'salt & light' in a major sphere of influence, or those who want to better understand the world view of the country or people to whom they are called.

Biblical Counseling, Introduction to

The purpose of this course is to introduce students to a biblical framework for Christian counseling. It will also help them discover God's foundational truths which shape their ability to relate to God, themselves, and those around them. Through this course, the students will learn the basic skills in helping others move towards wholeness.

Biblical Counseling, Methods and Models in

This course aims to provide a deeper understanding of

various models of biblical counseling and of the ways to help others understand and change particular hindrances of their spiritual growth. Emphasis is placed on applying the power of the Cross and the Holy Spirit to these hindrances. Issues on sexual identity are particularly addressed.

Biblical Studies, School of

A sequence of three courses (Interpreting the Scriptures I, II, III) each 3 months in length, covers the complete Bible, giving a comprehensive knowledge and thorough understanding and use of the inductive method.

Child and Youth Ministries, Principles in

This course used to be referred to as the Small Half Foundation Training School, since almost half of the population of the world is under the age of 18 (the "small half"). It is designed for people preparing to work with children and young people, both in evangelism and in the church.

Children In Need

An in depth study of the spiritual, emotional and physical needs of the child. Topics include: biblical mandate for ministry to children, emotional, sexual and physical abuse, substance abuse, child development, child assessment and counseling, and child evangelism.

Christian Community Education , Diploma in

This two year course is designed to train teachers/tutors to staff a new model of all-age community learning centers. In many parts of the world where educational infrastructures are weak or non-existent there is an urgent need for education for people of all ages.

Church Leadership, School of

This school is aimed at developing ministry giftings that naturally result in leadership in the Body of Christ. Special emphasis is given to conflict management, the Gospel and various cultural considerations and how to avoid disqualification. Pastors, elders, and others with leadership callings receive practical training in team leadership, church planting and growth, spiritual gifts in church life, and how to train and mobilize the church.

Church Ministries School

Students are trained to minister and serve local churches and pastors in the areas of discipleship and evangelism, music ministry, and leadership training seminars.

College Ministries, School of

A twelve week school aimed at those desiring to minister to college students on college campuses. Four weeks of classroom teaching on evangelism, relationships, leadership, and counseling. The training phase would involve on-campus work for a period of eight weeks.

Communication & The Biblical View of Man

This course emphasizes basics in the major areas of communication: writing, listening, public speaking and inter-personal communication; and is applicable to every vocational field. It helps the student evaluate the audience, re-think the message and apply the message to the audience.

Communication, Advanced Principles of

This course is designed to give the communication major a balance of theory and practice in each of the four major areas of study: interpersonal communication, public speaking, small group dynamics and persuasion.

Community Counseling School

The purpose of this course is to equip Christians to counsel people in need, particularly non-Christians in an urban situation. The desire is to serve them in their need and lead them to a saving relationship with Jesus Christ.

Community Development, Foundations in

This school equips students to implement a biblical standard for community life in less-developed countries. It includes a study of the role of development workers, the structures and systems of a community, sanitation, housing, nutrition, and health care.

Community Health, Principles of

This course explores a broad perspective of community life as well as biblical principles for development. Community health skills and models of community health strategies are applied to communities through such activities as: survey and assessment, development and management of health programs, and basic field laboratory for epidemiology reporting.

Crusade Style Evangelism, School of

This school will equip you with the skills needed for mass evangelism and crusade directing. The purpose is to develop crusade directors who can employ creative evangelism concepts and work within interdenominational and cross-cultural settings.

Culinary Arts School

Someone has to prepare food for hundreds of missionaries at mission centers all over the world. If you would like to learn more about the ministry of feeding large groups of missionaries in a delicious, cost-effective manner, consider attending this 12 month course. You will also learn food service management, nutrition, and bulk purchasing.

DTS Phase II

This is a course for DTS graduates consisting of a 3-month lecture phase and optional outreach. It is designed to assist the student in making an intelligent decision in regards to long term calling and direction by introducing them to several of the major areas of study and ministry opportunities available through the University of the Nations and more broadly, Youth With A Mission.

Discipling Kingdom Musicians School

To enable and equip Christian Musicians to fulfill the Great Commission while pursuing excellence in the art of music. The five month course will involve teaching on our identity as musicians, evangelism and communication through music, Christian philosophy of music, and discipling a nation through music.

Education, Biblical Foundations in

A general introduction to education in the context of missions. Topics included are: a biblical basis for education, the curriculum, the teacher and the child. A curriculum development project and a time of application round out the course.

Education I, II Early Childhood

These courses include an overview of the history of education and the biblical philosophy of education, together with biblical principles focusing on knowing God our Creator, knowing God our Father, knowing Jesus -- God with us, and knowing the scriptures. There is also an in-depth study of the materials and principles of the multi-sensory approach to education of young children.

Education I, II, III, Elementary

A series of courses providing a basic understanding of how children learn and develop in the areas of spiritual life, character, language, intercession, history, geography, political science, art, creation, science, mathematics, health, physical education, dance and drama. The 6 - 12 year age group is emphasized.

Evangelism, School of

An advanced training program for DTS graduates, usually 5-6 months long (language study programs are available at certain locations). The emphasis is upon the "message' and "method" of evangelism. Teaching includes areas such as: Christian philosophy and apologetics, friendship evangelism, cross-cultural communication, and leadership training in various aspects of world evangelism. The field trip affords direct opportunities for ministry and leadership experience.

Family DTS

A Discipleship Training School that targets families for the purpose of discipling and mobilizing them for world evangelism.

Family Ministries School

The purpose of this course is to train leaders for ministry

in the areas of marriage and family restoration from a biblical perspective. Areas such as relationships, communication, life-style, and sexual problems are considered.

Fine Arts, Foundation One

A general introduction to theater arts, music and dance from a Christian perspective.

Focus Nine Sixteen

This three-month specialized course focuses on the use of the arts in reaching young people between the ages of nine and sixteen. Their development, thinking, and culture are examined as an exciting and relevant vehicle for communicating truth.

Frontier Mission, School of

Equips missionaries to plant fellowships of believers among unreached people groups. Training includes evangelism, misology, cross-cultural studies and language acquisition.

Graphic Design I & II, School of

These two courses are designed for those who have a selective eye, a store-house of ideas, and a desire to express them creatively on paper. Graphic techniques, layout, illustration, and studio management are among the topics covered.

Health Care Course

This course is for health care professional who want to integrate their faith with their health care practices.

Humanities & Science: A Christian Perspective

A core course dealing with the traditional liberal arts disciplines of philosophy, history, biography, political science, literature, the fine arts, and languages. Topics include the determination of truth, science and human values, the lessons of history, the search for justice in government and law, creativity in literature, art and music, and the justification of the Christian missionary enterprise.

Illustration, School of

This school helps students develop the art of illustration in relation to God's principles of communication. Topics include: a Christian view of illustration, composition and color, conceptual techniques, training in the use of different media, nature and figure drawing, and illustration as it related to photography and graphic design.

Intercession, Worship and Warfare, School of

The school of intercession, worship and spiritual warfare is designed to train potential teachers/leaders in intercession, worship and spiritual warfare. The course is committed to target the major language groups of the world and see training established in the church in those languages.

Jewish Ministries, School of

Studies include the land, people and history of Israel, Messianic Judaism, Modern Hebrew I, and how to communicate faith.

Journalism: Mass Media, School of

Studies the systems and technologies of television, radio and print journalism, with special emphasis on print media. Students will be able to write in a journalistic fashion appropriate for each mode.

Language & Culture Training School

Many YWAM bases offer language study programs in the country where the language is spoken. Students begin to read and write the foreign language as well as understand the cultural values. Classroom teaching and discussion are combined with a series of self-paced learning units.

Leadership Training School

Designed mainly for those involved in leadership at YWAM bases or in a YWAM ministry, this course teaches management, communication, and spiritual leadership principles. The hands-on workshops enable students to acquire practical skills in computer applications, time management, planning, delegation, finances, and related topics for effective management and ministry leadership.

Lifework Consulting Training

Designed to equip in personal ministry and career guidance, this course incorporates the SIMA (System for Identifying Motivated Abilities) to assist students in understanding God-given strengths and motivations.

Marketing and Research, School of

This course develops the business aspect of communication including communication systems, public relations, audience research and communication management. Students learn to manage communication projects utilizing all the various communications technologies.

Mercy Ministry, School of

The course work in this school teaches mercy ministries as a way to impact frontier areas.

Mercy, Relief and Development, School of

This school is designed to equip and train personnel for working in the areas of mercy, relief and development. Biblical approaches to implementing mercy ministries in the areas of prisons, orphanages, refugees and natural/man-caused disasters will be studied.

Missions, School of

Trains pioneer missionaries to trailblaze and pioneer, especially among the unreached people groups of the world. There are also specialized SOM's that reflect their targeted people group in their name.

Operation Year

This program lasts 1 year and includes what is done during a DTS and a DTS field assignment. The goal is to provide an opportunity for young people, aged 18 - 25, to work with one of the YWAM evangelism teams in Britain.

Pastoral Support School

Supporting missions through pastoral care. This course is designed to train people to be able to give pastoral support to mission workers. The course will examine the biblical view of pastoral care as it is appropriate for a variety of mission settings.

Performing Arts, Foundations in

An overview school providing training and improvement in one's artistic skills, biblical perspective of the Arts, and the need for a clean heart and right motivation in ministering through the Arts.

Performing Arts, Phase I, Apprenticeship in

The apprenticeship phase allows students to study dance, music, theater arts, or teen and child evangelism, within the context of the Academy's full-time Performing Arts Companies. Working and studying alongside practicing artists, students will be exposed to a high level of excellence as they continue to pursue their chosen art form, through a very practical apprenticeship model.

Photography, School of

This is designed for acquiring more specialized knowledge and skill in the area of photography, to communicate with visual impact God's purposes in the world today. Topics will include photo journalism, camera techniques, composition and light, darkroom techniques, color and b/w photography, filing and presentation, Christian approach to photography, and stewardship and photography.

Primary Health Care, Applied

This advanced course is for health workers who already have understanding and experience in primary health care in Third World settings. It is designed to provide specific clinical skills of diagnosis and management of medical problems.

Primary Health Care, Introduction to

This course introduces the student to primary health care strategies in Third World settings. Basic but practical health care skills are discussed with these strategies to aid the student meet felt needs of the poor and needy in these environments.

Printing, School of

This course combines technical knowledge and practical experience to multiply Christian printers and publishers worldwide. You will complete major projects on tract, magazine and booklet production.

Project Development Leadership School

Effective leadership is the key element in accomplishing nearly every task. In the construction of relief and development facilities, leaders with special skills are vital to the successful planning, designing, building and managing of men and materials for these projects. There is a great need in missions for construction leaders who know how to integrate the spiritual, technical and professional for effective communication of the gospel through meeting felt needs as well as proclaiming the Good News.

Radio Broadcasting, School of

The purpose of this school is to help students develop the use of radio effectively as a medium. The intensive training includes hands-on experience in radio production and broadcasting. Topics include: radio production, broadcast journalism, and radio management.

Strategic Missions, School of

A course which teaches strategies for evangelizing unreached people groups.

Teacher Training

The school trains teachers in the Principle Approach to teaching.

Teaching of English to Speakers of Other Languages

Equips the student to teach English in non-English speaking countries, and prepares the student spiritually and emotionally for cross-cultural experiences.

Urban Health Care School

Similar to the Primary Health Care School, but focusing on urban related problems such as addiction, AIDS, prostitution and venereal diseases, homosexuality.

Video Production, School of

Involves intense training in video production. Along with classroom lectures, there are hands-on experiences in script writing, camera work, editing, post production, audio, lighting and multi and single camera production.

Worship, School of

This school is designed to train men and women to take worship into the nations as a tool for spiritual warfare and evangelism.

Writing for Public Relations School

Students are trained to develop a personal writing style that is informative and appropriate for communication within organizations and to the public. Writing assignments include: evangelism literature, newsletters, brochures, writing for public speaking, fund raising literature, business correspondence, media copy and promotional material.

What Must I Do To Apply?

1 You must have committed your life to Jesus Christ and desire to share Him with others.
2. The minimum age for training schools is usually 18, but we welcome older, dedicated Christians as well.
3. Prayerfully consider the list of schools found in this Manual.
4. Consult with your pastor or spiritual leader. Pray with him about your intentions.
5. After deciding which school you wish to attend, you should request an application form from that location. They will be able to provide you with more information on costs and dates.

NOTE

1. Successful completion of a DTS is required prior to attending any other type of school listed.
2. Many of these courses are part of the University of the Nations (U of N) system and grant university credit. Please contact the specific location to inquire if they are officially registered as a part of the U of N System.

3. Some of the above defined schools may not be available at the time of this printing.

University of the Nations

University of the Nations (U of N) is a global university dedicated to be a multiplier for missions in fulfilling Christ's Great Commission. It is one university but located on many continents. We have two types of faculty: highly skilled resident faculty, and resource professors who are either professional in their various fields or professors from other universities. U of N's modular approach to education means students concentrate on one course per term, enabling them to live and study with the same classmates and the school staff.

Many (but not all) of the courses in The Go Manual, are registered with the U of N. The prerequisite to any U of N course is a Discipleship Training School (DTS) or Crossroads Discipleship Training School (CDTS). The admonition from II Peter 1:5 stresses development of faith and character before other areas.

(The U of N is a degree-granting institution (Associate's, Bachelor's and Master's degrees), but it is not accredited by any accrediting agency or association recognized by the United States Commissioner of Education. Various accredited colleges throughout the USA accept transfer students and credits.)

School Listing

Explanation of Information in Section III

School:

Name of school being offered. Listed alphabetically.

Abbreviation:

The YWAM abbreviation for that school.

Ctry/City:

The country and city code indicating the location of the school. (See Appendix for code key.)

Beginning Month:

The starting month for that school. If two months are listed, the school starts in both of those months. (A school may start three times a year, but the third month will be listed separately.)

Length:

The total length of the school listed in weeks or months. (wk= week, mo=month) If a "+" sign appears after the length, the school may continue on for an optional amount of time longer than what is stated.

Language(s):

The primary language(s) to be used in this school. The main language will be listed first. The second language will be listed second. (See Appendix for explanation of language codes used.)

Abrev.	Ctry/City	Beg.Mon.	Length	Lang.
Addictive Behavior Counseling School				
ABC	NETH-NATL	Apr	6 mo	Eng/Dut
ABC	USA-HI-UN	varies	6 mo	Eng
Aquaculture Technology School				
ACTS	USA-HI-UN	Apr	6 mo	Eng
Arts In Ministry				
AIM	CAN-ONT-CAMB	Feb	5 mo	Eng
Author's Training School				
ATS	USA-TX-EDIT	Sep	3 mo	Eng
Basic Construction Technology School				
BCTS	USA-HI-UN	Jun	6 mo	Eng
Basic Leadership Course				
BLC	AUST-NSW-MT	Jan/Aug	14 mo	Eng
BLC	IRELAND	Apr/Oct	1 yr	Eng
BLC	MALAY-PENANG	Dec/Jun	1 yr	Eng
BLC	MALAY-PENANG	Mar	1 yr	Tam
BLC	NZ-NORTH	Jan/Sep	54 wk	Eng
BLC	SWITZ-BIEL	Dec/Mar	13 wk	Ger
BLC	SWITZ-BIEL	Jun	13 wk	Germ
BLC	SWITZ-BIEL	Sep	13 wk	Ger/Eng
BLC	UGANDA-NATL	Jan	12 mo	Eng
BLC	UK-ENG-CUCK	Jan/May	21 wk	Eng
BLC	UK-ENG-CUCK	Oct	21 wk	Eng
BLC	UK-ENG-HARP	Jan/Sep	6 mo	Eng
BLC	UK-ENG-PARR	Apr/Oct	20 wk	Eng
BLC	USA-FL-MIAMI	Mar/Sep	6 mo	Eng
Bible, School of the				
	USA-TX-MEX	Sep	5 mo	Spa
SOTB	USA-TX-TWIN	Sep	10 mo	Eng
Biblical Christian World View School				
BCWV	SWITZ-WILER	Jul	3 mo	Ger/Eng
Biblical Counseling, Intro				
IBC	AUST-ACT-WAT	Apr	3 mo	Eng
IBC	BRAZ-RECIFE	Jan	5 mo	Por/Spa
IBC	FRANCE-MONT	Sep	3 mo	Fre/Eng
IBC	NETH-NATL	Sep	6 mo	Eng/Dut
IBC	PHIL-ANT	Jan	6 mo	Eng
IBC	SAFR-MUIZ	Sep	6 mo	Eng
IBC	SWED-LJUN	Sep	3 mo+	Eng/Swe
IBC	SWITZ-WILER	Jan	3 mo+	Ger/Eng
IBC	USA-HI-UN	Jan/Apr	6 mo	Eng
IBC	USA-HI-UN	Sep	6 mo	Eng
IBC	ZIMB-BULAW	Apr	24 wk	Eng
Biblical Counseling, Methods & Models				
MMBC	SWITZ-WILER	Oct	6 mo	Ger/Eng
MMBC	USA-HI-UN	Jan	6 mo	Eng

Abrev.	Ctry/City	Beg.Mon.	Length	Lang.
Biblical Studies (I & II), School of				
SBS 1&2	USA-VA-UN	Sep	6 mo+	Eng
Biblical Studies (I), School of				
SBS I	ZIMB-BULAW	Oct	12 wk	Eng
Biblical Studies, School of				
SBS	AUST-ACT-WAT	Jan	9 mo	Eng
SBS	BOLIV-SANTA			
SBS	CAN-BC-WIN	Sep	9 mo	Eng
SBS	CHILE-SANT	Sep	9 mo	Spa
SBS	COLOM-BUCA	Sep	9 mo	Spa
SBS	FRANCE-MONT	Sep	3 mo	Fre
SBS	GERM-BISP	Jan	9 mo	Ger
SBS	GHANA	Feb	9 mo	Eng
SBS	GUAT-GUAT	Jan	9 mo	Spa
SBS	HONG-REG	Feb	5 mo	Can
SBS	INDO-JAVA	Jul	9 mo	Ind
SBS	ITALY-CADEG	Apr	9 mo	Ita/Eng
SBS	NZ-CHRIST	Mar	9 mo	Eng
SBS	SAFR-MUIZ	Mar	9 mo	Eng
SBS	SING-NATL	Sep	9 mo	Eng
SBS	TAIW-TAIPEI	Feb	9 mo	Eng/Man
SBS	UK-ENG-KINGS	Sep	9 mo	Eng
SBS	USA-HI-HONOL	Jan	9 mo	Eng
SBS	USA-HI-UN	Sep	9 mo	Eng
SBS	USA-MT-LAKES	Sep	9 mo	Eng
SBS	USA-TN-NASH	Sep	9 mo	Eng
Biblical Studies, School of (I)				
SBS (I)	SWED-LJUN	Sep	3 mo	Eng/Swe
SBS	SWITZ-WILER	Oct	3 mo	Ger/Eng
Biblical Studies, School of (part-time)				
SBS	UK-ENG-LOND	Jan	2 yr	Eng
Child & Youth Ministry, Principles in				
PCYM	AUST-TAS-SAN	Oct	12 wk+	Eng
PCYM	CAN-VAN-KK	Sep	12 wk	Eng
PCYM	INDIA-NEW	Jan	4 mo	Eng
PCYM	NETH-HEERDE	Sep	3 mo	Eng/Dut
PCYM	UK-SCOT-KK	Apr/Oct	5 mo	Eng
PCYM	UK-WAL-PONT	Sep	11 mo	Eng
PCYM	USA-GA-ATL	Sep	5 mo	Eng
Child & Youth Ministry:Principles in				
PCYM	DENMARK-COPE	Mar	5 mo	Sca/Eng
Child & Youth Ministry: Principles in				
PCYM	MALI	Jan	6 mo	Fre/Eng
Children In Need				
CIN	CAN-BC-WIN	Sep	3 mo	Eng
CIN	NZ-AUCK-URB	May	3 mo	Eng

Abrev.	Ctry/City	Beg.Mon.	Length	Lang.
Christian Character Development Program				
CCDP	UK-ENG-TOR	Apr/Sep	12 wk	Eng
Church Leadership, School of				
SCL	USA-HI-UN	Jun	6 mo	Eng
Church Ministries School				
CMS	USA-HI-UN	Apr	6 mo	Eng
Church Planting & Leadership, School of				
SCPL	BRAZ-RECIFE	Jul	9 mo	Por
SCPL	GHANA	Feb	3 mo	Eng
SCPL	INDIA-PUNE	Jan	Eng	
SCPL	SAFR-STIL	Feb	6 mo	Eng
SCPL	USA-VA-UN		3 mo+	Eng
College Ministries School				
	USA-FL-WAVES	Jan/Sep	12 wk	Eng
Communication & Biblical View of Man				
CBVM	AUST-ACT-WAT	Jul	3 mo	Eng
CBVM	USA-HI-UN	Sep	3 mo	Eng
Community Counseling School				
CCS	SWED-STOCK	Sep	6 mo	Swe/Eng
CCS	UK-ENG-PARR	Apr	24 wk	Eng
Community Development, Foundations in				
FCD	AUST-WA-PERTH	Jul	6 mo	Eng
FCD	BRAZ-RECIFE	Jul	5 mo	Por/Eng
FCD	INDIA-PUNE	Sep	6 mo	Eng
FCD	UGANDA-NATL	Sep	6 mo	Eng
FCD	USA-HI-UN	Apr	6 mo	Eng
FCD	USA-TX-MERCY	Apr/Sep	3 mo	Eng
Community Health Care - Internship				
	USA-CA-RICH	Jan	5 mo	Eng
Community Health, Principles of				
PCH	USA-HI-UN	Jun	6 mo	Eng
Counseling Training School				
CTS	CAN-QUE-DUN	Sep	3 mo	Fre
Creative Ministries, School of				
SOCM	UK-DERBY	Oct	6 mo	
Cross-cultural Education & Literacy				
CEL	BRAZ-ROND		3 mo	Por/Eng
Cross-cultural Missions, School of				
CCM	BOLIV-LAPAZ	Apr	9 mo	Spa
Crossroads DTS				
CDTS	AUST-ACT-WAT	Apr/Oct	3 mo	Eng
CDTS	AUST-WA-PERTH	Jan	6 mo	Eng
CDTS	BRAZ-REST	Jul	5 mo	Por/Sig
CDTS	CAN-BC-WIN	Jan	5 mo	Eng
CDTS	CAN-ONT-CAMB	Jun	3 mo+	Eng
CDTS	DENMARK-MORK	Apr	5 mo	Eng/Dan

Abrev.	Ctry/City	Beg.Mon.	Length	Lang.
CDTS	FRANCE-MONT	Apr	5 mo	Fre/Eng
CDTS	GERM-HURL			
CDTS	NZ-MATAM	Feb	24 wk	Eng
CDTS	SAFR-MUIZ	Apr	5 mo	Eng
CDTS	SAFR-STIL	Sep	3 mo	Eng
CDTS	SING-NATL	Jul	5 mo	
CDTS	SWED-LJUN	Jan	3 mo+	Eng/Swe
CDTS	SWITZ-WILER	Jul	6 mo	Ger/Eng
CDTS	UK-ENG-KINGS	Jan	5 mo	Eng
CDTS	USA-CA-BISH	Jan	6 mo	Eng
CDTS	USA-CA-RICH	Sep	5 mo	Eng
CDTS	USA-CO-FRONT	Sep	6 mo	Eng
CDTS	USA-FL-ORL	Apr	5 mo	Eng
CDTS	USA-HI-UN	Jan/Apr	6 mo	Eng
CDTS	USA-HI-UN	Jun/Sep	6 mo	Eng
CDTS	USA-MT-LAKES	Apr	5 mo	Eng
CDTS	USA-OR-SALEM	Jun	5 mo	Eng
CDTS	USA-PA-ROAR	Apr	12 wk	Eng
CDTS	USA-TX-MERCY	Mar/Sep	5 mo	
CDTS	USA-TX-TWIN	Jan/Jun	4 mo	Eng
Crusade Style Evangelism, School of				
CSE	USA-WI-NORTH	Sep	12 wk	Eng
Culinary School				
	USA-TX-LAST	Apr	12 mo	Eng
Desktop Communication, School of				
SDC	GERM-MEDIA	Sep	3 mo	Eng
Desktop Publishing, School of				
SDC	USA-TX-LAST	Jan	3 mo	Eng
Diploma in Christian Community Education				
DCCE	UK-ENG-SHEP	Apr	12 wk	Eng
Discipleship Program:Evenings				
	SIERRA	Mar/Sep	15 wk	Kri/Eng
Discipleship Training School				
DTS	AMSAMOA	Apr	5 mo	Eng
DTS	AUST-ACT-WAT	Jan	6 mo	Eng
DTS	AUST-NSW-ALB	Sep	6 mo	Eng
DTS	AUST-NSW-KOT	Mar	10 mo	Eng
DTS	AUST-NSW-MT	Jan/Sep	5 mo	Eng
DTS	AUST-NSW-MT	Jan	5 mo	Kor/Eng
DTS	AUST-QLD-CAR	Jan	6 mo	Eng
DTS	AUST-QLD-CAR	May/Sep	6 mo	Eng
DTS	AUSTRIA-WIEN	Sep	5 mo	Ger/Eng
DTS	AUST-TAS-SAN	Feb	22 wk	Eng
DTS	AUST-VIC-NATL	Jan/May	6 mo	Eng
DTS	AUST-VIC-NATL	Sep	6 mo	Eng
DTS	AUST-WA-PERTH	Jan/Sep	6 mo	Eng
DTS	BELIZE-BEL	Sep	6 mo	Eng
DTS	BOLIV-SANTA	Apr	5 mo	Spa

Abrev.	Ctry/City	Beg.Mon.	Length	Lang.
DTS	BOLIV-SANTA	Oct	5 mo	Spa/Eng
DTS	BRAZ-CURIT	Feb/Jul	5 mo	Por
DTS	BRAZ-MANAUS	Mar/Jul	5 mo	Por
DTS	BRAZ-NATL	Feb	5 mo	Por
DTS	BRAZ-PORTO	Feb/Jul	5 mo	Por
DTS	BRAZ-RECIFE	Jan	5 mo	Eng
DTS	BRAZ-RECIFE	Feb	5 mo	Por
DTS	BRAZ-ROND		5 mo	
DTS	BRAZ-SAO	Feb/Jul	5 mo	Por
DTS	CAN-ALB-TURN	Oct/Apr	6 mo	Eng
DTS	CAN-BC-WIN	Sep/Apr	5 mo	Eng
DTS	CAN-ONT-CAMB	Jan/Sep	5 mo	Eng
DTS	CAN-ONT-TOR	Apr	6 mo	Kor
DTS	CAN-QUE-DUN	Mar	5 mo	Fre
DTS	CHILE-SANT	Jan	6 mo	Spa
DTS	CISUK	Apr/Sep	5 mo	Eng/Ukr/Rus
DTS	COLOM-BOG	Jan/Jul	5 mo	Spa
DTS	COLOM-BUCA	Jul	6 mo	Spa
DTS	COLOM-CART	Jan	5 mo	Spa
DTS	COLOM-CART	Jul	5 mo	Spa/Eng
DTS	COOK-RARO	Apr/Sep	5 mo	Eng
DTS	DENMARK-MORK	Jan/Sep	5 mo	Eng/Dan
DTS	DOMIN-SANTO	Sep/Jun	5 mo	Spa
DTS	FRANCE-CHAT	Sep	6 mo	Fre/Eng
DTS	FRANCE-MONT	Jan	5 mo	Fre/Eng
DTS	GERM-ALTEN	Apr	6 mo	Ger/Eng
DTS	GERM-BISP	Oct	5 mo	Eng/Ger
DTS	GERM-HURL			
DTS	GHANA	Jan	3 mo	Eng
DTS	GREENLAND	Apr	20 wk	Eng/Gre
DTS	GRENADA	Mar/Sep	5 mo	Eng
DTS	GUAT-GUAT	May	6 mo	Spa
DTS	GUINEABIS		6 mo	Por
DTS	HAITI	Mar	5 mo	Eng
DTS	HONG-REG	Sep	5 mo	Can/Eng
DTS	HUNGARY	Sep	6 mo	Eng/Hun
DTS	INDIA-BANG	Jan/Jul	6 mo	Eng/Kan
DTS	INDIA-BHOPAL	Jan/May	5 mo	Hin
DTS	INDIA-BHOPAL	Sep	5 mo	Hin
DTS	INDIA-CALC	Jan/Jul	6 mo	Eng/Ben
DTS	INDIA-MADRAS	Jan/Jul	5 mo	Eng/Tam
DTS	INDIA-NEW	Jul	5 mo	Eng
DTS	INDIA-PUNE	Jan/Apr	5 mo	Eng/Mar
DTS	INDO-JATIM	Sep	6 mo	Ind/Eng
DTS	INDO-JAVA	Jul/Sep	6 mo	Eng/Ind
DTS	INDO-TIMOR	Sep	6 mo	Ind
DTS	IRELAND	Apr/Oct	6 mo	Eng
DTS	ITALY-CADEG	Jan	5 mo	Ita
DTS	JAMAICA	Sep	6 mo	Eng
DTS	JAPAN-HIGA	Sep	6 mo	Kor/Jap

Abrev.	Ctry/City	Beg.Mon.	Length	Lang.
DTS	JAPAN-NATL	Apr	23 wk	
DTS	JAPAN-NATL	Sep	24 wk	
DTS	JAPAN-OKIN	Apr/Oct	24 wk	Jap/Eng
DTS	KENYA-LIKONI	Mar/Sep	5 mo	Eng
DTS	KENYA-MOMB	Jul	5 mo	Eng
DTS	KOREA-PUSAN	Mar	6 mo	Kor
DTS	LATVIA	Sep	5 mo	Lat/Eng
DTS	MALAY-PENANG	Jan/Jul	5 mo	Eng
DTS	MALAY-PENANG	Apr	5 mo	Tam
DTS	MALI	Jul	6 mo	Fre
DTS	MALI	Nov	5 mo	Bam
DTS	MEX-GUADAL	Sep	5 mo	Spa
DTS	MEX-JUAR	Mar	5 mo	Spa
DTS	MEX-MAZAT	Sep	5 mo	Eng
DTS	MEX-MEXCITY	Oct	6 mo	Spa
DTS	MEX-OAX	Jan	5 mo	Spa
DTS	MEX-TEPIC	Jan	5 mo	Spa
DTS	NAMIB-WIND	Jan/Jul	5 mo	Eng
DTS	NEPAL-KATH		6 mo	Nep
DTS	NEPAL-POKH		6 mo	Nep
DTS	NETH-HEERDE	Jan/Sep	6 mo	Eng/Dut
DTS	NETH-NATL	Jan/Apr	6 mo	Eng/Dut
DTS	NETH-NATL	Sep	6 mo	Eng/Dut
DTS	NEWCAL	Sep	6 mo	Fre
DTS	NICAR	Sep	5 mo	Spa
DTS	NORTHMAR	Jul	6 mo	Eng
DTS	NORW-KRIS	Sep	6 mo	Nor
DTS	NORW-LENS	Sep	6 mo	Nor/Eng
DTS	NORW-OTT	Sep	6 mo	Nor/Eng
DTS	NZ-AUCK-URB	Sep	6 mo	Eng
DTS	NZ-MERCY	Apr/Jul	6 mo	Eng
DTS	NZ-NORTH	Jan/Sep	24 wk	Eng
DTS	NZ-OXFORD	Jan/Sep	6 mo	Eng
DTS	PARAGUAY	Apr	6 mo	Spa
DTS	PHIL-ANT	May/Sep	6 mo	Eng
DTS	PHIL-DAVAO	Oct	6 mo	Eng/Ceb
DTS	PHIL-PALAW	Apr		Vie
DTS	PNG-MTHAG	Jan/Jul	6 mo	Eng
DTS	POLAND	Apr	5 mo	Eng/Pol
DTS	PUERTO	Jan/Aug	5 mo	Spa/Eng
DTS	SAFR-MUIZ	Jan	5 mo	Eng
DTS	SAFR-STIL	Jan/Jul	6 mo	Eng
DTS	SAFR-WORC	Jan/Jul	5 mo	Eng/Afr
DTS	SENEGAL	Jan	6 mo	Fre
DTS	SING-NATL	Apr	6 mo	
DTS	SWED-LJUN	Jan/Sep	6 mo	Eng/Swe
DTS	SWITZ-BIEL	Jan/Apr	12 wk	Ger
DTS	SWITZ-BIEL	Jul	12 wk	Ger
DTS	SWITZ-BIEL	Oct	12 wk	Ger/Eng
DTS	TAIW-TAIN	Mar	6 mo	Man/Eng

Abrev.	Ctry/City	Beg.Mon.	Length	Lang.
DTS	TAIW-TAIPEI	Feb/Sep	6 mo	Eng/Man
DTS	TANZANIA	Mar/Sep	5 mo	Kis/Eng
DTS	UGANDA-NATL	Jan	6 mo	Eng
DTS	UK-ENG-CUCK	Jan/May	20 wk	Eng
DTS	UK-ENG-CUCK	Oct	20 wk	Eng
DTS	UK-ENG-KINGS	Apr/Sep	6 mo	Eng
DTS	UK-ENG-LOND	Sep	6 mo	Eng
DTS	UK-ENG-PARR	Apr/Oct	20 wk	Eng
DTS	USA-CA-BISH	Jan/Oct	6 mo	Eng
DTS	USA-CA-CHULA	Sep	6 mo	Spa/Eng
DTS	USA-CA-RICH	Mar	9 mo	Eng
DTS	USA-CA-SUN	Jan/Apr	5 mo	Eng
DTS	USA-CA-SUN	Sep	5 mo	Eng
DTS	USA-CENTRAL	Mar	5 mo	Eng
DTS	USA-CO-ARV	Jan/Apr	5 mo	Eng
DTS	USA-CO-ARV	Sep	5 mo	Eng
DTS	USA-CO-FRONT	Sep	6 mo	Eng
DTS	USA-FL-MIAMI	Apr/Sep	5 mo	Eng
DTS	USA-FL-MIAMI	Jan	5 mo	Spa
DTS	USA-FL-ORL	Sep	5 mo	Eng
DTS	USA-HI-HONOL	Jan/Apr	5 mo	Eng
DTS	USA-HI-HONOL	Sep	5 mo	Eng
DTS	USA-HI-MAUI	Jan/Apr	5 mo	Eng
DTS	USA-HI-MAUI	Oct	5 mo	Eng
DTS	USA-HI-UN	Jan/Apr	6 mo	Eng
DTS	USA-HI-UN	Jun/Sep	6 mo	Eng
DTS	USA-MA-SOMER	Sep	5 mo	Eng
DTS	USA-MT-LAKES	Jan/Apr	5 mo	Eng
DTS	USA-MT-LAKES	Sep	5 mo	Eng
DTS	USA-NC-CHAR	Apr/Sep	6 mo	Eng
DTS	USA-NY-ANT	Jan	5 mo	Eng/Kor
DTS	USA-NY-EAST	Sep	5 mo	Eng
DTS	USA-OR-SALEM	Mar/Sep	5 mo	Eng
DTS	USA-PA-PHIL	Sep	5 mo	Eng
DTS	USA-PA-TITUS	Mar/Sep	5 mo	Eng/Sig
DTS	USA-SOUTHAM		5 mo	Spa
DTS	USA-STCROIX	Mar/Sep	5 mo	Eng
DTS	USA-TN-NASH	Jan/Sep	5 mo	Eng
DTS	USA-TX-LAST	Jan/Apr	5 mo	Eng
DTS	USA-TX-LAST	Sep	5 mo	Eng
DTS	USA-TX-MERCY	Feb/May	5 mo	
DTS	USA-TX-MERCY	Aug/Nov	5 mo	
DTS	USA-TX-MEX	Sep/Mar	5 mo	Eng/Spa
DTS	USA-TX-TWIN	Jan/Mar	5 mo	Eng
DTS	USA-TX-TWIN	Sep	5 mo	Eng
DTS	USA-VA-INT	Apr	5 mo	Eng
DTS	USA-VA-UN	Apr/Sep	5 mo	Eng
DTS	USA-WI-WEYER	Sep	5 mo	Eng
DTS	VENEZ-CARAC	Jan	5 mo	Spa
DTS	WSAMOA-PION	Feb/May	5 mo	Eng/Sam

Abrev.	Ctry/City	Beg.Mon.	Length	Lang.
DTS	WSAMOA-PION	Aug	5 mo	Eng/Sam
DTS	WSAMOA-SAVA	Feb/May	5 mo	Sam/Eng
DTS	WSAMOA-SAVA	Aug	5 mo	Sam/Eng
DTS	ZIMB-BULAW	Jan/Jul	24 wk	Eng
Discipleship Training School (R&D)				
DBS	UK-ENG-HARP	Jan	6 mo	Eng
Discipleship Training School:Arabic				
DTS/A	UK-ENG-HARP	Sep	6 mo	Ara/Eng
Discipleship Training School:Arabic/Eng				
DTS	EGYPT	Jan	20 wk	Eng/Ara
DTS	UK-ENG-HARP	Sep	20 wk	Eng/Ara
Discipleship Training School:Business				
DTS/B	KOREA-PUSAN	Dec	10 mo	Kor
Discipleship Training School:Cambodian				
DTS/CAM	AUST-NSW-CABR	Sep	5 mo	Eng/Khm
Discipleship Training School:College				
DTS/C	KOREA-PUSAN	Jul	8 mo	Kor
Discipleship Training School:Japanese				
DTS/J	USA-HI-UN	Apr/Sep	6 mo	Jap
Discipleship Training School:Mini				
DTSmini	LATVIA	Jul	2 mo	Lat/Eng
DTSMini	TAIW-TAICH	Jul	3 mo	Chi/Eng
Discipleship Training School:Pacific				
DTS/P	GUAM	Sep	6 mo	Eng
DTS/P	USA-HI-UN	Apr/Sep	6 mo	
Discipleship Training School:Prison				
DTS	BRAZ-RECIFE	Feb	5 mo	Por
Discipleship Training School:Veitnamese				
DTS/V	AUST-NSW-CABR	Mar	5 mo	Eng/Vie
Discipling Kingdom Musicians School				
DKMS	AUST-TAS-SOR	Sep	5 mo	Eng
DTS: Cross-cultural				
CCDTS	AUST-WA-PERTH	Apr	6 mo	Eng
CCDTS	NZ-NORTH			
DTS Phase II				
DTSII	COLOM-BOG	Jul	3 mo	Spa
DTS II	USA-CO-ARV	Apr/Sep	3 mo+	Eng
DTS: Poor & Needy				
PNDTS	AUST-WA-PERTH	Apr	6 mo	Eng
DTS: Surfers for Missions				
	USA-HI-MAUI	Apr	5 mo	Eng
DTS:Impact World Tour				
DTS	USA-OR-SALEM	Mar	5 mo	Eng
DTS	USA-WI-NORTH	Sep	5 mo+	Eng

Abrev.	Ctry/City	Beg.Mon.	Length	Lang.
Early Childhood Education, Advanced				
	USA-HI-UN	varies	3 mo	Eng
Early Childhood Education, School of				
SECE	BRAZ-PORTO	Jul	18	Por
SECE	GERM-HURL			
SECE	UGANDA-NATL		3 mo+	Eng
SECE	UK-SCOT-WEE	Sep	3 mo	Eng
SECE	USA-HI-UN	Apr	18 mo	Eng
Early Childhood Teacher Training				
ECTT	NZ-AUCK-TAKA	Feb	3 yr	Eng
Ecology and Environmental Education				
	BRAZ-ROND		3 mo	
Elementary Education, Biblical Foundat				
BFE I	USA-HI-UN	Apr	3 mo	Eng
Elementary Teacher Training Course				
ETTC	AUST-ACT-WAT	Jan	11 mo	Eng
English Language and Culture				
ESL	USA-HI-UN	Sep	3 mo	Eng
Evangelism & Church Planting, School of				
SECP	NZ-OXFORD	Mar	6 mo	Eng
Evangelism, School of				
SOE	BRAZ-RECIFE	Jul	5 mo	Por/Eng
SOE	INDIA-BANG	Jan	6 mo	Eng
SOE	JAPAN-OKIN	Jan	24 wk	Eng/Jap
SOE	NORW-OTT	Apr	5 mo	Nor/Eng
SOE	QUST-QLD-CAR	Sep	6 mo	Eng
SOE	SAFR-MUIZ	Jun	5 mo	Eng
SOE	SAFR-WORC	Jul	5 mo	Eng/Afr
SOE	UK-DERBY	Oct	6 mo	
SOE	USA-HI-MAUI	Jan	5 mo	Eng
SOE	USA-NC-CHAR	Sep	6 mo	Eng
SOE	USA-PA-TITUS	Mar	5 mo	Eng/Sig
SOE	USA-TN-NASH	Apr/Jul	5 mo	Eng
SOE	USA-TX-TWIN	Mar/Jun	5 mo	Eng
SOE	USA-TX-TWIN	Sep	5 mo	Eng
Evangelism, School of (Strike A Light!)				
SOE	AUST-VIC-NATL	Mar/Sep	1 yr	Eng
Family DTS				
DTS	AUST-ACT-WAT	Jul	5 mo	Eng
FDTS	GERM-BUCH	Sep	4 mo	Ger/Eng
	NZ-FAMILY	Feb/Sep	5 mo	Eng
FDTS	USA-ID-RIGG	Sep	5 mo	Eng
Family Ministries School				
FMS	AUST-ACT-WAT	Jan	3 mo	Eng
FMS	NZ-FAMILY	Jul	6 mo	Eng
FMS	USA-WI-WEYER	Apr	5 mo	Eng

Abrev.	Ctry/City	Beg.Mon.	Length	Lang.
Family Therapy School				
FTS	AUST-ACT-WAT	Oct	3 mo	Eng
Focus Nine Sixteen				
F9-16	CAN-ONT-CAMB	Feb	6 mo	Eng
Foundational School of Biblical Studies				
FSBS	NEPAL-POKH	Apr	9 mo	Nep
Foundations For Leadership				
FFL	IRELAND	Mar	3 wk	Eng
Frontier Missions, School of				
SOFM	AUST-ACT-WAT	Oct	6 mo	Eng
SOFM	AUST-WA-PERTH	Jul	9 mo	Eng
SOFM	COLOM-BUCA	Jan	6 mo	Spa
SOFM	FRANCE-CHAT	Sep	6-9 mo	Fre/Eng
SOFM	GERM-BISP	Oct	3 mo	Ger/Eng
SOFM	INDIA-PUNE	Jul	3 mo+	Eng
SOFM	INDIA-VARAN	Jan	3 mo+	Hin
SOFM	INDO-JAVA	Jan	6 mo	Ind
SOFM	ISRAEL-JERUS	Jan	1 yr	Eng/Ara
SOFM	MEX-OAX	Sep	6 mo	Spa
SOFM	NEPAL-KATH			Eng/Nep
SOFM	NETH-HEERDE	Sep	3 mo	Eng
SOFM	NETH-NATL	Apr	3 mo	Eng/Dut
SOFM	NORW-OTT	Apr	5 mo	Nor/Eng
SOFM	PHIL-DAVAO	May	5 mo	Eng/Ceb
SOFM	SING-NATL	Jan	3 mo	
SOFM	SPAIN-TORR	Feb	5 mo	Eng
SOFM	SWED-LJUN	Sep	3 mo	Eng/Swe
SOFM	TAIW-MIA	Mar	1 yr	Eng
SOFM	TAIW-TAIPEI	Feb	2 yr	Eng
SOFM	THAIL-FRONT	Sep	2 yr	Eng
SOFM	UK-ENG-CUCK	Apr	12 wk	Eng
SOFM	UK-ENG-HARP	May	9 mo	Eng
SOFM	USA-CO-ARV	Jan		Eng
SOFM	VENEZ-CARAC	Aug	1 yr	Spa
Gifts & Ministry of the Holy Spirit				
GMHS	GERM-ALTEN	Nov	4 wk	Ger/Eng
Graphic Design I, School of				
SGD1	USA-HI-UN	Apr	3 mo	Eng
Graphic Design II, School of				
SGDII	USA-HI-UN	Jun	6 mo	Eng
Graphic Design III, School of				
SGDIII	USA-HI-UN	Jan	6 mo	Eng
Hospitality School				
	CAN-ASSOC	Apr	4 wk	Eng
	NETH-HEERDE	Apr	5 wk	Eng/Dut
Humanities & Science:A Christ Perspect				
HIS/SAT	AUST-ACT-CAN	Jan	3 mo	Eng

Abrev.	Ctry/City	Beg.Mon.	Length	Lang.
HS	AUST-ACT-WAT	Jan	3 mo	Eng
Humanities & Science:Christian Perspect				
HIS	USA-HI-UN	Apr	3 mo	Eng
Impact World Tour Outreach/Internship				
	USA-WI-NORTH	Dec	24 wk	Eng
Intensive Bible School				
	MEX-JUAR	Oct	3 mo	Spa
Intercession, School of				
SOI	JAPAN-NATL	Jul	12 wk	
SOI	USA-CO-ARV	Jan	3 mo	Eng
SOI	USA-CO-FRONT	May/Sep	6 mo	Eng
SOI	USA-VA-UN	Jan	6 mo	Eng
Intercession, Worship & Warfare:School				
SOI	AUST-QLD-ASH	Mar	12 wk	Eng
SOI	NORW-LENS	Jan	4 mo	Nor/Eng
SOI	TAIW-TAIPEI	Sep	3 mo	Eng/Man
SOI	USA-OR-SALEM	Jan	5 mo	Eng
Jewish Studies, School of				
SJS	USA-VA-UN	Sep	6 mo	Eng
Language & Culture School - Greenlandic				
GLCS	GREENLAND	Sep	12 wk	Eng
Language School - Russian/Ukrainian				
	CISRUS	Sep+	1 mo+	Eng/Rus/Ukr
Leadership & Ministry Skills School				
	USA-CA-SUN	Mar	3 mo	Eng
Leadership Development Internship				
LDI	USA-CO-MISS	Jan	11 mo	Eng
Leadership Training School				
LTS	USA-HI-UN	Jan	3 mo	Eng
Life Audit School				
LAS	AUST-NSW-DEE	Jan	10 mo	Eng
Lifework Consulting Training I & II				
LCT	USA-HI-UN	varies	6 mo	Eng
Linguistics School				
LIS	BRAZ-ROND		3 mo	Por/Eng
Marketing and Research, School of				
SMR	USA-HI-UN	Sep	6 mo	Eng
Medical Missions, Orientation to				
OMM	UK-ENG-HARP	Sep	3 mo	Eng
Mercy Ministry, School of				
SOMM	SWED-LJUN	Sep	3 mo+	Eng/Swe
Mission Bridge Training				
	USA-CO-FRONT	May/Sep	12 mo	Eng

Abrev.	Ctry/City	Beg.Mon.	Length	Lang.
Mission School				
MS	BRAZ-NATL	Jun	5 mo	Por
Missions & Evangelism, School of				
SOME	USA-HI-HONOL	Apr/Sep	5 mo	Eng
Missions & Evangelism, School of				
SOME	PNG-BOR			Eng
Missions, School of				
SOM	GRENADA	Sep	12 mo	Eng
SOM	URUGUAY	Apr	11 mo	Spa
Missions, School of (CCSOE, SOFM, SOM)				
SOM	USA-HI-UN	Jan	6 mo	Eng
Operation Year				
OP YEAR	SWED-STOCK	Jan	1 yr	Swe/Eng
OP YEAR	UK-DERBY	Oct	11 mo	
OP YEAR	UK-ENG-BRIST	Sep	1 yr	Eng
OP YEAR	UK-ENG-LIV	Sep	12 mo	Eng
OP YEAR	UK-ENG-LOND	Sep	1 yr	Eng
OP YEAR	UK-SCOT-EDIN	12 mo	Eng	
OP YEAR	UK-WAL-PONT	Oct	11 mo	Eng
PCYM Internship				
PCYM in	UK-SCOT-KK	Sep	1 yr	Eng
PCYM: Rescue and Restore Training School				
PCYM	BRAZ-REST	Apr	3 mo+	Eng/Por
Performing Arts, Foundations in				
	CHILE-SANT	Apr	3 mo	Spa
FPA	USA-HI-UN	Sep	6 mo	Eng
Performing Arts (II)				
PAII	CAN-ONT-CAMB	May	4 mo	Eng
Personnel Development School				
PDS	AUST-NSW-MT	May	3 mo	Eng
Photography, School of				
SOP	USA-HI-UN	Jan	6 mo	Eng
Pioneer Ministry, School of				
	VENEZ-CARAC	May	5 mo	Spa
Primary Health Care, Applied				
APHC	USA-HI-UN	Jan	6 mo	Eng
Primary Health Care, Directed Studies				
	USA-HI-UN	varies	3 mo	Eng
Primary Health Care, Intro				
PHC	AUST-WA-PERTH	Jan	6 mo	Eng
PHC	BRAZ-ROND	5 mo	5 mo	
PHC	GHANA	Oct	6 wk	Eng
PHC	GUAT-GUAT	Sep	6 mo	Spa/Eng
PHC	INDIA-PUNE	Jul	6 mo	Eng
PHC	KENYA-MOMB	May	7 mo	Eng

Abrev.	Ctry/City	Beg.Mon.	Length	Lang.
PHC	MALI	Oct	6 mo	Fre
PHC	SAFR-MUIZ	Sep	6 mo	Eng
PHC	USA-HI-UN	Jun	6 mo	Eng
PHC	USA-ID-RIGG	Sep	3 mo	Eng
Principles of Child & Youth Ministry				
PCYM	SWITZ-WILER	Apr	4 mo	Ger/Eng
Print Production School				
PPS	PARAGUAY	Sep	3 mo	Spa/Eng
PPS	USA-TX-LAST	Apr	3 mo	Eng
Project Development Leadership School				
PDLS	USA-HI-UN	Jan	6 mo	Eng
Radio Broadcasting, School of				
SRB	USA-HI-UN	Sep	6 mo	Eng
Reorientation in Education				
RIE	AUST-ACT-WAT	Jul	3 mo	Eng
School of Worship				
SOW	USA-HI-UN	Apr/Sep	6 mo	Eng
Small Groups, Principles of				
PSG	SING-NATL	Jul	2 mo	
Strategic Missions, School of				
SOSM	USA-CO-FRONT	Sep	6 mo	Eng
SOSM	USA-TX-TWIN	Sep	5 mo	Eng
Teacher Training				
TT	COLOM-LUZ	Feb	10 mo	Spa/Eng
	USA-TX-TWIN	Aug	10 mo	Eng
Teaching English Speakers of Other Lang				
TESOL	UK-DERBY	Jul/Sep	1 mo	
TESOL	USA-HI-UN	Jun	6 mo	Eng
Urban Health Care School				
	BRAZ-REST	Aug	3 mo+	Por/Eng
Video Production, School of				
SOP	BRAZ-REST		3 mo+	Por/Eng
SVP	USA-HI-UN	Apr	6 mo	Eng
Worship, School of				
SOW	AUST-WA-PERTH	Apr	6 mo	Eng
SOW	CHILE-SANT	Jul	3 mo	Spa
SOW	USA-MT-LAKES	Sep	5 mo	Eng
SOW	USA-TN-NASH	Jan	5 mo	Eng
Writing for Public Relations School				
WPR	USA-HI-UN	Jun	3 mo	Eng
Writing, School of				
	USA-TX-EDIT	Sep	3 mo	Eng

Section IV

YWAM Base Ministry Focus

This section will be helpful to those who know the ministry area(s) that they would like to serve in, but are unsure of exact geographic location. This list is *not* exhaustive, but a YWAM operating location will appear under the ministry title if they listed that ministry as one of their primary emphases. For instance, under "Kings Kids," all operating locations involved in Kings Kids ministry will not appear under "Kings Kids" heading, but only those bases that listed Kings Kids as one of their primary focuses.

Explanation of Information in Section IV

Ministry:

Ministry categories are listed alphabetically. (See information above for details.)

Ctry/City:

The country and location that listed this ministry as one of their primary focuses. (See Appendix for Ctry/City code key.)

Language 1:

The main language spoken at this location.

Language 2:

The secondary, helpful language for this location.

Language 3:

The third, helpful language for this location.

KING'S KIDS

MAUI-HAWAII

OUTREACH OPPORTUNITIES:

1994 "MISSISSIPPI RIVER TOUR"

JULY 5TH - AUGUST 15TH

1995 "SUMMER SAFARI TOUR" AFRICA

SHORT TERM OPPORRTUNIITIES

NIKO - Building your character in outdoor adventure.

SPORTS TEAMS - Using sports as a vehicle to reach out and minister.

H.A.N.D.S. - (Helping A Neighbor Develop and Serve) Mercy ministries

STAFF OPPORTUNITIES - Summer and Year round postions.

FOR MORE INFORMATION CONTACT US AT:

P.O. BOX 237 PAIA-MAUI, HI 96779

PH (808) 579-8402 FAX (808) 579-8405

Ctry/City	Lang 1	Lang 2	Lang 3
Administration			
ICELAND-REY	Icelandic		
INDIA-NATL			
KOREA-NATL	Korean		
Adoption Ministry			
JAPAN-NARITA	English	Japanese	
AIDS Victims			
BRAZ-REST	Portuguese	English	
CAN-QUE-MONT	French	English	
PHIL-OLONG	English	Tagolog	
THAIL-LIFE	Thai	English	
UGANDA-SOR	English		
UK-ENG-ACACIA	English		
UK-ENG-EARL	English		
Battered Women			
NORTHMAR	English		
Bible Study			
JAPAN-HIGA	Japanese	Korean	English
WSAMOA-SAVA	Samoan	English	
Campus Evangelism			
AUST-ACT-CAN	English		
AUST-QLD-TOWN	English		
CAN-QUE-MONT	French	English	
INDO-TIMOR	Indonesian		
JAPAN-NATL	English	Japanese	
TAIW-TAICH	Chinese		
UK-ENG-LIV	English		
USA-FL-WAVES	English		
USA-IL-CHIC	English		
USA-IL-URB	English		
USA-MA-SOMER	English		
USA-NY-ITH	English		
USA-PA-TITUS	English	Sign Language	
USA-SD-SPEAR	English		
USA-WI-MADIS	English		
WSAMOA-SAVA	Samoan	English	
Children's Home			
BRAZ-NATL	Portuguese		
MEX-JUAR	Spanish		
Children's Ministry			
AUST-TAS-SAN	English		
AUST-TAS-SOR	English		
CAMBODIA	English	Khmer	
COLOM-BUCA	Spanish		
GUINEABIS	Portuguese		
INDIA-PUNE	English	Marathi	
INDIA-SHIMLA	Hindi	English	
INDO-JATIM	Indonesian	English	Dutch

Ctry/City	Lang 1	Lang 2	Lang 3
JAPAN-CHIBA	English		
NICAR	Spanish	English	
NZ-AUCK-TAKA	English		
PHIL-CEBU	English	Cebuano	
PHIL-KK	Tagalog	English	
PHIL-SURIG	English	Cebuano	Tagalog
PNG-BOR	English	PNG Pidgin	
THAIL-LIFE	Thai	English	
UK-ENG-SHEP	English		
UK-WAL-PONT	English	Welsh	
USA-STCROIX	English		
Church Ministries			
AUST-TAS-SOR	English		
COLOM-BUCA	Spanish		
JAPAN-CHIBA	English		
JAPAN-OKIN	Japanese	English	
JAPAN-TOKYO	Japanese	English	
NEPAL-KATH	Nepali	English	
NEWCAL	French		
PHIL-BANG	English	Ilocano	
POLAND	English	Polish	
SIERRA	English	Creole	
UK-DERBY	English		
USA-WA-REVIVE	English		
WSAMOA-PION	Samoan	English	
Church Planting			
ALBANIA	Albanian	English	
AUST-NSW-MT	English		
BELG-GENT	Dutch	English	
BOLIV-LAPAZ	Spanish		
BRAZ-RECIFE	Portuguese	English	Spanish
BURUNDI	French	English	
CHILE-SANT	Spanish		
COLOM-BUCA	Spanish		
DOMIN-SANTO	Spanish		
EQUATOR	Spanish		
GHANA	English		
GREENLAND	English	Greenlandic	Danish
GUINEABIS	Portuguese		
HUNGARY	English	Hungarian	
INDIA-BHOPAL	Hindi	English	
INDIA-BOMB	English		
INDIA-PUNE	English	Marathi	
INDIA-SHIMLA	Hindi	English	
INDIA-VARAN	Hindi	English	
INDO-JAVA	Indonesian		
INDO-TIMOR	Indonesian		
JAPAN-AKASHI	English	Japanese	
JAPAN-CHIBA	English		

Ctry/City	Lang 1	Lang 2	Lang 3
JAPAN-NARITA	English	Japanese	
JAPAN-TOYO	Japanese	English	
MALI	French	Bambara	
MEX-MAZAT	Spanish	English	
MICRO-YAP	English		
MONG	English	Korean	
NAMIB-UIS	English	Afrikaans	Damara
NEPAL-KATH	Nepali	English	
NETH-NATL	Dutch	English	
NIGER	French	English	
NZ-OXFORD	English		
PANAMA	Spanish		
PARAGUAY	Spanish		
PHIL-BANG	English	Ilocano	
PHIL-CEBU	English	Cebuano	
PHIL-SURIG	English	Cebuano	Tagalog
PHIL-TAL	English	Filipino	Visaya
SENEGAL	French		
SPAIN-LAS	Spanish		
TAIW-MIA	English	Mandarin	
TAIW-TAICH	Chinese		
THAIL-FRONT	English	Thai	
UK-ENG-CUCK	English		
ZAIRE	French	English	
ZIMB-BULAW	English		
Coffee House			
JAPAN-NATL	English	Japanese	
JAPAN-TOKYO	Japanese	English	
USA-WI-MADIS	English		
Communication			
AUST-NSW-KOT	English		
AUST-QLD-TOWN	English		
FRANCE-MONT	French	English	
GERM-MEDIA	English	German	French
NORW-OTT	Norwegian	English	
PARAGUAY	Spanish		
SWITZ-POST	German	English	
USA-CO-RES	English		
USA-TX-LAST	English		
Community Development			
CAMBODIA	English	Khmer	
COLOM-RESTOR	Spanish	English	
DJIBOUTI	French	English	
KENYA-MOMB	English	Swahili	
NETH-NATL	Dutch	English	
NICAR	Spanish	English	
NIGER	French	English	
PHIL-BANG	English	Ilocano	
SIERRA	English	Creole	

Ctry/City	Lang 1	Lang 2	Lang 3
SOMALIA	English		
SUDAN	English		
THAIL-LIFE	Thai	English	
THAIL-NATL	English	Thai	
UGANDA-SOR	English		
USA-TX-MERCY	English		
WSAMOA-SAVA	Samoan	English	
Construction			
AUST-TAS-SAN	English		
JAPAN-IMPACT	Japanese	English	
MEX-MAZAT	Spanish	English	
MEX-TIJ	Spanish	English	
USA-CA-CHULA	English	Spanish	
Coordinating			
KENYA-AREA			
UK-ENG-HARP	English		
Counseling			
CAN-QUE-DUN	French		
FRANCE-MONT	French	English	
SWITZ-WILER	German	English	
USA-CA-SANTA	English		
USA-WA-REVIVE	English		
Country Towns			
AUST-NSW-ALB	English		
AUST-TAS-SOR	English		
Creative Arts			
CAN-ONT-CAMB	English		
COLOM-LUZ	Spanish	English	
INDO-JAVA	Indonesian		
SWITZ-POST	German	English	
UK-ENG-LIV	English		
USA-CA-SUN	English		
USA-FL-MIAMI	English	Spanish	
USA-FL-ORL	English	Spanish	
USA-MT-LAKES	English		
Cult Evangelism			
USA-HI-MAUI	English		
USA-UT-OGD	English		
Deaf Ministry			
USA-PA-TITUS	English	Sign Language	
Discipleship			
AMSAMOA	English	Samoan	
CAN-BC-VAN	English		
CISBEL	Russian	English	
CISRUS	Russian	English	
CISUK	Ukrainian	Russian	English
CZECH-PRAHA	Czech	English	
GUAM	English		

Ctry/City	Lang 1	Lang 2	Lang 3
IRELAND	English		
LATVIA	Latvian	English	
NAMIB-UIS	English	Afrikaans	Damara
NZ-NORTH	English		
PHIL-DAVAO	English	Cebuano	Tagolog
PHIL-TAL	English	Filipino	Visaya
SWED-STORM	English	Swedish	
TAIW-TAICH	Chinese		
UK-ENG-CUCK	English		
UK-SCOT-CAT	English		
USA-NY-ITH	English		
USA-OR-PORT	English		
USA-STCROIX	English		
USA-WI-MADIS	English		
Education			
BRAZ-MANAUS	Portuguese		
CAMBODIA	English	Khmer	
COLOM-LUZ	Spanish	English	
FINLAND-SCH	Finnish	English	
GUINEABIS	Portuguese		
NZ-AUCK-TAKA	English		
UGANDA-NATL	English		
USA-NY-LONG	English		
Evangelism			
ALBANIA	Albanian	English	
AUST-NSW-ALB	English		
AUST-NSW-CABR	English	Khmer	Vietnamese
AUST-NSW-DEE	English		
AUST-NSW-KOT	English		
AUST-NSW-MT	English		
AUST-NT-DAR	English		
AUST-QLD-CAR	English		
AUSTRIA-WIEN	German	English	
AUST-VIC-NATL	English		
BELG-GENT	Dutch	English	
BRAZ-MANAUS	Portuguese		
BRAZ-NATL	Portuguese		
BRAZ-RECIFE	Portuguese	English	Spanish
BRAZ-SAO	Portuguese		
BURUNDI	French	English	
CISBEL	Russian	English	
CISRUS	Russian	English	
CISUK	Ukrainian	Russian	English
COLOM-CART	Spanish	English	
COOK-RARO	English		
DENMARK-COPE	Danish	English	
DENMARK-MORK	English	Danish	
FRANCE-CHAT	French	English	
FRANCE-PARIS	French		

Ctry/City	Lang 1	Lang 2	Lang 3
GHANA	English		
GREECE	English	Greek	
GUAM	English		
HAITI	English		
HONG-REG	English	Cantonese	
HUNGARY	English	Hungarian	
ICELAND-REY	Icelandic		
INDIA-CALC	English	Bengali	
INDIA-MADRAS	English	Tamil	
INDIA-PUNE	English	Marathi	
INDIA-SHIMLA	Hindi	English	
INDIA-VARAN	Hindi	English	
INDO-JATIM	Indonesian	English	Dutch
INDO-LOMB	Indonesian	English	
INDO-TIMOR	Indonesian		
JAPAN-HIGA	Japanese	Korean	English
LATVIA	Latvian	English	
MALI	French	Bambara	
MEX-GUADAL	Spanish		
MEX-TEPIC	Spanish	English	
NAMIB-UIS	English	Afrikaans	Damara
NEPAL-KATH	Nepali	English	
NICAR	Spanish	English	
NORW-LENS	Norwegian	English	
NZ-AUCK-POLY	English	Saomoan	Maori
NZ-AUCK-URB	English		
PANAMA	Spanish		
PHIL-KK	Tagalog	English	
PHIL-SURIG	English	Cebuano	Tagalog
PHIL-TAL	English	Filipino	Visaya
PNG-LAE	English		
PNG-MTHAG	English	PNG Pidgin	
POLAND	English	Polish	
RWANDA	French	English	
SENEGAL	French		
SWED-STOCK	Swedish	English	
SWED-STORM	English	Swedish	
TAIW-MIA	English	Mandarin	
TANZANIA	Kiswahili	English	
UK-DERBY	English		
UK-ENG-BRIST	English		
UK-ENG-CUCK	English		
UK-ENG-HARP	English		
UK-ENG-LIV	English		
UK-ENG-TOR	English		
USA-HI-HONOL	English		
USA-HI-UN	English	Japanese	
USA-OR-PORT	English		
USA-TX-DALL	English		
USA-TX-MERCY	English		

Ctry/City	Lang 1	Lang 2	Lang 3
USA-TX-TWIN	English		
VENEZ-CARAC	Spanish		
WSAMOA-PION	Samoan	English	
ZAIRE	French	English	
ZIMB-BULAW	English		
Evangelism:Islands			
COOK-RARO	English		
NORTHMAR	English		
NZ-MERCY	English		
Evangelism:Mobile			
AUST-VIC-NATL	English		
AUST-WA-PERTH	English		
BOLIV-SANTA	Spanish	English	German
UK-ENG-KINGS	English		
Evangelism:Night Club			
NZ-AUCK-STEI	English		
Family Ministry			
AUSTRIA-WIEN	German	English	
BELG-GENT	Dutch	English	
CAN-QUE-DUN	French		
CAN-VAN-KK	English		
GERM-ALTEN	German	English	
GERM-BUCH	German	English	
ICELAND-EGI	Icelandic		
JAPAN-KK	English	Japanese	
NORW-OTT	Norwegian	English	
NZ-FAMILY	English		
PHIL-KK	Tagalog	English	
UK-ENG-KINGS	English		
USA-CA-SUMM	English	Korean	
USA-ID-RIGG	English		
USA-WI-WEYER	English		
Farming			
TANZANIA	Kiswahili	English	
Frontier Missions			
AUST-ACT-WAT	English		
AUST-WA-PERTH	English		
CAN-VAN-KK	English		
COLOM-BUCA	Spanish		
GRENADA	English		
NZ-OXFORD	English		
SAFR-WORC	English	Afrikaans	
UK-ENG-CUCK	English		
USA-CO-FRONT	English		
USA-HI-HONOL	English		
USA-NC-CHAR	English		
USA-TX-TWIN	English		

Ctry/City	Lang 1	Lang 2	Lang 3
Go Teams			
USA-CENTRAL	English		
USA-NY-EAST	English		
Homeless			
BRAZ-REST	Portuguese	English	
UK-ENG-EARL	English		
USA-WA-URB	English		
Homosexual Ministry			
CAN-QUE-MONT	French	English	
UK-ENG-ACACIA	English		
Hospitality			
PHIL-NEW	English	Tagalog	
PHIL-SURIG	English	Cebuano	Tagalog
Hosting Teams			
AUST-NT-DAR	English		
BRAZ-CURIT	Portuguese		
CAN-BC-VAN	English		
CROATIA	English	German	
MEX-GUADAL	Spanish		
MONG	English	Korean	
PHIL-NEW	English	Tagalog	
USA-TX-DALL	English		
Indigenous Groups			
AUST-NT-DAR	English		
BRAZ-ROND	Portuguese		
CAN-BC-WIN	English		
MEX-TEPIC	Spanish	English	
USA-ID-KAM	English		
USA-SD-SPEAR	English		
International Students			
USA-IL-CHIC	English		
USA-NY-ITH	English		
USA-VA-INT	English		
USA-WI-MADIS	English		
Internships:College			
USA-VA-INT	English		
Kings Kids			
AUST-NSW-ALB	English		
AUSTRIA-WIEN	German	English	
AUST-TAS-SAN	English		
AUST-VIC-NATL	English		
BELG-GENT	Dutch	English	
BOLIV-LAPAZ	Spanish		
CAN-ALB-CALG	English		
CAN-VAN-KK	English		
COLOM-LUZ	Spanish	English	
COOK-RARO	English		
GERM-ALTEN	German	English	

Ctry/City	Lang 1	Lang 2	Lang 3
GERM-BUCH	German	English	
GUINEABIS	Portuguese		
INDIA-PUNE	English	Marathi	
JAPAN-KK	English	Japanese	
MALI	French	Bambara	
NZ-AUCK-KK	English		
PARAGUAY	Spanish		
PHIL-DAVAO	English	Cebuano	Tagolog
PHIL-KK	Tagalog	English	
PNG-BOR	English	PNG Pidgin	
PNG-LAE	English		
PORTUGAL	Portuguese	English	
PUERTO	Spanish		
SAFR-WORC	English	Afrikaans	
SWITZ-POST	German	English	
SWITZ-WILER	German	English	
UK-ENG-LIV	English		
UK-ENG-TOR	English		
UK-WAL-PONT	English	Welsh	
USA-CA-HOLL	English		
USA-FL-ORL	English	Spanish	
USA-GA-ATL	English		
USA-ID-RIGG	English		
USA-MT-LAKES	English		
USA-NY-EAST	English		
USA-PA-TITUS	English	Sign Language	
USA-WA-KK	English		
USA-WA-REVIVE	English		
Leadership Training			
CAN-VAN-KK	English		
GHANA	English		
NZ-NORTH	English		
POLAND	English	Polish	
USA-CA-SUN	English		
USA-CENTRAL	English		
USA-FL-MIAMI	English	Spanish	
Literacy			
INDIA-PUNE	English	Marathi	
INDIA-SHIMLA	Hindi	English	
Media			
AUST-TAS-SOR	English		
GERM-ALTEN	German	English	
GERM-MEDIA	English	German	French
USA-TX-LAST	English		
Medical Ministry			
CAMBODIA	English	Khmer	
INDIA-SHIMLA	Hindi	English	
INDO-LOMB	Indonesian	English	
MALI	French	Bambara	

Ctry/City	Lang 1	Lang 2	Lang 3
MEX-MAZAT	Spanish	English	
MEX-TEPIC	Spanish	English	
MEX-TIJ	Spanish	English	
PHIL-BALUT	English	Tagalog	
PNG-LAE	English		
THAIL-LIFE	Thai	English	
UGANDA-SOR	English		
USA-CA-CHULA	English	Spanish	
USA-TX-MERCY	English		
USA-TX-TWIN	English		
Men's Ministry			
USA-MA-SOMER	English		
Mercy Ministry			
AUST-NSW-ALB	English		
AUST-NSW-CABR	English	Khmer	Vietnamese
AUST-NSW-DEE	English		
AUST-QLD-MERCY	English		
BRAZ-MANAUS	Portuguese		
BRAZ-NATL	Portuguese		
BRAZ-RECIFE	Portuguese	English	Spanish
BRAZ-REST	Portuguese	English	
CAN-BC-VAN	English		
CAN-BC-WIN	English		
CISBEL	Russian	English	
CISRUS	Russian	English	
CISUK	Ukrainian	Russian	English
COLOM-CART	Spanish	English	
COLOM-RESTOR	Spanish	English	
CROATIA	English	German	
EQUATOR	Spanish		
ETHIOPIA	English	Amharic	
GUAT-GUAT	Spanish		
INDIA-VARAN	Hindi	English	
INDO-JATIM	Indonesian	English	Dutch
JAPAN-HIGA	Japanese	Korean	English
JAPAN-TOKYO	Japanese	English	
LATVIA	Latvian	English	
MEX-JUAR	Spanish		
MEX-TEPIC	Spanish	English	
NETH-NATL	Dutch	English	
NIGER	French	English	
NZ-MERCY	English		
PANAMA	Spanish		
PARAGUAY	Spanish		
PHIL-BALUT	English	Tagalog	
PHIL-DAVAO	English	Cebuano	Tagolog
SENEGAL	French		
TAIW-TAIN	English	Madarin	
UGANDA-SOR	English		

Ctry/City	Lang 1	Lang 2	Lang 3
UK-ENG-ACACIA	English		
UK-ENG-BIRM	English		
UK-ENG-EARL	English		
UK-ENG-HARP	English		
UK-SCOT-CAT	English		
USA-HI-UN	English	Japanese	
USA-ID-KAM	English		
USA-NY-LONG	English		
USA-TX-MERCY	English		
USA-TX-MEX	Spanish	English	
Ministry to Pastors			
RWANDA	French	English	
USA-SD-SPEAR	English		
Missions Service Center			
NORW-OTT	Norwegian	English	
USA-NY-EAST	English		
Mobilization			
AUST-NSW-CABR	English	Khmer	Vietnamese
AUST-NSW-KOT	English		
AUST-QLD-ASH	English		
CZECH-PLZEN	English	Czech	
CZECH-PRAHA	Czech	English	
DOMIN-SANTO	Spanish		
NAMIB-WIND	English	Afrikaans	
NETH-HEERDE	English	Dutch	
PNG-BOR	English	PNG Pidgin	
UK-DERBY	English		
USA-CO-FRONT	English		
USA-NC-CHAR	English		
Music			
AUST-TAS-SOR	English		
COLOM-LUZ	Spanish	English	
CZECH-PLZEN	English	Czech	
ICELAND-REY	Icelandic		
NZ-AUCK-STEI	English		
USA-FL-ORL	English	Spanish	
USA-MT-LAKES	English		
USA-TN-NASH	English		
USA-TX-LAST	English		
National Revival			
USA-WA-REVIVE	English		
Olympic Outreach			
JAPAN-TOYO	Japanese	English	
Orphanage			
HONG-REG	English	Cantonese	
INDO-JATIM	Indonesian	English	Dutch
Outdoor Adventure			
USA-CA-SUMM	English	Korean	

Ctry/City	Lang 1	Lang 2	Lang 3
Pastoral Care:YWAM			
PHIL-RIZAL	English		
USA-CENTRAL	English		
Pioneering			
AUST-QLD-ASH	English		
CZECH-PRAHA	Czech	English	
KENYA-AREA			
NAMIB-WIND	English	Afrikaans	
NIGER	French	English	
USA-HI-HONOL	English		
USA-NC-CHAR	English		
Prayer Networking			
AUST-QLD-ASH	English		
USA-NY-ITH	English		
Preschool			
BRAZ-NATL	Portuguese		
HONG-REG	English	Cantonese	
KENYA-LIKONI	English	Swahili	
NORTHMAR	English		
PHIL-SURIG	English	Cebuano	Tagalog
PNG-BOR	English	PNG Pidgin	
SAFR-WORC	English	Afrikaans	
WSAMOA-PION	Samoan	English	
Prison Ministry			
CHILE-SANT	Spanish		
COOK-RARO	English		
DOMIN-SANTO	Spanish		
UK-ENG-KINGS	English		
USA-NY-LONG	English		
Pro-Life			
USA-TX-TWIN	English		
Prostitution Recovery			
PHIL-OLONG	English	Tagolog	
USA-NY-LONG	English		
Publishing			
NORW-OTT	Norwegian	English	
SWITZ-POST	German	English	
USA-TX-LAST	English		
USA-WA-PUBL	English		
Rehab:Drug/Alcohol			
FINLAND-SIU	Finish		
GUAM	English		
NETH-SILOAM	Dutch	English	
UK-ENG-ACACIA	English		
UK-ENG-BETH	English		
UK-ENG-EARL	English		
USA-CA-SANTA	English		
USA-LA-NEW	English		

Ctry/City	Lang 1	Lang 2	Lang 3
USA-WA-URB	English		
Relief			
CAMBODIA	English	Khmer	
COLOM-RESTOR	Spanish	English	
CROATIA	English	German	
DJIBOUTI	French	English	
KENYA-AREA			
KENYA-MOMB	English	Swahili	
NETH-NATL	Dutch	English	
NIGER	French	English	
PHIL-BANG	English	Ilocano	
SIERRA	English	Creole	
SOMALIA	English		
SUDAN	English		
THAIL-LIFE	Thai	English	
THAIL-NATL	English	Thai	
UGANDA-SOR	English		
USA-TX-MERCY	English		
Research			
GERM-MEDIA	English	German	French
Retirees			
USA-FL-ORL	English	Spanish	
Retreats			
USA-ID-RIGG	English		
Seminars			
COLOM-LUZ	Spanish	English	
ICELAND-EGI	Icelandic		
ICELAND-REY	Icelandic		
RWANDA	French	English	
USA-FL-ORL	English	Spanish	
Short Term			
ALBANIA	Albanian	English	
DOMIN-SANTO	Spanish		
MEX-JUAR	Spanish		
MEX-MAZAT	Spanish	English	
MEX-TIJ	Spanish	English	
PORTUGAL	Portuguese	English	
SWED-LJUN	English	Swedish	
SWED-STORM	English	Swedish	
USA-CA-BISH	English		
USA-CA-CHULA	English	Spanish	
USA-CA-SUN	English		
USA-IL-URB	English		
USA-MT-LAKES	English		
USA-NC-CHAR	English		
USA-STCROIX	English		
USA-TX-MEX	Spanish	English	

Ctry/City	Lang 1	Lang 2	Lang 3
Sports Ministry			
HONG-REG	English	Cantonese	
Street Kids			
BOLIV-SANTA	Spanish	English	German
BRAZ-MANAUS	Portuguese		
BRAZ-REST	Portuguese	English	
BRAZ-SAO	Portuguese		
CAN-QUE-MONT	French	English	
PHIL-DAVAO	English	Cebuano	Tagolog
USA-WA-URB	English		
Surfers			
MEX-MAZAT	Spanish	English	
USA-HI-MAUI	English		
Teambuilding			
USA-CA-SUMM	English	Korean	
Tentmaking			
MOROCCO			
Training			
ALBANIA	Albanian	English	
AMSAMOA	English	Samoan	
AUST-ACT-CAN	English		
AUST-ACT-WAT	English		
AUST-NSW-ALB	English		
AUST-NSW-CABR	English	Khmer	Vietnamese
AUST-NSW-KOT	English		
AUST-NSW-MT	English		
AUST-QLD-CAR	English		
AUST-TAS-SAN	English		
AUST-VIC-NATL	English		
AUST-WA-PERTH	English		
BOLIV-SANTA	Spanish	English	German
BRAZ-MANAUS	Portuguese		
BRAZ-NATL	Portuguese		
BRAZ-RECIFE	Portuguese	English	Spanish
BRAZ-REST	Portuguese	English	
BURUNDI	French	English	
CAN-BC-WIN	English		
CAN-ONT-CAMB	English		
CHILE-SANT	Spanish		
CISBEL	Russian	English	
CISRUS	Russian	English	
CISUK	Ukrainian	Russian	English
COLOM-BUCA	Spanish		
COLOM-CART	Spanish	English	
COOK-RARO	English		
CROATIA	English	German	
CZECH-PRAHA	Czech	English	
DENMARK-MORK	English	Danish	

Ctry/City	Lang 1	Lang 2	Lang 3
ETHIOPIA	English	Amharic	
FRANCE-CHAT	French	English	
FRANCE-MONT	French	English	
GERM-ALTEN	German	English	
GERM-MEDIA	English	German	French
GREECE	English	Greek	
GREENLAND	English	Greenlandic	Danish
GRENADA	English		
GUAM	English		
GUAT-GUAT	Spanish		
HAITI	English		
HONG-REG	English	Cantonese	
ICELAND-EGI	Icelandic		
INDIA-CALC	English	Bengali	
INDIA-MADRAS	English	Tamil	
INDIA-NEW	English		
INDO-JATIM	Indonesian	English	Dutch
INDO-JAVA	Indonesian		
INDO-TIMOR	Indonesian		
IRELAND	English		
ITALY-CADEG	Italian	English	French
JAMAICA	English		
JAPAN-NATL	English	Japanese	
JAPAN-OKIN	Japanese	English	
KENYA-LIKONI	English	Swahili	
KENYA-MOMB	English	Swahili	
LATVIA	Latvian	English	
MALAY-PENANG	English	Bahasa Malaysia	Tamil
MALI	French	Bambara	
MEX-JUAR	Spanish		
MEX-TEPIC	Spanish	English	
MEX-TIJ	Spanish	English	
NEPAL-KATH	Nepali	English	
NEPAL-POKH	Nepali	English	
NETH-HEERDE	English	Dutch	
NEWCAL	French		
NICAR	Spanish	English	
NORW-LENS	Norwegian	English	
NZ-AUCK-POLY	English	Saomoan	Maori
NZ-AUCK-URB	English		
NZ-MATAM	English		
NZ-NORTH	English		
NZ-OXFORD	English		
PHIL-ANT	Tagalog	English	
PHIL-DAVAO	English	Cebuano	Tagolog
PHIL-TAL	English	Filipino	Visaya
PNG-MTHAG	English	PNG Pidgin	
POLAND	English	Polish	
PORTUGAL	Portuguese	English	
PUERTO	Spanish		

Ctry/City	Lang 1	Lang 2	Lang 3
RWANDA	French	English	
SAFR-WORC	English	Afrikaans	
SENEGAL	French		
SWED-LJUN	English	Swedish	
SWED-STOCK	Swedish	English	
SWED-STORM	English	Swedish	
SWITZ-BIEL	German	English	
SWITZ-WILER	German	English	
TAIW-TAIN	English	Madarin	
TAIW-TAIPEI	English	Mandarin	
TANZANIA	Kiswahili	English	
THAIL-FRONT	English	Thai	
UGANDA-NATL	English		
UK-ENG-HARP	English		
UK-ENG-KINGS	English		
UK-ENG-LIV	English		
UK-ENG-LOND	English		
UK-ENG-PARR	English		
UK-ENG-TOR	English		
URUGUAY	Spanish		
USA-CA-BISH	English		
USA-CA-CHULA	English	Spanish	
USA-CA-SANTA	English		
USA-CA-SUN	English		
USA-CENTRAL	English		
USA-FL-MIAMI	English	Spanish	
USA-FL-ORL	English	Spanish	
USA-GA-ATL	English		
USA-HI-HONOL	English		
USA-HI-MAUI	English		
USA-HI-UN	English	Japanese	
USA-ID-KAM	English		
USA-MA-SOMER	English		
USA-MT-LAKES	English		
USA-NC-CHAR	English		
USA-NY-EAST	English		
USA-PA-PHIL	English		
USA-PA-ROAR	English		
USA-PA-TITUS	English	Sign Language	
USA-STCROIX	English		
USA-TN-NASH	English		
USA-TX-LAST	English		
USA-TX-MERCY	English		
USA-TX-MEX	Spanish	English	
USA-TX-TWIN	English		
USA-WI-WEYER	English		
VENEZ-CARAC	Spanish		
ZAIRE	French	English	
ZIMB-BULAW	English		

Ctry/City	Lang 1	Lang 2	Lang 3
Training:Church			
AUST-NSW-DEE	English		
BOLIV-SANTA	Spanish	English	German
MEX-JUAR	Spanish		
PHIL-SURIG	English	Cebuano	Tagalog
USA-SD-SPEAR	English		
Training:Teacher			
COLOM-LUZ	Spanish	English	
NZ-AUCK-TAKA	English		
UK-ENG-SHEP	English		
Tutoring			
USA-PA-PHIL	English		
Unreached Peoples			
BRAZ-ROND	Portuguese		
DOMIN-SANTO	Spanish		
GRENADA	English		
INDIA-BANG	English	Kannada	
NETH-HEERDE	English	Dutch	
PHIL-CEBU	English	Cebuano	
THAIL-FRONT	English	Thai	
Unwed Mothers			
USA-LA-NEW	English		
Urban Ministry			
AUST-NSW-KOT	English		
AUST-NSW-MT	English		
BOLIV-LAPAZ	Spanish		
BRAZ-CURIT	Portuguese		
BRAZ-REST	Portuguese	English	
BRAZ-SAO	Portuguese		
CAN-ALB-EDM	English		
CAN-BC-VAN	English		
CAN-ONT-TOR	Korean	English	
CAN-QUE-MONT	French	English	
DENMARK-COPE	Danish	English	
JAPAN-TOKYO	Japanese	English	
MEX-MEXCITY	Spanish	English	
NETH-NATL	Dutch	English	
NZ-AUCK-URB	English		
SWED-STOCK	Swedish	English	
TAIW-TAIPEI	English	Mandarin	
UK-ENG-ACACIA	English		
UK-ENG-BIRM	English		
UK-ENG-EARL	English		
UK-ENG-LOND	English		
UK-ENG-PARR	English		
UK-ENG-TOR	English		
USA-GA-ATL	English		
USA-HI-HONOL	English		

Ctry/City	Lang 1	Lang 2	Lang 3
USA-IL-CHIC	English		
USA-LA-NEW	English		
USA-NY-EAST	English		
USA-OR-PORT	English		
USA-PA-PHIL	English		
USA-TX-TWIN	English		
USA-WA-URB	English		
Women's Ministry			
JAPAN-CHIBA	English		
THAIL-LIFE	Thai	English	
USA-NY-LONG	English		
Worship/Prayer			
BRAZ-SAO	Portuguese		
CZECH-PLZEN	English	Czech	
CZECH-PRAHA	Czech	English	
DENMARK-COPE	Danish	English	
GREECE	English	Greek	
ICELAND-REY	Icelandic		
JAPAN-HIGA	Japanese	Korean	English
NORW-LENS	Norwegian	English	
PHIL-TAL	English	Filipino	Visaya
USA-CA-SUN	English		
USA-CO-FRONT	English		
USA-TN-NASH	English		
Youth Ministry			
AUST-NSW-KOT	English		
AUST-NSW-MT	English		
AUSTRIA-WIEN	German	English	
AUST-TAS-SAN	English		
AUST-TAS-SOR	English		
BELG-BRUSS	French	Dutch	English
CAN-VAN-KK	English		
COLOM-BUCA	Spanish		
DENMARK-MORK	English	Danish	
HAITI	English		
HUNGARY	English	Hungarian	
ICELAND-EGI	Icelandic		
INDO-TIMOR	Indonesian		
IRELAND	English		
IRELAND	English		
JAPAN-CHIBA	English		
JAPAN-HIGA	Japanese	Korean	English
JAPAN-KK	English	Japanese	
NEWCAL	French		
NORW-OTT	Norwegian	English	
PHIL-BALUT	English	Tagalog	
PHIL-KK	Tagalog	English	
PNG-BOR	English	PNG Pidgin	
PUERTO	Spanish		

Ctry/City	Lang 1	Lang 2	Lang 3
UK-WAL-PONT	English	Welsh	
USA-CA-SUMM	English	Korean	
USA-ID-RIGG	English		
USA-LA-NEW	English		
USA-MA-SOMER	English		
USA-STCROIX	English		
USA-WA-URB	English		
WSAMOA-SAVA	Samoan	English	

Section V

YWAM Short-Term Outreach Information

The short-term outreaches listed are open to the public with no DTS required. Some restrictions may apply. Please write to the location you are interested in for further details.

Explanation of Information in Section V

Name:

The name of the outreach listed alphabetically.

Ctry/City:

The country and city code indicating the YWAM ministry sponsoring the outreach. (See Appendix for Ctry/City code key.)

Destination:

The destination of the outreach. This may be a city, country or other geographic location.

Beginning Month:

The month that the outreach will begin. If a "+" sign appears after the month, the outreach begins in that month, but may begin in several months following that initial month listed. If two months are listed, the outreach will begin in both of those months. (any = anytime or on-going)

Length:

The total length of the outreach in days, weeks or months. (wk= week, mo=month, wkend=weekend) The "+" sign will be listed after the length for those outreaches that are on-going and the maximum length of involvement is optional.

Language(s):

The primary language to be spoken on this outreach is listed first. If a secondary language would be helpful, that will be listed second. (See Appendix for Language code key.)

Minimum Age:

The minimum age requirement for participants. Restrictions other than age may apply. Please contact the operating location for information and requirements.

Ctry/City	Destination	Beg. Mon.	Length	Lang.	Min. Age
A Tale of Two Kingdoms					
UK-SCOT-NATL	Scotland & Ukraine	Jun	2 mo	Eng/Rus	18
Action '94					
UK-SCOT-NATL	European Countries	Jul	1 wk+	Eng/Fre	17
Back Packers for Missions					
USA-HI-MAUI	Maui, Hawaii	Jun	1 wk	Eng	
Bike International					
USA-TX-TWIN	USA/Canada	Jun	2 mo	Eng	16
Boomerang Teams					
AUST-WA-PERTH	Asia	Dec	1 mo	Eng	18
Cap Blanc (Prayer)					
SPAIN-TORR	Tunisia	Jun	2 wk	Eng/Ara	18
Cardinal Points					
AUST-QLD-TOWN	Australia	Jun	3 wk	Eng	18
Cardinal Pts Prayer					
AUST-QLD-ASH	All continents	Jun	4 wk		18
Christmas Outreach					
USA-LA-NEW	New Orleans	Dec	1 wk	Eng	
Church Teams					
BELIZE-BEL	Belize	any	10 days+	Eng/Spa	
College Campus Outreach					
USA-FL-WAVES	5 Campuses, Florida	Sep	4 wk	Eng/Spa	18
Commonwealth Games					
CAN-BC-WIN	Victoria, BC	Jul	2 mo	Eng	15
CAN-VIC-COMM	Victoria, BC	Aug	3 wk	Eng	15
Cross-Cult. Teach/Evang.					
WSAMOA-PION	Samoa Capitol	May	2 wk	Eng	18
Desert (Prayer)					
SPAIN-TORR	W. Sahara	Oct	1 mo	Eng/Ara	18
Easter Festival					
BRAZ-RECIFE	NE Brazil	Mar	1 wk		18
Eco Tours/Amazon Basin					
BRAZ-ROND	Madeira River	any	2 wk	Eng/Spa	16
Evangelism					
BRAZ-RECIFE	Recife	Feb	1 wk		18
USA-TN-NASH	Hung/Austria/Slov	Jul	3 wk	Eng	15
Evangelism Outreach					
USA-WI-MADIS	Belize	Mar	10 days	Eng/Spa	18
Evangelism/Intercession					
USA-TN-NASH	Kazakhstan	Aug	2 wk	Eng	18
Evangelism/Mercy Ministry					
USA-TN-NASH	Peru/Chile	Sep	3 wk	Eng/Spa	18
USA-TN-NASH	Ukraine	Mar	3 wk	Eng	18
USA-TN-NASH	Honduras	Jan	1 wk+	Eng/Spa	18

Ctry/City	Destination	Beg. Mon.	Length	Lang.	Min. Age
Exposure Tours					
USA-CO-FRONT	10/40 Window	Jun+	2 wk	Eng	18
FEET Teams					
HONG-REG	SE Asia	Jul	5 mo	Eng	18
Go Europe					
UK-ENG-CUCK	All Europe Countries	Jul	3 wk	Eng	16
UK-ENG-HARP	All Europe Countries	Jul	3 wk	Eng	16
UK-ENG-LOND	All Europe Countries	Jul	3 wk	Eng	16
Go Festival					
SWED-LJUN		Jul	3 wk	Eng/Swe	16
Go Teams					
NETH-NATL		Jun/Jul	3 wk	Eng/Dut	17
USA-NY-EAST	Ukraine	any	2 wk+	Rus/Ukr	17
Go-Festival					
NORW-OTT		Jul	2 wk	Nor/Eng	15
Good Samaritan Ship					
USA-TX-MERCY	Caribbean Islands	Jun+	2 wk+	Eng/Spa	18
Grenada Outreach Teams					
GRENADA	Grenada	Jun/Aug	2 wk	Eng	12
Health Care Outreach					
USA-HI-UN	Asia	Apr/Sep	3 wk+	Eng	18
High Country Outreach					
CAN-BC-WIN	Fountain Valley	Jul	1 mo	Eng	15
High Sierra Expedition					
USA-CA-SUMM	S.N. Mtn, Nevada	Jun+	2 wk	Eng	14
Impact Evangelism					
BRAZ-NATL	Brazil	Jan	2 wk	Por/Spa	18
BRAZ-NATL		Jun	2 wk	Por/Spa	18
Impact Team					
UK-ENG-EARL	Major Cities...		3 wk		18
Inner City Outreach					
USA-CO-ARV	Denver, CO USA	Aug	1 wk	Eng	16
Intercession/Education					
USA-TN-NASH	Israel	Oct	2 wk	Eng	18
International Trips					
USA-CA-SUN	various	Jun	5 wk	Eng	18
Japan Church Construction					
USA-HI-UN	Japan	Mar+	6 wk	Eng/Jap	18
Kauai Hurricane Recovery					
USA-HI-UN	Kauai, Hawaii	any	1 wk+	Eng	0
King's Kids					
AUST-NSW-KK	NSW, Australia	Dec	3 wk	Eng	5
AUST-NSW-KK	Samoa	Jun	4 wk	Eng	5
BELG-BRUSS		Jul/Aug	4 wk	Dut/Eng	7
BELG-BRUSS		Jul/Aug	4 wk	Fre/Eng	7

Ctry/City	Destination	Beg. Mon.	Length	Lang.	Min. Age
BELG-GENT	Belgium/E.Europe	Jul	4 wk	Eng/Dut	12
BRAZ-CURIT		Jan	2 mo	Por	
BRAZ-MANAUS	Brazil	Jan/Jul	6 wk	Por/Eng	6
BRAZ-PORTO	Brazil	Jan	5 wk	Por/Spa	1
COLOM-LUZ	Peru, Equador	Jan/Feb	3 wk	Spa/Eng	
COLOM-LUZ	USA	Jun/Jul	1 mo	Spa/Eng	
DOMIN-SANTO		Jun		Spa	
GREENLAND	Greenland	Jul	4 wk	Eng	11
GRENADA	Grenada/Guyana	Jul	3 wk	Eng	12
GUAM		Jun	2 mo	Eng	12
INDIA-NEW	Pune/Madras	May	36 days	Eng/Tam	10
IRELAND		Jun	2 mo	Eng	10
JAPAN-HIGA		Aug	15 days	Jap/Kor	
MEX-JUAR	Juarez, Mexico	Jun	2 wk	Eng/Spa	12
MEX-MEXCITY	Mex/Central Amer	Jul	6 wk	Spa/Eng	12
MEX-TEPIC	Mexico/Cent Amer	Jul	5 wk	Spa/Eng	8
NEWCAL		Jan	3 wk	Fre	
NZ-AUCK-KK	Tonga/Somoa	May	4 wk	Eng	
NZ-AUCK-KK	South Island, N.Z.	Aug	3 wk	Eng	
PNG-LAE	Papua New Guinea	Jun	6 wk	Eng/Pid	12
POLAND	Poland	Aug	4 wk	Eng/Pol	9
PORTUGAL	Portugal	Jul	3 wk	Por/Eng	10
UK-ENG-HARP	Europe	Jul	3 wk	Eng	
UK-ENG-TOR	local	Jul	3 wk	Eng	10
URUGUAY	Uruguay	Jan	2 days	Spa/Por	5
USA-CO-ARV	Russia	Jun	6 wk	Eng/Rus	12
USA-FL-MIAMI	USA	Jul	3 wk	Eng/Spa	8
USA-FL-ORL	USA	Jul	3 wk	Eng/Spa	8
USA-GA-ATL		Jun	5 wk	Eng	6
USA-ID-RIGG			5 wk	Eng	13
USA-PA-PHIL	Philadelphia, USA	Jun	5 wk	Eng/Spa	12
USA-SD-SPEAR		Jun	5 wk	Eng	18
USA-TX-MEX	Mexico	Jun	Eng/Spa	12	
USA-TX-TWIN		Jun	6 wk	Eng	
USA-WA-REVIVE	Chile	Jul	3 wk	Eng/Spa	12
USA-WA-REVIVE	Commonwealth Games		Jul	3 wk	Eng 12
VENEZ-CARAC		Aug	1 mo	Spa	
King's Kids Boot Camp					
PNG-BOR				Eng	
SWITZ-POST		Jul	5 wk	Ger/Eng	8
King's Kids Camp					
BOLIV-LAPAZ	Bolivian Cities	Jan	4 wk	Spa	12
King's Kids Family Team					
CAN-ALB-CALG	Dominica, Carib.	Dec	2 wk	Eng	10
King's Kids Go Camp					
PHIL-DAVAO	Cebu/Mindanao	Apr	1 mo	Eng/Tag	10
King's Kids HANDS					
CAN-ALB-CALG	Native Communities	Jul	3 wk	Eng	10

Ctry/City	Destination	Beg. Mon.	Length	Lang.	Min. Age
King's Kids HANDS					
AUST-NT-DAR	Indonesia	Jan/Mar	2 mo	Eng/Ind	13
King's Kids HANDS					
USA-MT-LAKES		Jun	3 wk	Eng	
King's Kids HANDS					
USA-HI-UN	Iraq	Jul	6 wk	Eng/Kur	13
King's Kids Health Team					
COLOM-RESTOR	Amazon/Bogota	Jun	1 mo	Spa/Eng	13
King's Kids Int'l Tour					
USA-PA-TITUS		Jul	4 wk	Eng	
King's Kids Local Tour					
USA-PA-TITUS	local cities	Jun	3 wk	Eng	0
King's Kids Mega Camp					
SWED-KK	various	Jul	4 wk	Eng/Sca	
King's Kids Multicultural					
NZ-AUCK-KK	New Zealand	Dec	4 wk	Eng	
King's Kids Outreach					
PHIL-KK	Cebu/Manila/Mind.	Apr	1 mo	Eng/Tag	10
UK-SCOT-KK	U.K. & Ireland	Jul	3 wk	Eng	10
UK-SCOT-KK	various	Jul	4 wk	Eng/Fre	10
King's Kids Perf. Arts					
USA-MT-LAKES	Crow Reservation	Aug	3 wk	Eng	
King's Kids Slavic					
CAN-ALB-CALG	Eastern Europe	Jul	4 wk	Eng/Rus	10
King's Kids Sports					
CAN-ALB-CALG	Alberta Towns	Jul	2 wk	Eng/Fre	10
GERM-HURL	Albania	Jul	1 mo	Eng/Ger	9
King's Kids					
CAN-VAN-KK	China	Jul	Eng/Man		13
King's Kids:Urban					
USA-VA-UN		Jun	6 wk	Eng	10
KK - Impact World Tour					
USA-MT-KK	Northwest USA	Apr	6 mo	Eng	
USA-MT-KK	Northwest USA	May	6 mo	Eng	
USA-MT-LAKES	Northwest USA	Jun	6 mo	Eng	
USA-OR-SALEM	Rural America	Apr	2 mo	Eng	10
USA-WI-NORTH	Rural America	Apr/May	6 wk	Eng	
KK Bootcamp/Outreach					
JAPAN-KK	Japan	Aug	1 mo	Jap/Eng	10
KK Canadian Torch run					
USA-MT-KK	Canada	Jun	3 mo	Eng/Fre	
KK Int'l Alumni Team					
USA-MT-KK	Northwest USA	Apr	3 mo	Eng	
KK Performing Arts					
AUST-TAS-SAN	Melbourne, Aust.	Jan/Feb	4 wk	Eng	10

Ctry/City	Destination	Beg. Mon.	Length	Lang.	Min. Age
AUST-TAS-SAN	Canada (Games)	Aug	4 wk	Eng	10
KK Sports Surfing Team					
AUST-TAS-SAN	Port Macquerie	Jan	3 wk	Eng	12
KK Summer Perform. Arts					
CAN-ALB-CALG	Sask/Manitoba	Jul	3 wk	Eng/Fre	10
KK-Mississippi River Tour					
USA-HI-MAUI		Jul	6 wk	Eng	
Literature Distribution					
USA-OR-SLAVIC	Russ/Ukr/Latvia	Sep/May	2 wk+		
USA-OR-SLAVIC	Slavic Countries	Sep+	2 wk+	Eng/Rus	
Love Mexico					
USA-CO-MISS	Mexico City	Apr/Dec	varies	Eng/Spa	14
Love S.Africa Outreach					
NAMIB-UIS	Damaraland	Jul	3 wk	Eng/Afr	17
Made to Order Outreach					
USA-TX-TWIN	various	any		Eng	
March For Jesus					
SPAIN-TORR	Morocco	Jun	3 wk	Eng/Ara	18
Mardi Gras Outreach					
USA-LA-NEW	New Orleans	Feb	1 wk	Eng	
MED AIR Operation					
SWITZ-MED	Somalia/Armenia	Jan	12 mo	Eng	25
Medical					
USA-TN-NASH	Jamaica/Guat/El Sal	Jul	1 wk	Eng/Spa	18
Medical & Mercy Outreach					
USA-TX-TWIN	Haiti	Jan	3 wk	Eng	16
USA-TX-TWIN	Brazil	Jan	2 wk	Eng	16
USA-TX-TWIN	Peru	Apr/Jun	2 wk	Eng	16
USA-TX-TWIN	Peru	Oct	2 wk	Eng	16
Medical Boomerang					
AUST-WA-PERTH	Asia	Sep/Jan	1 mo	Eng	18
Medical Outreach					
MEX-MEXCITY	Oaxaca	Jan	4 wk	Spa/Eng	20
NZ-MERCY	Islands	Jul	2 wk+	Eng	
USA-FL-MIAMI	Haiti	Mar	2 wk	Eng/Cre	17
USA-FL-MIAMI	Sophia Bulgaria	May	2 wk	Eng	17
USA-FL-MIAMI	Panama	Aug	2 wk	Eng/Spa	17
USA-FL-ORL	Haiti	Mar	2 wk	Eng/Cre	17
USA-FL-ORL	Sophia Bulgaria	May	2 wk	Eng	17
USA-FL-ORL	Panama	Aug	2 wk	Eng/Spa	17
Medical/Construction/Dev.					
USA-TX-MERCY	West Africa	Nov	4 wk	Eng/Fre	18
Medical/Dental Outreach					
USA-HI-UN	Asia	Apr/Sep	3 wk+	Eng	18

Ctry/City	Destination	Beg. Mon.	Length	Lang.	Min. Age
Medical/Healthcare					
THAIL-LIFE	various	any	2 wk+	Eng/Tha	22
Mercy Ministry					
THAIL-LIFE	Handicapped Child.	any	1 mo+	Eng/Tha	20
USA-OR-SLAVIC	Russ/Ukr/Latvia	Jun/Jul	7 days+		
USA-OR-SLAVIC	Slavic Countries		2 wk+	Eng/Rus	
Mexican Outreaches					
CAN-BC-VAN	Mexico	Jan/Feb	1 wk+	Eng/Spa	13
CAN-BC-VAN	Mexico	May/Jun	1 wk+	Eng/Spa	13
CAN-BC-VAN	Mexico	Jul/Aug	1 wk+	Eng/Spa	13
Mini DTS					
NZ-NORTH	local	May	2 wk	Eng	15
UK-ENG-KINGS	English City	Jul	2 wk	Eng	16
Mission Builder Team					
SWITZ-POST	Peru	Jan	3 mo	Eng/Spa	18
Mission to Mexico					
USA-IL-URB	Mexico	Jan/Mar	1 wk	Eng/Spa	16
USA-IL-URB	Mexico	Apr/Jul	1 wk	Eng/Spa	16
USA-IL-URB	Mexico	Aug	1 wk	Eng/Spa	16
Mission Trip					
INDO-TIMOR	Timor Province	Mar/Jul	2 wk	Ind/Eng	17
INDO-TIMOR	Timor Province	Sep	2 wk	Ind/Eng	17
Mountain Bike Island Team					
USA-HI-MAUI	Maui, Hawaii	Jun	1 wk	Eng	
Music to Mexico					
USA-TN-NASH	Mexico	Jun	2 wk	Eng/Spa	15
Music/Drama Presentation					
JAPAN-TOYO	Toyoshina Town	Jul	3 wkend	Eng	0
Musicians Summer of Serv.					
USA-MT-LAKES	various	Jun	10 wk	Eng/Spa	0
USA-TX-TWIN	Brazil	Jun	2 mo	Eng	16
Najeevan Evangelism Team					
INDIA-PUNE	India	Jan/Jul	4 wk	Eng/Hin	18
New Year in New York					
USA-TN-NASH	New York City	Dec	1 wk	Eng	15
New York City Outreaches					
USA-NY-EAST	New York City	any	2 wkend	Eng/Spa	16
Nine Worlds Tour					
AUST-QLD-TOWN	SE Asia/China	Aug	3 wks	Eng	16
Northern Exposure					
CAN-ALB-TURN	NW Territories/Can.	Jul	4 wk	Eng	15
Olympic Outreach					
NORW-OTT	Winter Olympics	Feb	3 wk	Nor/Eng	16
Operation Nineveh					
CAN-QUE-MONT	Montreal	Jul	4 wk	Eng/Fre	18

Ctry/City	Destination	Beg. Mon.	Length	Lang.	Min. Age
Outreach					
CISBEL	Belarus	Jul	4 wk	Eng/Rus	
CISRUS	Krasnodar	Jul	4 wk	Eng/Rus	
CISRUS	Krasnoyarsk	Jul	4 wk	Eng/Rus	
CISUK	Ukraine	Jul	4 wk	Eng/Rus	
LATVIA	Latvia	Jul	4 wk	Eng/Rus	
TAIW-TAICH	Naning China	Aug	1 mo	Chi/Eng	18
Project Kurdistan/Medical					
USA-HI-UN	Northern Iraq	Apr+	3 wk+	Eng/Kur	18
Rare Jewels					
USA-HI-MAUI	Maui, Hawaii	Jun	1 wk	Eng	
Renovation:M/V Anastasis					
NETH-ROTT	Holland	Jul	2 mo	Eng	18
Sao Paulo Urgente					
BRAZ-SAO	Sao Paulo/Brazil	Jul	2 wk	Por/Eng	18
Season of Service					
HAITI	Haiti	Jun	2 wk	Eng/Fre	14
Short Term Mission					
USA-WI-WEYER	Mexico	Feb+	10 days	Eng/Spa	15
USA-WI-WEYER	Cuba/El Sal/Nicar	Jul	16 days	Eng/Spa	16
Short Term Mission					
USA-CA-CHULA	Tijuana	Mar/Apr	1 wk	Spa	16
Short Term Mission					
MEX-MAZAT	Nayarit, Mexico	any	10 days+	Eng/Spa	15
USA-CA-CHULA	Tijuana	Jun/Jul	9 days	Spa	16
USA-CA-CHULA	Tijuana	Aug	9 days	Spa	16
Short Term Outreach					
USA-CO-ARV	Juarez, Mexico	Jul	10 days	Eng	16
USA-CO-ARV	Russia	Jul	2 wk	Eng	16
Short Term Service					
BELIZE-BEL	Belize	any	2 wk+	Eng	18
GUAM	Micronesia Games	Mar	2 wk	Eng	18
Short Term Teams					
USA-STCROIX	St. Croix	May+	1 wk+	Eng/Spa	14
Small Team					
UK-ENG-TOR	Ghana	Sep	3 wk	Eng	18
Specialized S.O.S.					
AUST-NSW-ALB	Thailand	Jan/Feb	6 wk	Eng/Tha	
Sports Outreach/HK Youth					
HONG-REG	Hong Kong/China	Jun	2 mo	Eng/Can	17
Spring Break Outreach					
USA-TN-NASH	Atlanta	Mar	1 wk	Eng	13
USA-TN-NASH	Nashville	Mar	1 wk	Eng	13
SST: Amazon					
USA-CO-ARV	Brazil	Aug	3 wk	Eng/Por	16

Ctry/City	Destination	Beg. Mon.	Length	Lang.	Min. Age
SST: Nepal/India					
USA-CO-ARV	India/Nepal	Jul	3 wk	Eng/Hin	16
SST: Russia					
USA-CO-ARV	Moscow, Russia	Jul	3 wk	Eng/Rus	16
SST: Seirra Madre/Mexico					
USA-CO-ARV	Mexico	Jun	3 wk	Eng/Spa	16
Strat. Outreach Leaders					
USA-CENTRAL	Morocco	Oct	2 wk	Eng/Spa	18
Summer Impact					
BRAZ-SAO	Flor/Brazil	Jan	2 wk	Por/Eng	18
Summer Missions					
BOLIV-LAPAZ	Bolivian Cities	Jan	4 wk	Spa	15
Summer Missions Impact					
USA-NY-ANT	Native Amer.-NWest	Jun	7 wk	Eng/Kor	18
Summer of Missions					
BOLIV-SANTA	South Bolivia	Jan	4 wk	Spa/Eng	16
USA-HI-HONOL	Pacific/Asia	Jul	3 wk	Eng	16
USA-HI-MAUI	Maui, Hawaii	Jul/Aug	3 wk	Eng	
USA-HI-MAUI	Fiji Islands	Jul	5 wk	Eng/Fij	
USA-HI-MAUI	Japan	Jul	5 wk	Eng/Jap	
USA-UT-OGD	Utah	Jun	4 wk	Eng	13
USA-UT-OGD	Israel/Egypt	Aug	3 wk	Eng/Heb	15
Summer of Service					
AUST-ACT-WAT	Central Australia	Jul	1 mo	Eng	18
AUST-NSW-DEE	Malaysia	Nov	6 wk	Eng/Mal	18
AUST-NSW-KOT	India	Jan	4 wk	Eng	18
AUST-NSW-MT	Com.wealth Games	Aug	3 wk	Eng/Fre	16
AUST-NT-DAR	SE Asia/Indonesia	3 mo	Eng/Ind	16	
AUST-QLD-CAR	Gold Coast	Dec	2 wk	Eng	18
CAN-ALB-TURN	Mexico	Jul	6 wk	Eng/Spa	15
CAN-ALB-TURN	Com.wealth Games	Jul	4 wk	Eng	15
DENMARK-MORK	Peru/Tibet	May/Jun	2 wk	Eng	17
DENMARK-MORK	Peru/Tibet	Jul	2 wk	Eng	17
FRANCE-CHAT	Marseille	Jul	2 wk	Fre/Ara	16
FRANCE-PARIS	Paris	Jul	2 wk	Fre/Ara	18
HUNGARY	Romania/Turkey	Jul	6 wk	Eng/Hun	16
KENYA-LIKONI		May	3 mo		18
NETH-NATL	Amsterdam	Jul	8 wk	Eng/Dut	17
NZ-AUCK-URB	Dec/Jan		4 wk	Eng	18
NZ-NORTH	various	May/Dec	3 wk+	Eng	17
PARAGUAY	Asuncion	Feb	2 wk	Spa	16
POLAND	Russia/Poland	Jul	2 mo	Eng/Pol	18
TAIW-TAIPEI	China	Jul	4 wk	Eng/Man	18
URUGUAY	Uruguay	Jan	2 wk	Spa/Por	16
USA-CA-BISH	Croatia	Jun	7 wk	Eng/Ger	18
USA-CA-BISH	Croatia	Jul	7 wk	Eng/Ger	18
USA-CA-RICH		Jun	5 wk	Eng	15
USA-CA-RICH		Jun	4 wk	Eng	15

Ctry/City	Destination	Beg. Mon.	Length	Lang.	Min. Age
USA-CO-FRONT	Mexico...	Jun+	9 days	Eng/Spa	13
USA-FL-MIAMI	Guatemala	Jun	5 wk	Eng/Spa	16
USA-FL-MIAMI	Jamaica	Jun	5 wk	Eng	16
USA-FL-MIAMI	Panama	Jun	5 wk	Eng/Spa	16
USA-FL-MIAMI	Guadalajara	Jun	5 wk	Eng/Spa	16
USA-FL-MIAMI	Costa Rica	Jun	5 wk	Eng/Spa	16
USA-FL-ORL	Guatemala	Jun	5 wk	Eng/Spa	16
USA-FL-ORL	Jamaica	Jun	5 wk	Eng	16
USA-FL-ORL	Panama	Jun	5 wk	En/Spa	16
USA-FL-ORL	Guadalajara	Jun	5 wk	Eng/Spa	16
USA-FL-ORL	Costa Rica	Jun	5 wk	Eng/Spa	16
USA-NC-CHAR	Bulgaria	Jul	3 wk	Eng	16
USA-NC-CHAR	Central America	Jul	3 wk	Eng/Spa	16
USA-OR-PORT	Portland, OR	Jun	2 wk+	Eng	18
USA-OR-SALEM	C.I.S. (Russia)	Jun/Jul	3 wk	Eng/Rus	16
USA-OR-SALEM	C.I.S. (Russia)	Aug	3 wk	Eng	16
USA-TX-TWIN	Romania	Jan/Jun	3 wk+	Eng	16
USA-TX-TWIN	Romania	Jul	3 wk	Eng	16
USA-TX-TWIN	Albania	Jun	1 mo	Eng	16
USA-TX-TWIN	Russia	Jul	3 wk	Eng	16
USA-TX-TWIN	Peru	Jun/Jul	3 wk	Eng	16
USA-TX-TWIN	Bulgaria	Jun/Jul	3 wk	Eng	16
USA-TX-TWIN	Brazil	Jun	1 mo	Eng	16
USA-TX-TWIN	Mongolia	Jun	1 mo	Eng	16
USA-TX-TWIN	Nepal	Jul	1 mo	Eng	16
Summer of Service:Dance					
USA-MT-LAKES	various	Jun	10 wk	Eng	
Summer of Service:Sports					
USA-MT-LAKES	China	Jun	6 wk	Eng	
Summer Outreach					
NETH-HEERDE	Albania				
Summer School					
BRAZ-CURIT	Parana State:Beach	Jan	4 wk	Por/Ger	18
Summer School of Training					
HAITI	Haiti	Jul	1 wk	Eng/Cre	14
HAITI	Haiti	Jul	1 wk	Cre/Eng	14
PHIL-DAVAO	Mindanao	Apr	1 mo	Eng/Ceb	18
USA-IL-CHIC	Chicago	Jun	2 wk	Eng/Spa	13
Summer Short Term					
USA-CA-SUN	Mexico	Jun	9 days	Eng/Spa	
Summer Teams Internships					
USA-VA-INT	various	Jun	6 wk	Eng/Spa	18
Surfers for Missions Intl					
USA-HI-MAUI	Hawaii/Indonesia	Jul	4 wk	Eng	
Take Action Teams					
USA-TN-NASH	Mexico	Jun/Jul	2 wk	Eng/Spa	13

Ctry/City	Destination	Beg. Mon.	Length	Lang.	Min. Age
Tell Boulder					
USA-CO-ARV	Boulder, CO USA	Jul	1 wk	Eng	16
The Atlas					
SPAIN-TORR	Morocco	Jul	3 wk	Eng/Ara	18
Torch Run					
JAPAN-OKIN	Tokyo	Jan	4 wk	Eng/Jap	10
Training for Gov't Leader					
USA-HI-UN	Albania	Apr/Jun	3 wk	Eng/Alb	22
USA-HI-UN	Albania	Jul/Sep	3 wk	Eng/Alb	22
University Campus					
USA-WI-MADIS	Univ. of Wisconsin	Jun	8 wk	Eng	18
Unreached Areas					
ZAIRE		Sep	2 wk	Fre/Swa	18
Urban Mission Adventures					
CAN-BC-VAN	Greater Vancouver	any	1 wk+	Eng	13
Urban Neighbor Internship					
USA-VA-INT	Richmond, VA	Jun	3 mo	Eng/Spa	18
Village Outreach					
BURUNDI		Sep	2 wk	Fre/Swa	18
RWANDA		Sep	2 wk	Fre	18
Water Festival Outreach					
SWED-STOCK	Stockholm	Aug	3 wk	Swe/Eng	
Winter of Service					
CAN-ALB-TURN	Dominica, Carib.	Jan	2 wk	Eng	18
CAN-ALB-TURN	NW Territories/Can.	Jan	3 wk	Eng	15
Winter School					
BRAZ-CURIT	Brazil Cities	Jul	4 wk	Por/Ger	18
World Cup Soccer Games					
USA-IL-CHIC	Chicago	Jun	4 wk	Eng/Spa	16
USA-TN-NASH	Orlando	Jun	2 wk	Eng	13
USA-TX-DALL	Dallas	Jun	6 wk	Eng/Spa	13
Youth Evangelistic					
AUSTRIA-WIEN	Vienna	Jul/Aug	8 wk	Ger/Eng	18

Section VI

YWAM Camp Information

The camps listed in this section are open to the public. Some restrictions may apply. Please write to the location sponsoring the camp for further details.

Explanation of Information in Section VI

Ctry/City:

The country and city code indicating the YWAM ministry sponsoring the camp. (See Appendix for Ctry/City code key.)

Camp:

The name of the camp.

Destination:

If the camp includes an outreach, the destination of that outreach will be listed.

Beginning Month:

The month the camp begins. If two months are listed, the camp will begin in both of those months.

Length:

The total length of the camp in weeks or days. (wk=week, wkend=weekend)

Language(s):

The primary language to be spoken at this camp will be

listed first. If there is a secondary language that would be helpful, that will be listed second.

Minimum Age:

The minimum age requirement for the camp. Restrictions other than age may apply. Please write the operating location for information and requirements.

Camp	Dest.	Beg. Mon.	Length	Lang.	Min. Age
AUST-QLD-CAR					
Lifestyle Discipleship		Dec	1 wk	Eng	18
AUSTRIA-WIEN					
Sports Camps	Austria	Jul	1 wk	Ger/Eng	18
AUST-TAS-SAN					
King's Kids Youth Camps	Tasmania, Aust.	Mar/Apr	wkend	Eng	12
King's Kids Youth Camps	Tasmania, Aust.	Nov	wkend	Eng	12
BELG-GENT					
Family Camp		Jul	1 wk	Dut	18
BRAZ-PORTO					
Teenage Camp		Jan	2 wk	Por/Spa	12
CAN-ALB-CALG					
King's Kids Boot Camp		Jul	10 days	Eng	
NIKO Adventure Camps		Mar	4 days	Eng	13
CAN-ASSOC					
In Touch Renewal Camp	Texas, USA	May	1 wk	Eng	
In Touch Renewal Camp	California, USA	Jun	1 wk	Eng	
In Touch Renewal Camp	Holland	Jun	1 wk	Eng	
In Touch Renewal Camp	Idaho, USA	Jul	1 wk	Eng	
In Touch Renewal Camp	Switzerland	Jul	1 wk	Eng	
In Touch Renewal Camp	BC, Canada	Jul	1 wk	Eng	
In Touch Renewal Camp	Minnesota, USA	Aug	1 wk	Eng	
In Touch Renewal Camp	Hawaii, USA	Nov	1 wk	Eng	
In Touch Renewal Camp	South Africa	Dec	1 wk	Eng	
CAN-ONT-TOR					
King's Kids Summer Camp		Jul	4 wk	Eng	
GERM-BUCH					
King's Kids/Family Camp		Jul	10 days	Ger/Eng	
INDO-TIMOR					
Youth Camp	Island/Timor	Mar/Jul	1 wk	Eng/Ind	17
IRELAND					
Youth Camp		Jul	3 mo	Eng	16
JAPAN-HIGA					
Kings Kids	Kyushu, Japan	Aug		Jap/Kor	
Mini DTS Camp	Japan	May	1 wk	Kor/Eng	18
MALAY-PENANG					
Carry the Light	Malay/Thailand	Nov	2 wk	Eng	17
Carry the Light (Tamil)	Malay/Thailand	Nov	2 wk	Tam/Eng	17
MEX-MAZAT					
Surf Camp	Oaxaca, Mexico	Mar/Aug	2 wk	Eng/Spa	18
NAMIB-UIS					
Evangelism/Discipleship	Damaraland	Dec	3 wk	Eng/Afr	17
NAMIB-WIND					
Discipleship Training	Namibia	Dec	1 wk	Eng	15
King's Kids Go Camp	Namibia/S.Africa	May/Sep	2 wk	Eng/Afr	10
NZ-ASSOC					
In Touch Renewal Camp		Dec/Jan	1 wk	Eng	

Camp	Dest.	Beg. Mon.	Length	Lang.	Min. Age
PARAGUAY					
King's Kids Winter Camp		Jul	2 wk	Spa	12
PUERTO					
King's Kids Boot Camp	Puerto Rico	Jul	3 wk	Spa/Eng	13
SWED-LJUN					
Family Camp		Jul	10 days	Swe/Eng	
King's Kids Go Camp		Jun/Jul	1 wk+	Eng/Sca	6
UK-ENG-KINGS					
Family Ministries Camp		Jul	1 wk	Eng	18
USA-CA-HOLL					
King's Kids Go Camp	Local	Jul	3 wk	Eng/Spa	10
USA-CA-RICH					
Doing it! 'Kamp' 94		Aug	6 days	Eng	15
Easter Perf Art/Disciple.		Mar	3 days	Eng	13
'Kidz Kamp' #1		Jul	5 days	Eng	8
'Kidz Kamp' #2		Jul	5 days	Eng	8
Radicals Only Teen #1		Jul	5 days	Eng	13
Spring Gauntlet '94		Apr	4 days	Eng	15
Summer of Service -'Kamp'	Calif, Mexico	Jun	9 wk	Eng/Spa	15
Teen Camp #2		Aug	6 days	Eng	15
Winter 'Kidz' Camp		Feb	3 days	Eng	8
Winter Teen Camp		Jan	3 days	Eng	12
USA-CA-SUMM					
Rockclimbing Camp	Sierra Nevada Mtn		Jun+	1 wk	Eng 14
USA-CO-ARV					
Rocky Mtn Family Camp	Colorado USA	Aug	1 wk	Eng	16
USA-HI-HONOL					
Surf Camp	Oahu, Hawaii	Jul/Aug	2 wk	Eng	13
USA-HI-MAUI					
NIKO Adventure Camps	Maui, Hawaii	Mar/Jun	1 wk	Eng	
Surfer for Missions Camps	Maui, Hawaii	Jun	1 wk	Eng	
USA-ID-RIGG					
Family Camp		Aug	2 wk	Eng	
Youth Camp	Mexico	Jun	2 wk	Eng/Spa	13
USA-MT-LAKES					
NIKO Adventure Camps	Montana	May/Jul	5 days	Eng	
NIKO Adventure Camps	Montana	Aug	5 days	Eng	
Speed & Strength Camp		Jun	1 wk	Eng	
Vacation With A Mission		Jul	1 wk	Eng	0
Youth A.T.T.A.C.	Mexico		4 wk	Eng/Spa	
USA-OR-SLAVIC					
Youth Camps	Russ/Ukr/Latvia		2 wk+		
Youth Camps	Slavic Countries	Jun+	1 wk+	Eng/Rus	
USA-STCROIX					
Youth Discipleship Camps	Caribbean Islands	Jun/Jul	2 wk	Eng/Spa	16
Youth Discipleship Camps	Caribbean Islands	Aug	2 wk	Eng/Spa	16
USA-TX-TWIN					
SST	Mexico	Jun/Jul	3 wk	Eng/Spa	13
SST Phase 2		Jun/Jul	4 wk	Eng	13

Camp	Dest.	Beg. Mon.	Length	Lang.	Min. Age
USA-WI-NORTH					
Vacation With A Mission		Jul	1 wk	Eng	
VENEZ-CARAC					
Vacation With A Purpose		Aug	1 mo	Spa	
WSAMOA-PION					
Church Leadership Role		Sep	1 wk	Eng	18

Section VII

YWAM Seminar/Conference Information

The seminars and conferences listed in this section are open to the public. Some restrictions may apply. Please write the operating location you are interested in for further details.

Explanation of Information in Section VII

Ctry/City:

The country and city code indicating the YWAM ministry sponsoring the seminar or conference. (See Appendix for Ctry/City code key.)

Conference/Seminar:

The name of the conference or seminar.

Beginning Month:

The month that the conference will begin. If the conference will be held twice, both starting months will appear.

Length:

The total length of the conference or seminar in days or weeks. (wk=week, wkend=weekend) If there is an option to continue the conference or seminar for a longer amount of time than specified, a "+" sign will appear after the length.

Language(s):

The primary language to be spoken at the conference or

seminar will be listed first. If a secondary language would be helpful, it will be listed second.

Minimum Age:

The minimum age requirement for the conference or seminar. Some restrictions other than age may apply. Please write to the YWAM location for specific information and requirements.

Conf/Seminar	Beg Mon	Length	Lang	Min. Age
AUST-ACT-CAN				
Building a Biblical Worldview	Jan	1 day+	Eng	18
AUST-ACT-WAT				
Counselling (Plumbline)	Apr	1 wk	Eng	18
Discipleship	Feb	2 wk	Eng	
AUST-QLD-ASH				
Cindy Jacobs (Gates/Enemy)	Jun	1 wk	Eng	
George Otis, Jr. (Terr/Spirit)	Apr	1 wk	Eng	
Go Fest	Jun	4 days	Eng	16
Linda Cowie (Reach/City)	May	1 wk	Eng	
AUST-TAS-SAN				
Kings Kids National Conference	Jul	1 wk	Eng	18
Kings Kids Principles/Values	May/Jun	2 days	Eng	18
Kings Kids Principles/Values	Jul/Nov	2 days	Eng	18
AUST-WA-PERTH				
Teaching English/2nd Language	Oct	4 wk	Eng	18
BRAZ-PORTO				
National Seminar of Education	Jul	1 wk	Por	
BRAZ-RECIFE				
Go Fest	Jul	3 days	Por/Eng	
Go Fest	Jul	4 days	Por/Eng	13
Leadership Conference	Aug	5 days	Por/Eng	18
BURUNDI				
Mini DTS	Jul	2 wk	Fre/Eng	18
CAN-ALB-CALG				
King's Kids Introductory Sem.	Nov	2 days	Eng	18
KK Outreach Leaders Seminar	Feb	4 days	Eng	18
NIKO Leaders Training Weekend	Feb	4 days	Eng	18
CAN-BC-WIN				
Go Fest	Jun	4 days	Eng	0
CAN-QUE-MONT				
Redeeming/Church's Sexuality	Oct	3 days	Eng/Fre	13
CAN-VIC-COMM				
Go Fest	Aug	4 days	Eng	
CISBEL				
Go Fest	Jul	3 days	Eng/Rus	
CISRUS				
Go Fest	Jul	3 days	Eng/Rus	
CISUK				
Go Fest	Jul	3 days	Eng/Ukr	
COLOM-LUZ				
Educational	Jan	2 wk	Spa	
FINLAND-SCH				
Christian Education	Jun	2 wk	Eng	20

Conf/Seminar	Beg Mon	Length	Lang	Min. Age
FRANCE-MONT				
Nouvel Essor	Aug	4 wk	Fre	30
GERM-BUCH				
Couples, Rettenbachiallgau	Mar	3 days	Ger	
Couples Seminar, Sachsen	Apr	3 days	Ger	
GERM-HURL				
European Teenager Congress	Jul	4 days	Eng/Ger	12
GHANA				
Leadership Seminar	Nov	10 days	Eng	18
GUINEABIS				
National Missionary Conference	Apr	4 days	Por	0
HUNGARY				
Exchange Life	Feb/Jul	3 days	Eng	16
Exchange Life	Sep	3 days	Eng	16
INDIA-BHOPAL				
Literacy Seminar		2 wk	Hin/Eng	21
SBS Seminar	Oct	3 wk	Hin/Eng	
INDO-JAVA				
Go Fest	Oct	3 days	Eng/Ind	18
INDO-TIMOR				
Missions Conference	Aug	4 days	Ind/Eng	
JAPAN-HIGAN				
Spiritual Warfare	Oct	5 days	Jap/Kor	18
JAPAN-NATL				
Frontier Missions Seminar	Feb	5 wk		
JAPAN-TOKYO				
Discipleship Seminar	Feb	3 days	Eng	0
Taking Your City (Dawson)	Sep	3 days	Eng	0
KENYA-LIKONI				
Mini DTS	Apr/Aug	2 wk	Eng/Swa	18
Mini DTS	Dec	2 wk	Eng/Swa	18
LATVIA				
Go Fest	Jul	3 days	Eng/Lat	
MEX-TEPIC				
Destiny '94 Youth Conf.	Apr	5 days	Spa	13
Spiritual Warfare	Feb	5 days	Eng/Spa	0
NETH-HEERDE				
Mini DTS		3 wk	Dut	
NETH-NATL				
Urban Frontiers Conference	Mar	1 wk	Eng	18
NORW-OTT				
Easter Festival	Mar	5 days	Nor/Eng	15
New Year Olympic Conference	Dec	5 days	Nor/Eng	15
Worship Seminar	Mar	2 wk		

Conf/Seminar	Beg Mon	Length	Lang	Min. Age
NZ-AUCK-KK				
King's Kids Intro/Training	Jul	1 wk	Eng	16
PARAGUAY				
Desktop Communications	Jun	2 wk	Spa/Eng	18
Seminar of Authors	Nov	2 wk	Spa/Eng	
Seminar of Illustration	Sep	3 wk	Spa	18
POLAND				
Small Group Leading	Mar	3 days	Eng	18
RWANDA				
Mini DTS	Jul	2 wk	Fre	18
Pastor's Seminar	Jul	2 wk	Fre	18
SWED-KK				
Choreography Seminar		4 days	Swe	
National Conference		4 days	Swe	
SWED-LJUN				
"Focus" Counselling Course	Jul	2 wk	Swe/Eng	18
Prayer Seminar	Apr	2 wk	Swe/Eng	17
SWED-STOCK				
Counseling		wkend	Swe/Eng	
Evangelism		wkend	Swe/Eng	
Spiritual Growth		wkend	Swe/Eng	
SWED-STORM				
Leadership Training Course	Mar	6 days	Eng/Swe	
SWITZ-MED				
MEDAIR Crisis Situation Sem.	Mar	10 days	Eng/Fre	25
SWITZ-POST				
Politics (Dennis Peacocke)	May	1 wk	Ger/Eng	20
UK-ENG-EARL				
Urban Missions		1 day+	Eng	18
UK-ENG-HARP				
Muslim Awareness	Apr/Oct	1 wk	Eng	18
UK-ENG-LOND				
TESOL	Apr	4 wk	Eng	18
UK-SCOT-KK				
King's Kids National Conf.	Jun	3 days	Eng	
UK-SCOT-NATL				
Families Alive	Jul	1 wk	Eng	17
URUGUAY				
Urban Missions Seminar	Oct	5 days	Spa	
USA-CA-CHULA				
Medical Seminar	Oct	4 days	Eng	18
USA-CA-RICH				
Primary Health/Develop Nations	Mar	2 days	Eng	
USA-CA-SUMM				
Parent & Child Wilderness Sem.	Jun+	5 days	Eng	8

Conf/Seminar	Beg Mon	Length	Lang	Min. Age
USA-CENTRAL				
Leadership Development Seminar	Apr	6 days	Eng/Spa	18
USA-CO-ARV				
School of Worship	Sep	1 wk	Eng	16
USA-CO-FRONT				
N.A. Frontier Missions Conf.	May	3 days	Eng	
USA-CO-MISS				
Leadership Conference	varies		Eng	
Prayer Conference	varies		Eng	
USA-FL-MIAMI				
Health Care/Developing Nations	Nov	2 days	Eng	
King's Kids Seminar	Jan	2 days	Eng	16
USA-HI-UN				
Advanced Project Planning	Feb	16 days	Eng	0
Aquaculture Tech. Symposium	Jun	6 days	Eng	0
Blessing of Authority	Feb	3 days	Eng	0
Color Photography	Feb	5 days	Eng	0
Elderhostel	Feb/May	1 wk	Eng	0
English Language Seminar	Jul	1 wk	Jap	0
Generation at Rist	Mar	1 day	Eng	0
Gifts of the Holy Spirit	Mar	4 days	Eng	0
Hospitality Seminar	Jan	2 wk	Eng	0
Indonesian DTS Seminar	Oct	2 wk	Eng	0
Int'l Business Seminar	Mar	8 days	Eng	0
Japanese Exchange Students	Jan	3 days	Eng	0
Living Free	Apr	10 days	Eng	0
Love, Acceptance, Forgiveness	May	5 days	Eng	0
Marriage Plus Seminar	Apr/Aug	4 days	Eng	0
Messenger International	Jan	1 wk	Eng	0
Pastor's Seminar	Aug	11 days	Eng	0
Project Develop/Leadership	Jan	3 wk	Eng	0
Redeeming the Arts	Jan	4 days	Eng	0
Restoring Christian Identity	Feb	11 days	Eng	0
Singles Plus Seminar	Mar/Jun	4 days	Eng	0
Teacher's Seminar	Jul	12 days	Eng	0
Team Leadership Seminar	Jan	2 wk	Eng	0
Team Leadership Seminar	Jan	2 wk	Eng	0
The Father Heart of God	Jan/Apr	5 days	Eng	0
The Love of God	Feb/May	4 days	Eng	0
Walking in Financial Freedom	Feb	1 day	Eng	0
Writers Workshop	Jan	3 days	Eng	0
Youth Leader's Seminar	May	1 day	Eng	0
USA-IL-URB				
Personal Witnessing:Learn/Do	Mar/Apr	3 days+	Eng	16
Personal Witnessing:Learn/Do	Sep+	3 days+	Eng	16
USA-MT-LAKES				
Women In Ministry	Aug	1 wk	Eng	

Conf/Seminar	Beg Mon	Length	Lang	Min. Age
USA-OR-SALEM				
Crossroads Seminar	Jan/May	2 wk	Eng	16
USA-PA-ROAR				
Crossroads Seminar	Nov	2 wk	Eng	
USA-SD-SPEAR				
Discipleship Institute Seminar	Jan	4 days	Eng	18
Intercession/Worship Seminar	Jan	2 wk	Eng	18
USA-TX-EDIT				
Advanced Writer's Training	various	1 wk	Eng	
Basic Writers		2 wk	Eng	16
Writer's Training Seminar	various	2 wk	Eng	
USA-TX-LAST				
Desktop Publishing Seminar			Eng	
Graphic Design Seminar			Eng	
Writer's Conference			Eng	
USA-TX-MERCY				
Agriculture/Developing Nations	Jul	3 wk	Eng	18
Medical Mission/Devel Nations	Apr/Aug	4 days	Eng	18
Orientation to Medical Mission	Oct	4 wk	Eng	18
USA-TX-TWIN				
Jesus Go-Fest	Apr	1 day	Eng	
Living Alternatives Seminar	Mar/Oct	1 wk	Eng	18
Take Action Seminar	Mar	1 day	Eng	0
USA-UN-HI				
Seminar for Japanese	Aug/Sep	10 days	Jap	0
USA-UT-OGD				
Mini DTS Jan	5 days	Eng	18	
USA-WI-MADIS				
Mission Bridge	Feb	8 wk	Eng	16
USA-WI-NORTH				
Marketing to Reach the Lost	Oct	1 wk	Eng	
Minstry & Partner Mail Seminar	Nov	2 wk	Eng	
USA-WI-WEYER				
Outreach Leadership Training	Jan/May	1 day	Eng	18
WSAMOA-PION				
Active Ex-YWAMers for Christ	Nov	1 wk	Eng	18
ZAIRE				
Mini DTS	Jul	2 wk	Fre/Kis	18
Pastor's Seminar	Jul	2 wk	Fre/Kis	18

Country/City Codes

ALBANIA	Albania
AMSAMOA	American Samoa
ANGOLA	Angola
ARGEN-BA	Argentina - Buenos Aires
ARGEN-CHACO	Argentina - Chaco
AUST-ACT-CAN	Australia - Canberra
AUST-ACT-WAT	Australia - Watson
AUST-NSW-ALB	Australia - Albury
AUST-NSW-CABR	Australia - Cabramatta
AUST-NSW-DEE	Australia - Dee Why
AUST-NSW-GOUL	Australia - Goulburn
AUST-NSW-KK	Australia - Sydney - (K Kids)
AUST-NSW-KOT	Australia - Kotara
AUST-NSW-MT	Australia - Mt. Druitt
AUST-NSW-RYDE	Australia - Ryde
AUST-NT-DAR	Australia - Darwin
AUST-QLD-ASH	Australia - Ashgrove
AUST-QLD-CAR	Australia - Carbrook
AUST-QLD-MERCY	Australia - (Mercy Ships)
AUST-QLD-TOWN	Australia - Townsville
AUST-SA-ADEL	Australia - Adelaide
AUST-TAS-SAN	Australia - Sandy Bay
AUST-TAS-SOR	Australia - Sorrell
AUST-VIC-COLL	Australia - Collingwood
AUST-VIC-IB	Australia - (Island Breeze)
AUST-VIC-NATL	Australia - Surrey (Nat'l)
AUST-WA-PERTH	Australia - Perth
AUSTRIA-WIEN	Austria - Wien
AZERBAIJAN	Azerbaijan
BANGLA-CHITT	Bangladesh - Chittagong
BANGLA-DHAKA	Bangladesh - Dhaka
BELG-BRUSS	Belgium - Brussels
BELG-GENT	Belgium - Gent
BELIZE-BEL	Belize - Belmopan
BOLIV-BENI	Bolivia - Beni
BOLIV-LAPAZ	Bolivia - La Paz
BOLIV-SANTA	Bolivia - Santa Cruz
BRAZ-BLUMEN	Brazil - Blumenau
BRAZ-CT	Brazil - Ct. Valorizcao
BRAZ-CURIT	Brazil - Curitiba
BRAZ-DAY	Brazil - Belo H. (Day Care)
BRAZ-FLOR	Brazil - Florianopolis
BRAZ-LAR	Brazil - Lar de Criancas
BRAZ-LUZ	Brazil - Belo H. (Luzeiro)
BRAZ-MANAUS	Brazil - Manaus
BRAZ-MAUES	Brazil - Maues
BRAZ-NATL	Brazil - Belo Horiz. (Nat'l)
BRAZ-PARA	Brazil - Belem, Para
BRAZ-PORTO	Brazil - Porto Alegre
BRAZ-REC	Brazil - Belo H. (Recanto)
BRAZ-RECIFE	Brazil - Recife
BRAZ-RESCUE	Brazil - Belo H. (Rescue)
BRAZ-REST	Brazil - Belo H. (Restorat.)
BRAZ-RIO	Brazil - Rio de Janeiro
BRAZ-ROND	Brazil - Rondonia
BRAZ-SAO	Brazil - Sao Paulo

BRAZ-TAP	Brazil - Tapaua
BULGARIA	Bulgaria
BURKINA	Burkina Faso
BURUNDI	Burundi
CA	Central America (c/o USA)
CAMBODIA	Cambodia
CAMEROON	Cameroon
CAN-ALB-CALG	Canada - Alb - Calgary
CAN-ALB-EDM	Canada - Alb - Edmonton
CAN-ALB-TURN	Canada - Alb - Turner Valley
CAN-ASSOC	Canada - (YWAM Assoc.)
CAN-BC-VAN	Canada - BC - Vancouver
CAN-BC-WIN	Canada - BC - Winfield
CAN-NOVA	Canada - Nova Scotia
CAN-ONT-CAMB	Canada - Ont - Cambridge
CAN-ONT-TOR	Canada - Ont - Toronto
CAN-QUE-DUN	Canada - Que - Dunham
CAN-QUE-MONT	Canada - Que - Montreal
CAN-VAN-KK	Canada - Vancouver (KK)
CAN-VIC-COMM	Canada - Vic (Games)
CHILE-CALBUCO	Chile - Calbuco
CHILE-CAST	Chile - Castro
CHILE-PUERT	Chile - Puerto Montt
CHILE-PUNTA	Chile - Punta Arenas
CHILE-SANT	Chile - Santiago (Nat'l)
CHILE-TEMUCO	Chile - Temuco
CIS-RUS-BAR	C.I.S. - Russia - Barnaul
CIS-RUS-MUR	C.I.S. - Russia - Murmansk
CISBEL	C.I.S. - Belarus
CISRUS	C.I.S. - Russia
CISUK	C.I.S. - Ukraine
COLOM-BOG	Colombia - Bogota DTS
COLOM-BUCA	Colombia - Bucaramanga
COLOM-CART	Colombia - Cartagena
COLOM-CHILD	Colombia - (Street Children)
COLOM-LUZ	Colombia - (Light/Nations)
COLOM-RESTOR	Colombia - (Restoration)
COOK-RARO	Cook Islands - Rarotonga
CROATIA	Croatia
CYPRUS-NIC	Cyprus - Nicosia
CYPRUS-WEE	Cyprus - Nic. (Wee Care)
CZECH-PLZEN	Czech Republic - Plzen
CZECH-PRAHA	Czech Republic - Praha
DENMARK-COPE	Denmark - Copenhagen
DENMARK-MORK	Denmark - Morke
DJIBOUTI	Djibouti
DOMIN-SANTO	Dominican Republic
ECUADOR	Ecuador
EGYPT	Egypt
EQUATOR	Equatorial Guinea
ESTONIA	Estonia
ETHIOPIA	Ethiopia
FAROE	Faroe Islands
FIJI-ADMIN	Fiji-Nadi (Administration)
FIJI-DTS	Fiji-Nadi (DTS)
FIJI-MARAN	Fiji-Nadi (Maranatuna)

FIJI-PRE	Fiji-Nadi (Preschool)
FINLAND-HELS	Finland - Helsinki
FINLAND-SCH	Finland - Hels (School)
FINLAND-SIU	Finland - Siuntio
FRANCE-BOOK	France - Paris (Bookshop)
FRANCE-FRENCH	France - (French Ministries)
FRANCE-MONT	France - Le Gault
FRANCE-PARIS	France - Paris (Nat'l)
FRENCH	French Polynesia
GERM-ALTEN	Germany - Altensteig
GERM-BISP	Germany - Bispingen
GERM-BUCH	Germany - Buchholz
GERM-HURL	Germany - Hurlach
GERM-MEDIA	Germany - (Media Plus)
GERM-RELL	Germany - Rellingen
GERM-TUEB	Germany - Tuebingen
GHANA	Ghana - Tema
GREECE	Greece - Thessaloniki
GREENLAND	Greenland
GRENADA	Grenada - Sauteurs
GUAM	Guam - Agana
GUAT-GUAT	Guatemala - Guatem. City
GUINEABIS	Guinea Bissau
GUYANA	Guyana - Georgetown
HAITI	Haiti - St. Marc
HONDURAS	Honduras - Tegucigalpa
HONG-KOWL	Hong Kong - Kowloon
HONG-REG	Hong Kong - (Regl/Nat'l)
HONG-TRAIN	Hong Kong - (Chinese Trng)
HONG-YUEN	Hong Kong - Yuen Long
HUNGARY	Hungary - Budapest
ICELAND-EGI	Iceland - Egilsstadir
ICELAND-REY	Iceland - Reykjavik (Nat'l)
INDIA-BANG	India - Bangalore
INDIA-BENG	India - West Bengal
INDIA-BHOPAL	India - Bhopal
INDIA-BOMB	India - Bombay
INDIA-CALC	India - Calcutta
INDIA-DEHR	India - Dehradun
INDIA-KALIM	India - Kalimpong
INDIA-MADRAS	India - Madras
INDIA-MAN	India - Manali
INDIA-NATL	India - Madras (Nat'l)
INDIA-NEW	India - New Delhi
INDIA-PUNE	India - Pune
INDIA-SECUN	India - Secunderabad
INDIA-SHIMLA	India - New Shimla
INDIA-VARAN	India - Varanasi
INDO-AMBON	Indonesia - Ambon
INDO-BALI	Indonesia - Bali - Kuta
INDO-JAK	Indonesia - Jakarta
INDO-JATIM	Indonesia - Jember - E.Java
INDO-JAVA	Indonesia - Surabaya
INDO-LOMB	Indonesia - Lombok
INDO-MANADO	Indonesia - Manado
INDO-PONT	Indonesia - Pontianak
INDO-SING	Indonesia - Bali - Singaraja
INDO-TIMOR	Indonesia - Timor
INDO-UJUN	Indonesia - Ujungpandang
IRAQ	Iraq (c/o Netherlands)
IRELAND	Republic of Ireland
ISRAEL-COORD	Israel - (Coordinating Off.)
ISRAEL-JERUS	Israel - Jerusalem
ITALY-CADEG	Italy - Cadegliano
ITALY-ROME	Italy - Rome
JAMAICA	Jamaica - Manchester
JAPAN-AKASHI	Japan - Akashi
JAPAN-CHIBA	Japan - Chiba
JAPAN-HIGA	Japan - Higashi Osaka
JAPAN-IMPACT	Japan - Osaka (Impact)
JAPAN-ITAB	Japan - Itabashi

JAPAN-KK	Japan - Tokyo - (Kings Kids)
JAPAN-KOBE	Japan - Kobe
JAPAN-KODAI	Japan - Kodaira
JAPAN-MAEB	Japan - Maebashi
JAPAN-NARITA	Japan - Narita
JAPAN-NATL	Japan - Takatsuki (Nat'l)
JAPAN-NODA	Japan - Noda
JAPAN-OKIN	Japan - Okinawa
JAPAN-SHIN	Japan - Shinano
JAPAN-TOKYO	Japan - Tokyo
JAPAN-TOYO	Japan - Toyoshina
JAPAN-YACH	Japan - Yachiyo
JAPAN-YOKO	Japan - Yokohama
KENYA-AREA	Kenya - Nairobi (Area Off.)
KENYA-LIKONI	Kenya - Likoni-Mombasa
KENYA-MOMB	Kenya - Mombasa
KENYA-NATL	Kenya - Nairobi (Nat'l Off.)
KOREA-CHUN	Korea - Chunchon
KOREA-FARM	Korea - (Farm for Nations)
KOREA-KK	Korea - Seoul - (King's Kids)
KOREA-KWANG	Korea - Kwangju
KOREA-MOKPO	Korea - Mokpo City
KOREA-NATL	Korea - Seoul - (Nat'l)
KOREA-PRAISE	Korea - Seoul (P/W Team)
KOREA-PUSAN	Korea - Pusan
KOREA-SEOUL	Korea - Seoul
KOREA-TRNG	Korea - Seoul - (Trng)
LATVIA	Latvia
LESOTHO	Lesotho - Ketane
LIBERIA	Liberia - Monrovia
MACAU	Macau
MALAWI	Malawi - Blantyre
MALAY-PENANG	Malaysia - Penang
MALAY-PERAK	Malaysia - Perak
MALI	Mali - Kouhala
MEX-GUADAL	Mexico - Guadalajara
MEX-JUAR	Mexico - Juarez
MEX-MAZAT	Mexico - Mazatlan
MEX-MEXCITY	Mexico - Mexico City
MEX-OAX	Mexico - Oaxaca
MEX-TEPIC	Mexico - Tepic
MEX-TIJ	Mexico - Tijuana
MICRO-YAP	Micronesia, Yap
MONG	Mongolia - (c/o Korea)
MOROCCO	Morocco (c/o Spain)
MOZAMB	Mozambique - Beira
NAMIB-UIS	Namibia - Uis
NAMIB-WIND	Namibia - Windhoek
NEPAL-KATH	Nepal - Kathmandu
NEPAL-POKH	Nepal - Pokhara
NETH-ARNHEM	Netherlands - Arnhem
NETH-CLEFT	Netherlands - (The Cleft)
NETH-DEPOORT	Netherlands - De Poort
NETH-HEERDE	Netherlands - Heerde
NETH-NATL	Netherlands - (Nat'l)
NETH-ROTT	Netherlands - Rotterdam
NETH-SILOAM	Netherlands - (Siloam)
NETH-WESTER	Netherlands - Westervoort
NEWCAL	New Caledonia - Noumea
NICAR	Nicaragua - Managua
NIGER	Niger - Niamey
NORTHMAR	North Marianas - Saipan
NORW-HALDEN	Norway - Halden
NORW-KRIS	Norway - Kristiansand
NORW-OTEREN	Norway - Oteren
NORW-OTT	Norway - Ottestad (Nat'l)
NORW-TONS	Norway - Tonsberg
NZ-ASSOC	New Zealand - (Associates)
NZ-AUCK-IB	New Zealand - (Island Brz)
NZ-AUCK-KK	New Zealand - (Kings Kids)
NZ-AUCK-MEDIA	New Zealand - (Media Plus)

NZ-AUCK-NATL	New Zealand - (Nat'l Office)
NZ-AUCK-POLY	New Zealand - (Polynesian)
NZ-AUCK-STEI	New Zealand - Steiger
NZ-AUCK-TAKA	New Zealand - (Early Child)
NZ-AUCK-URB	New Zealand - (Heine)
NZ-CHRIST	New Zealand - Christchurch
NZ-DUNEDIN	New Zealand - Dunedin
NZ-FAMILY	New Zealand - (Family Min.)
NZ-HAST	New Zealand - Hastings
NZ-MATAM	New Zealand - Matamata
NZ-MERCY	New Zealand - (Mercy Ship)
NZ-NORTH	New Zealand - Northland
NZ-OXFORD	New Zealand - Oxford
NZ-TEPUKE	New Zealand - Te Puke
PAKISTAN	Pakistan - Lahore
PANAMA	Panama - Panama City
PARAGUAY	Paraguay - Asuncion
PERU	Peru - Cuzco
PHIL-ANT	Philippines - Antipolo (DTS)
PHIL-BAGUIO	Philippines - Baguio City
PHIL-BALUT	Philippines - Manila - Balut
PHIL-BANAUE	Philippines - Banaue
PHIL-BANGUED	Philippines - Bangued
PHIL-BATANG	Philippines - Batang
PHIL-BONTOC	Philippines - Bontoc
PHIL-CEBU	Philippines - Cebu City
PHIL-DAVAO	Philippines - Davao City
PHIL-KK	Philippines - Manila (K Kids)
PHIL-NATL	Philippines - Manila (Nat'l)
PHIL-NEW	Philippines - New Manila
PHIL-OLONG	Philippines - Olongapo City
PHIL-PALAW	Philippines - Palawan
PHIL-RIZAL	Philippines - Rizal (Pastoral)
PHIL-SKOP	Philippines - Manila(Skopun)
PHIL-SURIG	Philippines - Surigao City
PHIL-TAL	Philippines - Talisay - Cebu
PHIL-ZAMB	Philippines - Zomboanga
PNG-BOR	Papua NG - Boroko
PNG-LAE	Papua New Guinea - Lae
PNG-MTHAG	Papua NG - Mt. Hagen
POLAND	Poland - Krakow
PORTUGAL	Portugal - Sintra
PUERTO	Puerto Rico
REUNION	France - Reunion Island
RWANDA	Rwanda
SA	South America (c/o USA)
SAFR-HAMM	South Africa-Hammanskraal
SAFR-JOZINI	South Africa - Jozini
SAFR-KUILS	South Africa - Kuils River
SAFR-MUIZ	South Africa - Muizenberg
SAFR-STE	South Africa - Stellenbosch
SAFR-STIL	South Africa - Stilfontein
SAFR-WORC	South Africa - Worcester
SAOTOME	Sao Tome & Principe
SENEGAL	Senegal - Dakar
SIERRA	Sierra Leone - Freetown
SING-CREATE	Singapore - (Create Int'l)
SING-NATL	Singapore - (Nat'l Office)
SOMALIA	Somalia
SPAIN-BARC	Spain - Bercelona
SPAIN-HOSP	Spain - (Hospitality Ctr)
SPAIN-LAS	Spain - Las Palmas
SPAIN-NATL	Spain - Torrejon (Nat'l)
SPAIN-SEVIL	Spain - Sevilla
SPAIN-TORR	Spain - Torremolinos
SRILANKA	Sri Lanka - Kandy
SUDAN	Sudan
SWED-KK	Sweden - (Kings Kids)
SWED-LAXA	Sweden - Laxa
SWED-LJUN	Sweden - Ljungskile
SWED-NATL	Sweden - Stockholm (Nat'l)

SWED-STOCK	Sweden - Stockholm
SWED-STORM	Sweden - (STORM)
SWITZ-BIEL	Switzerland - Calvinweg
SWITZ-BURT	Switzerland - Burtigny
SWITZ-CHAT	Switzerland - Chatel
SWITZ-EIN	Switzerland - Einigen
SWITZ-LAUS	Switzerland - Lausanne
SWITZ-MED	Switzerland - (MedAir)
SWITZ-MERCY	Switzerland - (Mercy Ships)
SWITZ-POST	Switzerland - Poststrasse
SWITZ-WILER	Switzerland - Wiler
SWITZ-YVER	Switzerland - Yverdon
TAIW-MIA	Taiwan - Miaoli, Toufen
TAIW-TAICH	Taiwan - Taichung
TAIW-TAIN	Taiwan - Tainan
TAIW-TAIPEI	Taiwan - Taipei
TANZANIA	Tanzania - Dar-es-Salaam
THAIL-CHRIST	Thailand - Bang. (Christjak)
THAIL-FRONT	Thailand - Bang. (Frontier)
THAIL-LIFE	Thailand - Bang. (Proj. Life)
THAIL-NAKH	Thailand - Nakhon Si Tham.
THAIL-NATL	Thailand - Bang. (Nat'l Off.)
THAIL-PHAN	Thailand - Phanat Nikhom
THAIL-REFUGE	Thailand - Bang. (Refuge)
THAIL-SITE2	Thailand - (Site 2)
THAIL-SLUM	Thailand - Bang. (Slum)
THAIL-TAPH	Thailand - (Church Plant.)
TOGO-ANEHO	Togo - Aneho
TOGO-KETAO	Togo - Ketao
TOGO-KPAL	Togo - Kpalime
TOGO-LOME	Togo - Lome (Nat'l)
TONGA-UN	Tonga - (U of N South Pac.)
TURKEY	Turkey - (c/o Netherlands)
UGANDA-HOPE	Uganda - Kampala (Hope)
UGANDA-KAM	Uganda - Kampala (Jinja)
UGANDA-NATL	Uganda - Kampala (Nat'l)
UGANDA-SOR	Uganda - Soroti
UK-ACACIA	UK - Acacia
UK-DERBY	United Kingdom - Derby
UK-ENG-BETH	UK - England - (Beth Shal.)
UK-ENG-BIRM	UK - England - Birmingham
UK-ENG-BRIST	UK - England - Cuckfield
UK-ENG-DAR	UK - England -(Dar Al Aman)
UK-ENG-DUN	UK - England - (Dunamis)
UK-ENG-EARL	UK - England - (Earl's Ct)
UK-ENG-HARP	UK - England - Harpenden
UK-ENG-KINGS	UK - England - (King Lodge)
UK-ENG-LIV	UK - England - Liverpool
UK-ENG-LOND	UK - England - London (Off.)
UK-ENG-ORCH	UK - England - (Orchard)
UK-ENG-PARR	UK - England - Parr Mt.
UK-ENG-SHEP	UK - England - (Shepherd's)
UK-ENG-THIRD	UK - England - (Third Wave)
UK-ENG-TOR	UK - England - Torquay
UK-SCOT-CAT	UK - Scotland - Catrine
UK-SCOT-DUMB	UK - Scotland - Dumbarton
UK-SCOT-EDIN	UK - Scotland - Edinburgh
UK-SCOT-GLAS	UK - Scotland - Glasgow
UK-SCOT-KK	UK - Scotland - (Kings Kids)
UK-SCOT-NATL	UK - Scotland - (Nat'l Off.)
UK-SCOT-OY	UK - Scotland - (Oper. Year)
UK-SCOT-PAIS	UK - Scotland - Paisley
UK-SCOT-WEE	UK - Scotland - (Pre-school)
UK-WAL-PONT	UK - S. Wales - Pontyclun
UK-WALES	UK - Wales - Porth
URUGUAY	Uruguay - Montevideo
USA-AR-ELM	USA - AR - Elm Springs
USA-CA-BISH	USA - CA - Bishop
USA-CA-CHULA	USA - CA - Chula Vista
USA-CA-HOLL	USA - CA - Hollywood
USA-CA-IDY	USA - CA - Idyllwild

USA-CA-RICH	USA - CA - Richard. Springs
USA-CA-SAN	USA - CA - San Francisco
USA-CA-SANTA	USA - CA - Santa Barbara
USA-CA-SULT	USA - CA - Sultana
USA-CA-SUMMIT	USA - CA - SB - (Summit)
USA-CA-SUN	USA - CA - Sunland
USA-CA-TUJ	USA - CA - Tujunga
USA-CENTRAL	USA - (Central Am/Caribb.)
USA-CO-ARV	USA - CO - Arvada
USA-CO-CIM	USA - CO - Cimarron
USA-CO-FRONT	USA - CO - (Strat. Frontiers)
USA-CO-MISS	USA - CO - (Mission Village)
USA-CO-RES	USA - CO - (Communication)
USA-FL-MIAMI	USA - FL - Miami
USA-FL-ORL	USA - FL - Orlando
USA-FL-WAVES	USA - FL - (Waves)
USA-GA-ATL	USA - GA - Atlanta
USA-HI-HONOL	USA - HI - Honolulu
USA-HI-KK	USA - HI - (Kings Kids)
USA-HI-MAUI	USA - HI - Maui
USA-HI-PRES	USA - HI - (President Off.)
USA-HI-REGL	USA - HI - (Pacific Reg'l)
USA-HI-UN	USA - HI - (Univ. Nations)
USA-ID-KAM	USA - ID - Kamiah
USA-ID-RIGG	USA - ID - Riggins
USA-IL-CHIC	USA - IL - Chicago
USA-IL-URB	USA - IL - Urbana
USA-LA-HOPE	USA - LA - (New Hope)
USA-LA-LIVING	USA - LA - (Living Alt.)
USA-LA-NEW	USA - LA - New Orleans
USA-LA-TARGET	USA - LA - (Target N.O.)
USA-MA-SOMER	USA - MA - Somerville
USA-ME-CAM	USA - ME - Camden
USA-MT-CROW	USA - MT - Crow Reserv.
USA-MT-KK	USA - MT - (King's Kids)
USA-MT-LAKES	USA - MT - Lakeside
USA-MT-SBS	USA - MT - (SBS Int'l)
USA-NC-CHAR	USA - NC - Charlotte
USA-NC-TR	USA - NC - (Charlotte Trng)
USA-NY-ANT	USA - NY - (Antioch Conn.)
USA-NY-EAST	USA - NY - Islip (East Coast)
USA-NY-ITH	USA - NY - Ithaca
USA-NY-LONG	USA - NY - Long Island City
USA-NY-RIVER	USA - NY - Riverhead
USA-OR-PORT	USA - OR - Portland
USA-OR-SALEM	USA - OR - Salem
USA-OR-SLAVIC	USA - OR - (Slavic Min.)
USA-PA-PHIL	USA - PA - Philadelphia
USA-PA-ROAR	USA - PA - Roaring Branch
USA-PA-TITUS	USA - PA - Titusville
USA-SD-SPEAR	USA - SD - Spearfish
USA-SOUTH	USA - (South Amer. Off.)
USA-SPANISH	USA - (Spanish Coord.)
USA-STCROIX	USA - St. Croix
USA-TN-NASH	USA - TN - Nashville
USA-TX-BUILD	USA - TX - (YWAM Bldg)
USA-TX-DALL	USA - TX - Dallas
USA-TX-EDIT	USA - TX - (Editorial)
USA-TX-LAST	USA - TX - (Last Days)
USA-TX-MERCY	USA - TX - (Mercy Ships)
USA-TX-MEX	USA - TX - (Mexico)
USA-TX-TWIN	USA - TX - (Twin Oaks)
USA-UT-OGD	USA - UT - Ogden
USA-VA-ARM	USA - VA - (ARM)
USA-VA-INT	USA - VA - (UN Internship)
USA-VA-UN	USA - VA - (U of N)
USA-WA-KK	USA - WA - (Kings Kids)
USA-WA-MB	USA - WA - (Miss. Builders)
USA-WA-NATL	USA - WA - (Nat'l & NA Off.)
USA-WA-PUBL	USA - WA - (Publishing)
USA-WA-REVIVE	USA - WA - (Revive Amer.)
USA-WA-TAC	USA - WA - Tacoma
USA-WA-URB	USA - WA - (Urban Min.)
USA-WI-MADIS	USA - WI - Madison
USA-WI-NORTH	USA - WI - (Northwoods)
USA-WI-WEYER	USA - WI - Weyerhaeuser
VENEZ-CARAC	Venezuela - Caracas
VENEZ-CASA	Venezuela - (Casa Hogar)
VENEZ-MER	Venezuela - Merida
WSAMOA-APIA	Western Samoa - (Preschool)
WSAMOA-PION	Western Samoa - (Pioneer)
WSAMOA-SAVA	Western Samoa - Savaii
ZAIRE	Zaire
ZAMBIA	Zambia
ZIMB-BULAW	Zimbabwe - Bulawayo
ZIMB-HARARE	Zimbabwe - Harare

Language Codes

Afr	Afrikaans
Alb	Albanian
Ara	Arabic
Bam	Bambara
Ben	Bengali
Can	Cantonese
Ceb	Cebuano
Chi	Chinese
Cre	Creole
Dan	Danish
Dut	Dutch
Eng	English
Fij	Fijian
Ger	German
Gre	Greenlandic
Heb	Hebrew
Hin	Hindi
Hun	Hungarian
Ind	Indonesian
Ita	Italian
Jap	Japanese
Kan	Kannada
Khm	Khmer
Kis	Kiswahili
Kri	Krio
Kur	Kurdish
Lat	Latvian
Mal	Malay
Man	Mandarin
Mar	Marathi
Nep	Nepali
Pid	Pidgin (PNG)
Pol	Polish
Por	Portuguese
Rus	Russian
Sca	Scandinavian
Sig	Sign Language
Spa	Spanish
Swa	Swahili
Swe	Swedish
Tag	Tagolog
Tam	Tamil
Tha	Thai
Tur	Turkish
Ukr	Ukrainian
Vie	Vietnamese

Miscellaneous Abbreviations/Codes (Commonly Used in this Manual)

(bi)	Bi-lingual
Admin.	Administration
Asst.	Assistant
CDTS	Crossroads Discipleship Training School
Coord.	Coordinator
Devel.	Development
Dir.	Director
DTS	Discipleship Trainig School
EMA	Europe, Middle East, Africa
Evang.	Evangelism
HANDS	Helping A Neighbor Develop and Serve
Int'l	International
KK	King's Kids
Maint.	Maintenance
Mgr.	Manager
Min.	Ministry
Mo	Month
Nat'l	National
P.R.	Public Relations
Publ.	Publishing
Reg'l	Regional
SOS	Summer of Service
Trng	Training
U of N	University of the Nations
Wk	Week
Wkend	Weekend
Wrkr	Worker

Month Abbreviations

JAN	January
FEB	February
MAR	March
APR	April
MAY	May
JUN	June
JUL	July
AUG	August
SEP	September
OCT	October
NOV	November
DEC	December

State/Province Abbreviations

Australia:	
NSW	New South Wales
NT	Northern Territory
QLD	Queensland
VIC	Victoria
Canada:	
BC	British Columbia
USA:	
AL	Alabama
AK	Alaska
AZ	Arizona
AR	Arkansas
CA	California
CO	Colorado
CT	Connecticut
DE	Deleware
DC	District of Columbia
FL	Florida
GA	Georgia
HI	Hawaii
ID	Idaho
IL	Illinios
IN	Indiana
IA	Iowa
KS	Kansas
KY	Kentucky
LA	Louisiana
ME	Maine
MD	Maryland
MA	Massachusetts
MI	Michigan
MN	Minnesota
MS	Mississippi
MO	Missouri
MT	Montana
NE	Nebraska
NV	Nevada
NH	New Hampshire
NJ	New Jersey
NM	New Mexico
NY	New York

NC	North Carolina	TN	Tennessee
ND	North Dakota	TX	Texas
OH	Ohio	UT	Utah
OK	Oklahoma	V.I.	Virgin Islands
OR	Oregon	VT	Vermont
PA	Pennsylvania	VA	Virginia
PR	Puerto Rico	WA	Washington
RI	Rhode Island	WV	West Virginia
SC	South Carolina	WI	Wisconsin
SD	South Dakota	WY	Wyoming

Chart Your Course to Impact the World!

The Personal Prayer Diary Planner, It's not just a Daily Planner...

It's a Global Adventure!

>Daily Journal/Planner	>Daily Bible Reading Guide
>Prayer Journal/Notes Section	>Overview of Each Nation
>2 Year-At-A-Glance	>World Maps (Regionally)
>Address/Telephone Section	>World Prayer Guide

Choose from 4 Great Covers:
Navy Blue, Rose, Burgundy, and Gray

Organize your schedule, Record important dates, Journal your prayer times and Bible reading, Systematically pray for the nations; All in one easy to use format!

reg. ~~$12.99~~
sale $10.00

Intercession Special!!

The Intercessors Special!
Purchase both **THE PERSONAL PRAYER DIARY/DAILY PLANNER & OPERATION WORLD**
for only $18.00
and Save a total of $8.98

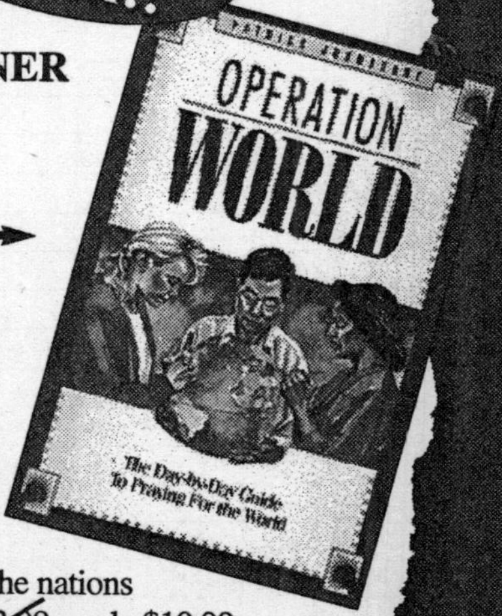

OPERATION WORLD

by Patrick Johnstone

The most widely used reference book for missions in the world. When used in conjunction with the YWAM Personal Prayer Diary /Daily Planner, you will have at your fingertips two important and effective tools of intercession for the nations and for journaling your prayer times. reg. ~~$13.99~~ sale $10.00

IF GOD HAS A PLAN FOR MY LIFE, WHY CAN'T I FIND IT?

BY RON BOEHME

You do have a destiny! God's plan for your life is not as far away as you might think it is. Here is a real "hands on" look at getting yourself lined up with God's highest purposes for your life. "Does God really have a plan for my life?" "Is it really possible to find out what God wants me to do?" Here are *real* answers for the *real* questions!

reg. ~~$7.99~~ sale $5.00

THROUGH THE DUST

by Denny Gunderson

Youth With A Mission's North American director, Denny Gunderson, beautifully draws leadership principles from the life of Jesus. This refreshingly candid book walks us alongside the Master. We observe Jesus through the eyes of people who experienced him firsthand. Through their eyes we discover many suprising insights into Jesus' leadership style. You will be challenged to re-think typical leadership stereotypes.

reg. ~~$6.99~~ sale $5.00

Qty.	Item		Total
	DARING TO LIVE ON THE EDGE	$5.00	
	FANNING THE FLAME	$5.00	
	FRIENDRAISING	$6.00	
	IF GOD HAS A PLAN...	$5.00	
	IS THAT REALLY YOU, GOD?	$5.00	
	OPERATION WORLD	$10.00	
	PERSONAL PRAYER DIARY...	$10.00	
	** PRAYER DIARY & OPER. WRLD	$18.00	
	RE-ENTRY	$5.00	
	STEPPING OUT	$5.00	
	THROUGH THE DUST	$5.00	
	Postage & Handling	$3.00	$3.00
	Total Amount Due (U.S. funds)		

Mail to:
Youth With A Mission
P.O. Box 55787
Seattle WA 98155
or call
1-800-922-2143 (U.S. only)
for Visa/Mastercard orders only

PRINT NAME ______

ADDRESS ______

CITY/STATE ______

ZIP ______ PHONE ______

Make checks payable to: Youth With A Mission Payments in U.S. funds only